DISCARDED

PORTRAITS OF THE EIGHTIES

(*From a photograph by Elliott and Fry.*)

PORTRAITS OF THE EIGHTIES

BY

HORACE GORDON HUTCHINSON

WITH 28 ILLUSTRATIONS

Essay Index Reprint Series

BOOKS FOR LIBRARIES PRESS
FREEPORT, NEW YORK

First Published 1920
Reprinted 1970

STANDARD BOOK NUMBER:
8369-1441-4

LIBRARY OF CONGRESS CATALOG CARD NUMBER:
72-105020

PRINTED IN THE UNITED STATES OF AMERICA

PREFACE

IT is curious, as one tries to bring into a picture gallery some of the chief actors in the Eighties, to find how naturally all the political portraits fall into a regular sequence. All the first half, and more, of the decade, up to 1886 and the new Parliament of that year, is the story of Ireland and of the Home Rule agitation. To be sure, there were by-plays, wherein the scene shifted to Egypt, with Arabi Pasha in a leading rôle, and later to the national shame of Khartoum and the tragedy of Gordon's death, but the main drama was domestic, in so far as we may speak of Ireland as domesticated. The leading actors are Mr. Gladstone and Mr. Parnell. Hero and villain, I presume most of the audience will regard them, but much depends on the point of view. Then, a little after the middle of the decade, "Puff!" like the magician's blow on the wand, comes the General Election. Like a single candle out goes the Liberal Party; in comes Lord Salisbury. Now the originals of all that were on the scene before the great extinguishing "Puff" seem to me, by comparison, to be easy to realise. I can, at least, form mental visions of them—much mistaken, it may be, but fairly clear in outline. But when it comes to Lord Salisbury; no, I have not, in my mind's eye, the slightest idea of the real man. Of course his massive physical outlines and certain surface manners were strikingly plain, but they count for very little.

And as for the lines and hues which do count in the presentment of the real inner man, I never gleaned any conception of them either from the very little that I saw of him, or from the very much that I heard of him. I knew one of his private secretaries rather intimately, yet I never extracted any information from him about the real man who was his chief. I do not think it was there to extract. He knew nothing of him, as it seemed to me, although he reverenced him deeply—and he was not a young man much given over to reverence.

Mercifully it does not fall on me to attempt a portrait of Lord Salisbury. I should refuse the attempt if it did. He is the most perfect enigma to me of all the statesmen, though I share very much of that private secretary's reverence for his great work and his great personality. I admit, however, that I do not know what manner of man it is that I reverence in him. But Mr. George Russell has done his outlines in the "Portraits of the Seventies." They are strictly outlines, however, as I deem, and nowhere inner lines in any sense. Some of his portraits that practised but alas! dead hand has done most vividly. I cannot, however, think that he has made the real Lord Salisbury live. Some of the portraits that he drew I have been obliged to try to retouch, because of the active rôle that the originals played in the Eighties ; but so far as possible I have not ventured to meddle with what he has done so well. I need not say that I expect no unanimity in my readers about the fidelity of the likenesses. Our chief interest in discussing character arises from our differing views and estimates. Least of all do I anticipate ready acceptance of the key which I have ventured to put forward to the secret of the strange, the repellent, yet the extraordinarily interesting character of Parnell.

I will say no more than this : that if mine is not indeed the right key, it is at least the only one which I have heard of which fits the hard lock at all. Even Mr. O'Brien, Parnell's own familiar friend, in his most able and sympathetic biography, offers no solution, no theory of the inner motives of this cold and aloof personality. He does but leave us wondering.

To return to that sequence of events and actors strung on the thread of Irish interests through all the first part of the Eighties. There was, of course, Mr. Gladstone, the great leader, with his henchmen, Morley, Harcourt, Hartington, Chamberlain, and so on, the first two to remain faithful to the end, the others, with many more, to fall away. Then, in opposition, Lord Salisbury, with Lord Randolph Churchill most persistent in the Commons, Mr. A. J. Balfour, and the rest. Most of these Mr. Justin McCarthy, in his *Portraits of the Sixties*, has given us; or, if not he, then Mr. G. W. E. Russell in his gallery of the Seventies. Both writers travel outside their respective briefs too, and gossip of the Eighties, beyond their borders. Therefore much of what I might have said I do not say, to avoid repetition of what has been better said already. For the rest, I have tried to fill in, where there were vacant places, some of the old portraits, besides drawing those original actors in the drama of the Eighties whom they have not touched.

I am rather painfully conscious that I have not done any justice at all to the ladies who were active in the period. Those were days when we first began to hear the cry of " Votes for Women " which was to swell to such a volume until the measure for which it was clamant was granted, almost as if part of the peace following the Great War. It was a concession which could scarcely be withheld from them in reward

for the amazing service which our British women
rendered in that awful struggle. But such a thing
as " militant suffragism " was unknown in the peaceful years of the Eighties, when Mrs. Fawcett was
perhaps the chief and most able figure in the ranks
of women demanding, by all constitutional means,
the vote. One at least of the most powerful of her
adjutants lives to celebrate the triumph which Mrs.
Fawcett was not spared to share—Lady Frances
Balfour. She was indeed most militant, though
never coming into open conflict with the police.
Well do I remember, in the Eighties, or a little later,
attending a meeting at which she gallantly declared,
" I hope not to die—I was almost saying that I do
not intend to die—until women get the vote." It
is an intention triumphantly fulfilled, for happily
she lives to fight many another day yet, and to witness
and enjoy the spectacle of women voting, to achieve
which she gave very much of her time and of her
uncommon ability. She may witness also, I am not
so sure with what measure of enjoyment, the spectacle
of women standing for Parliament, and of one
actually seated.

The lady whose name was a " household word,"
as is said, in all the British Empire, and was never
mentioned without a silent blessing, Florence Nightingale, was still living, as indeed she lived for another
score of years further, through all this period, but the
work that had made her name was done. She lived,
in a semi-regal seclusion, in her house at 10, South
Street, just off Park Lane, a seclusion imposed on
her by the indifferent health which she had broken
in her strenuous Crimean hardships and labours ; but
still she followed political and social movements with
much vivid interest. Greatly favoured persons were
summoned, almost as by royal command, to call on

her, and many in high places sought her counsel.
The healthy breath of contradiction never fell upon
her, and for lack of its corrective influence there is
little doubt that she began to look on her own judgment as infallible. A high official in the India Office
told me that he had been summoned to " talk over
Indian matters with her," as the summons said.
The talk, which lasted an hour, was entirely on Miss
Nightingale's part, although its first five minutes
demonstrated her nearly complete ignorance of the
subject. But no woman in all history has deserved
better of her country. Another lady who was still
active in her many good works at that time was the
Baroness Burdett Coutts.

Death, the Reaper, was very busy with his scythe
at the beginning of the Eighties, and culled some very
choice sheaves. George Eliot died at the very opening
of 1880 ; Carlyle early in 1881. There followed
Froude's biography of the Sage of Chelsea which
raised so great a storm. The very duty of a biographer became in question. Virtually the question
resolved itself into very simple form : " Is it the
biographer's duty to show us the man as he really is,
or the man as he ought to have been and as we imagined that he was ? " Froude had tacitly answered
the question, as it addressed itself to him, by writing
the biography with the former aim in view. The
public was shocked, who had believed in Carlyle as a
strong heroic soul, mentally suffering in philosophical
silence for the sins of the world. Froude presented
us with the picture of a poor mortal thing incessantly
complaining of its dyspepsia. The public had
figured Carlyle as possessed of all the virtues that he
commended to it and that he castigated it for not
possessing. It might have been grateful for a revelation that this was a poor fellow-being of like weak-

nesses with its own, only seeing into the core of those weaknesses perhaps a little more clearly, and having at command the most searching rhetoric for their condemnation. But as for the really right answer to the biographer's problem, it is surely this : " Give us the truth, so far as it is in you, about the man you describe to us ; or, if you cannot do this without offence, throw up your brief, quit telling the story." There is no right middle course.

1881 saw the death of Disraeli, most strangely gifted genius and especially strange figure to lead the country squires of England. In the same year died Arthur Stanley, the greatly loved Dean of Westminster ; James Spedding, the literary critic (with the " dome," as Edward Fitzgerald used disrespectfully to describe his naturally high forehead, still loftier elevated by his baldness). George Borrow, too, ceased his gipsyings in this year, a man who came from that East Anglia which Fitzgerald frequented, though a little more northerly than Fitzgerald. They should have met, for they would have had much in common : much, too, in violent antipathy, for while Borrow was an inveterate fraterniser with all and sundry, " Old Fitz " must have been as prickly and inaccessible as a solitary and misanthropical hedgehog. But I cannot recall any hint of such meeting from the writings of either—not even as given in those best of English letters of Fitzgerald's, in which such an encounter would scarcely have escaped record.

The work of all these and several more of note, whom death took in the first two years of the decade, was already done : they were not really of the Eighties, though their lives stretched into the period.

I believe I should say a word of defence, apology, excuse, or what you will, for the use of the term

" decade." Purists, I understand, object to it,
as a " coined " word, a word with no legitimate
ancestry or derivation. So be it. I accept it as a
coined word. The objectors may object and be happy.
It is too convenient for my present purpose to be
discarded in deference to their objection. Nor do
I entirely realise what bar sinister they can find in
the derivation from the Greek word for the numeral
" ten."

One caution I must give to prevent misapprehen-
sion : I have not portioned numbers of words and
pages in exact correspondence with the importance
of the persons whom the words and pages were meant
to portray. Of some, who have done the greater
work, there yet seemed less to say—less detail, that
would not be tiresome, to put into the picture—than
about others whose labour has been of less worth to
the world. Moreover it is the greater ones of whom
more has been written already, and I have tried to
avoid re-telling a known tale.

CONTENTS

xiii

CONTENTS

LIST OF ILLUSTRATIONS

PORTRAITS OF THE EIGHTIES

CHAPTER I

G. W. E. RUSSELL

TRIBUTE is due in the first instance to the memory of George Russell, author of those *Portraits of the Seventies* to which this is the intended sequel. George Russell knew everybody, and everybody knew George Russell. There never was a man better equipped to be the gossip of his day and to draw pen-portraits of the people prominent in his time. He might well have done the Eighties also, in which case the portraits in this volume would have been much bettered by his master hand, for he died only the other day, as I write in 1919. *Portraits of the Sixties* would have been a little too early for him, even had not Mr. Justin McCarthy gone ahead of him with them, for he was born only in the middle Fifties.

I think that it was quite a surprise to most people who did not already know his age, and were informed, to learn that he was comparatively so young at his death. For years his health had not been good, and he had the weighty figure and walk of a man far older than he was. He looked quite the part of the "heavy father" on the stage. He always appeared to regard himself, moreover, as old enough to be his own father, for he had the ways of one twenty years older. Men who were his senior by fully that span have told me that he always addressed them just as if he were their contemporary. More than that, his venerable aspect so impressed people of his own age that they were disposed to pay him the regard due to one a score of years older. He began to wear this air of dignity at the beginning of middle age, or even earlier.

His mind did not age in like measure, and kept a youth that contradicted his physical look. It was never a very original mind nor a very forceful mind; but it had remarkable gifts of storing information and of giving it pleasantly forth. He made a considerable success in life, but it is certain that he disappointed the high political hopes that had been formed of him. The heads of his Parliamentary record run as follows: Entry into the House in 1880, where he sat, as Member for Aylesbury, till 1885. Then, following Mr. Gladstone's fortunes, he was out of Parliament till 1892, when he came back as Member for North Bedfordshire. He was Parliamentary Secretary to the Local Government Board from 1883 to 1885, Under-Secretary for India from 1892 to 1894, and Under-Secretary for the Home Department from 1894 to 1895. He was made a Privy Councillor in 1907. Thus he went far, but, with his fine natural abilities and his heritage as a scion of the great Whig family, more might have been, and more was, expected of him.

George Russell, however, had a place of his own in the world distinct from any that political honours could confer. He was a ready and agreeable writer, as his *Portraits of the Seventies*, even if that volume stood alone, would testify. And it stands only as one in a goodly company of books rather similar to it, from his pen. Moreover he was a great conversa-

tionalist in a certain sense ; that is to say, that he
was a very agreeable and well-informed talker on a
wide variety of subjects. He knew men and manners.
He had a fine memory, and I expect that he must have
kept full and well-indexed note-books. He was not
a witty or an original talker, but he had a great store
of stories in his mind, and he told them well. Possibly he told rather too many, giving his enemies
opportunity to quote, in connection with him, the
ingenious word " anecdotage " which they would
not have had the wit to invent. As a matter of
fact his talk never fell into any kind of dotage, but
it might perhaps, without offence, be called anecdotal.

Enough is said to account for that " place of his
own " which I have claimed for George Russell,
but the principal ground on which it rested remains
still to be named : he was a great lay Churchman.
Most laymen in high position, however deep their
interest be in Church matters, are too busy in mun-
dane ways to give the Church much active help.
That is true to-day, and it was yet more true in the
Eighties. A layman zealous for the Church and
willing and anxious to lavish time and work and
thought on her service was a rarity, and one who
combined with this zeal the comparative leisure of
George Russell, save for the few years that he was
in Parliament and in office, was hardly to be found.
His support was of greatest value to the Church, just
because he was a layman. The high ecclesiastics
naturally welcomed him into their councils, and he
loved to assist in them. He loved, too, to take part
in the services of the Church, and almost the last
time that I saw him was on the occasion of his reading
the lessons, which he always did most beautifully,
at the Sunday morning service in St. Peter's, Eaton
Square.

Does it not become obvious how large his acquaintance must have been ? He was educated at Harrow and at Oxford. His natural place was in the " great world " of society and politics as one of the famous Russell family ; his gifts were just those which would make him welcome there ; all the leading Churchmen were his friends, because he was the zealous friend of the Church ; he wrote voluminously, so all the literary circles were open to him ; he even plied the busy pen of the journalist, and until nearly the end of his life he wrote the London letter for the *Manchester Guardian.*

So he was known, and I think that he liked being known. He used to drive about London in a carriage picked out in colours which did not suggest that he sought seclusion or would feel offence if people should say, as he passed : " That's George Russell." It would have pleased him, probably, to be so noticed, and so noticed, and pleased, he was. In a word he was one of the most sociable of men, interested in his fellow-kind and pleased that they should take an interest in him. It was a disposition as far as possible remote from that of the recluse and the misanthrope, and it qualified him remarkably well to be the portrayer of eminent men and women of his time.

CHAPTER II

W. E. GLADSTONE

THE decade of the Eighties was a period of political stir in England, and it was very largely dominated by the extraordinary and masterful figure of Mr. Gladstone. That is a statement which may be made equally without fear of contradiction as without avowal of Party bias, for it needs only to look at the record of those years to read that during the first half and more he was Premier and also leader of the House of Commons. Presumably it is of advantage to the Government and to the country that the Prime Minister should lead in the Lower House, but it is an advantage which did not favour Mr. Gladstone's successor. Lord Salisbury followed him as Prime Minister, and of necessity sat in the Upper House, with, at first, Sir M. Hicks Beach, next Lord Randolph Churchill, and then Mr. W. H. Smith, leading the Commons.

The result of the Election which brought Mr. Gladstone into power at the beginning of the Eighties came as a surprise to all the prophets. If they had anticipated a Liberal majority at all, it is certain that none nearly so large had been predicted by the accredited judges of the passing event. The Liberals had not been in office for many years, and the long interval made Mr. Gladstone's task in forming his Cabinet peculiarly difficult.

Happily it is not my task to relate the political

5

story of those years, nor is it my part to put a hand
to an attempt so venturesome as the sketch of a full-
length portrait of the actors who figured in it most
largely. Their portraits, at length, have been limned
by many deft masters, and notably by Mr. Justin
McCarthy in his *Portraits of the Sixties,* and by Mr.
G. W. E. Russell, who took up his parable with *Portraits of the Seventies.* Thus, Gladstone, Hartington,
Salisbury, and others of the great ones have already
had indifferent justice done to the lineaments of their
characters. To tell truth, these predecessors of mine,
McCarthy and Russell, did not stick any too strictly by
their text. They travelled gaily outside their decades, transgressing their self-set boundaries with a
laxity that was almost immoral. And of course
political life and energies are commonly prolonged to
far more than a ten years' measure. The men who were
active in the Sixties may be found still active, and
perhaps reinforced with an added wisdom and maturity, in the Eighties. They may be the same men,
playing different parts, in the one scene as in the
other, or it may happen again that they are essentially
different men, with an outlook, a judgment, and almost
a character profoundly changed. Nor are those
characters the most generally interesting which are
the most self-consistent. Growth is change, and
growth is the law of life : the man therefore who does
not change is, so far, dead. As living man, and so
" the noblest study of mankind," it no longer amuses
us to consider him.

The whole history of Mr. Gladstone's career and
administration has been written, as everybody knows
and as everybody ought to have read, by his friend
and follower who is now Lord Morley. Lord Morley's
high literary abilities and political sympathies, as
well as his personal attachment, marked him as a
right man for the great task, and by general consent

W. E. GLADSTONE.

he has more than justified his selection ; but it is to be
regretted that he was so little in real touch with the
earnest religious faith and principles which meant
so very much to Mr. Gladstone. Lord Morley's
own agnosticism, if I do him no wrong in attaching
to him this label of rather negative description, of
necessity shut off all sympathy with that side of the
nature of his great subject ; and his own engrossment
with politics inclined him perhaps to find in them an
even more exclusive interest for Mr. Gladstone than
they really had. He gives us a splendid picture of
Mr. Gladstone the statesman : we get from him
scarcely a glimpse of Mr. Gladstone as the human
being. And quite human he was, even in a family
circle which would almost insist in regarding him as
super-human. I regret that my personal knowledge
of him was next to nothing, but of and about him
I used to hear a great deal from various relations.
No man, I imagine, ever has inspired quite equal
veneration in his own household. A little farther from
the actual centre and source of this worship—that is
to say, among nephews and nieces—an occasional
breath of something which bordered upon criticism
might be permitted to intrude, but still only in the
hushed and rather awe-struck whisper in which it
used to be deemed proper, in Victorian days, to speak
of the Deity. Of course one of the greatest, perhaps
we are justified in saying the very greatest, event
of our domestic politics which happened in the
Eighties was Mr. Gladstone's announcement, which
fell like a thunderbolt on those who were outside
the circle that knew of its coming and in which it
was actually prepared, of his conversion to a Home
Rule Government for Ireland. It had an explosive
force which blew the Liberal Party into two distinct
halves, of which one, coalescing with the more progressive of the Conservatives, became a new Party

with a new name, the " Unionists," while the other, with Mr. Gladstone at its head, stood for Home Rule as it was defined in the Bill of '86. The issues cannot be forgotten : the rejection of the Bill by a sufficient majority in the House, the resignation of the Government, and the eventual return to office of the Unionists by a large majority of the electors' votes.

Mr. Alfred Lyttelton, the famous cricketer, afterwards Colonial Secretary and perhaps the most popular man of his generation, differed from the policy of Mr. Gladstone, who was his uncle. I believe he had " devilled " in his younger days for Henry James, the great lawyer ; at all events they had been closely associated. Henry James, then Attorney-General and one of Gladstone's most trusted henchmen before the delivery of the thunderbolt, had conceived it his duty to part company with his illustrious captain. It may have been in some measure due to his influence and example that Alfred Lyttelton went the same way.

Nothing remarkable in that we may say ! It has happened to all of us, we may suppose, to have uncles from whom in our youth we differed in opinion, and followed courses which were not their course. Likewise, in later life, there are few to whom it has not occurred to have nephews—and nieces, no less— and to find them, too, conducting themselves in a manner which does not appear to our ancient wisdom to be all that is to be wished.

But then, in neither case was the uncle Mr. Gladstone ! That is the difference. The secession of his nephew Alfred from the faithful of his train over this highly debatable question of Home Rule was looked on in the more immediate family circle as nothing less than a tragedy. Nay, worse : it was regarded as a crime, and a crime of the most heinous kind, approaching the deadly sin of sacrilege.

It is difficult to hear, or to read, without a smile, of the terrible solemnity, the fear of the awful consequences, with which the breaking of the shocking news to Mr. Gladstone was contemplated. Alfred had to travel down to Hawarden in person, probably at some considerable inconvenience, to do it. We are given to understand an awed hush pervading the house so soon as he had entered it upon his terrific errand, rather as if some criminal condemned to immediate execution had crossed the threshold. Breaths were tensely held when he went into the study, as though to his last confessional. One gathers that there was a certain subconscious surprise in all the household that the world, to all appearance, had changed so little, that no catastrophic stroke had fallen, when he came out from the avuncular presence after unbosoming himself of his guilt. There is an extraordinarily unreal atmosphere about it all. It is hardly as if it were a mere matter of statement of opinion, and of a course of action to be pursued, between two human beings both of mature years, although of course one much older and more experienced than the other. We cannot imagine that any such tragic emotion could have been kindled in the Cecil or the Cavendish family by the diversion of a nephew from the uncle's line in politics. Surely it is remarkable, and a high testimony to the splendid balance of Mr. Gladstone's great mental qualities, that, living in an atmosphere of adulation such as all this implies, elevated to an altitude in the estimation of those most near to him that clearly was above that of the natural human being, he should still have kept his clarity of judgment and a reasonable estimate of his own powers and character.

Mrs. Gladstone, it is true, in spite of the almost motherly care with which she guarded her illustrious husband, was able to take at times a view which

I think would have been deemed quite impious on the part of any other member of the family. " William would be a great bore, if he were not a genius," is a saying recorded of her which testifies to her shrewd insight. She had indeed an uncommon dower of profound and sympathetic wisdom which was not always credited to her on account of the perfect simplicity which veiled it. Her gift of humorous tact was never turned to better account than when she met, unexpectedly, one of Mr. Gladstone's most trusted followers who had just deserted him in his Home Rule campaign. She held up a rebuking finger, saying, " Naughty ! Naughty ! " and inevitably the laugh cleared all the electricity from the air.

I do not think that the warmth of Mr. Gladstone's affection for his greatly erring nephew was seriously diminished by his truancy ; and that is a testimony the more valuable to the goodness of his heart and his depth of feeling, because it is tolerably certain that this Irish Bill meant far more to him at the moment than any other of the great measures which he succeeded in writing on the Statute Book from time to time during his long career. I remember the then Lord Southesk, father of the present bearer of the title, telling me that he met Mr. Gladstone in the Parliament Yard, soon after he had made his great speech on the Bill. Lord Southesk had listened to it with the greatest attention and admiration. " A wonderful effort," he said it was, " for a man of Mr. Gladstone's years, on the physical side, to say nothing of its intellectual force." Naturally he welcomed the chance of congratulating the speaker. And then he told me that Mr. Gladstone raised his eyes to heaven, with almost a rapt look in them, and said earnestly : " Yes, I believe that God has designed that I shall be the saviour of Ireland."

He did not foresee the long and stony road which that unfortunate island is still travelling in search of its salvation. Yet he spoke in pious faith, and it is not for us, even now, to say that he spoke in self-delusion. It was not his destiny that either that Home Rule Bill, nor another which he attempted later, should be added to the number of those measures which I wrote of just now as placed by his hand on the Statute Book; but what his championship of the Home Rule cause did was to bring the idea of its possibility, as a piece of practical politics, to the minds of Englishmen as it never had been brought before. If the ultimate salvation of Ireland is to be ground out of the Home Rule mill, it is quite sure that the machine is less rapid in action than Mr. Gladstone imagined, but his may yet prove in the end, for all we know, to have been the master-milling hand, though it was not his to give, as he expected, the final turn to the wheel.

The ultimate secret of Mr. Gladstone's success in carrying through so very much of the vast business to which he set himself was, I am quite sure, his deadly earnestness. Of course, all his gifts of intellect, his grasp of the essential, his faculty for detaching the incidental details and concentrating on the core of the question, his marvellous memory, his rare eloquence—all these are to be understood. They always have been understood; they have been attributed to him in a thousand " appreciations." So, too, of his moral qualities, his high purpose, his working for what he believed to be the good of humanity, regardless of his personal interest, his accountability to God for his acts, and his indifference to the verdict of man—all these, too, are to be granted. He was thus supremely gifted. But, even so, with all this moral and intellectual wealth he would have achieved only a tithe of what he did but for that resistless driving force which his terrific earnestness supplied to set all in vigorous and almost perpetual motion. It was an earnestness unimpeded, unmollified by any of the unction, so valuable for the smooth working of the mechanism of life as in many ways it is, of humour. I do not think that Mr. Gladstone possessed a scintilla of it. As his nephews would say, " You can never quite tell how Uncle William is going to take a joke. It isn't quite safe to make one with him. It may just go to the right place with him, but again, it mayn't ; and if it doesn't, he lets you know it."

Generalisations are very dangerous things to hazard, and it constantly happens that, having ventured on some general statement, the immediate experience of the next few hours brings to your notice an instance utterly refuting it, but I do believe that very few instances can be cited in disproof of the general statement that no man of affairs has really achieved greatness, and carried through measures of the first importance, who has been gifted with a sense of humour at all keen and ready. The man who would be taken seriously must take himself and his mission very seriously first, and this is just the point of view which the sense of humour will not permit. It is continually at hand to suggest that, after all, " all the world's a play," and a comedy at that, and all the men and women, at the best, high-class comedy actors.

No such light view of life and its purpose ever interfered between Mr. Gladstone and the work which his hand found to do. Always, he did it with his might. I do not think that we find anywhere, in the many records of him, nor have heard in the many tales about him in which most of us must have taken part, a story of any joke, any humorous hint even, of his own making or suggestion. I do

remember indeed hearing of a joke, of the practical
nature, which he perpetrated, quite unintentionally
and unconsciously, at the expense of an unfortunate
footman in a house where he was dining. It happened that the young fellow was the son of old tenants
on the Hawarden estate. Mr. Gladstone caught
sight of him, and recognised him as he went round
the table with the dishes. The next time that he
came to Mr. Gladstone it was with a dish of peas.
Mr. Gladstone, taking no notice of the proffered
vegetable, held out his hand, turning half round
in his chair, and said in the most kindly and
hearty tones of his deep voice : " How are you,
Henry ? Very glad to see you ; father and mother
well ? "

The poor fellow, in his agitation, having to dis-
engage a right hand to shake that of the Prime
Minister extended to him, very naturally poured
most of the peas in an avalanche over the head of the
next sitter at table, after which, Mr. Gladstone,
unconscious or uncaring that he had done anything
at all unusual, turned in his chair to his dinner again
and took up his knife and fork and the threads of the
general conversation just where he had laid them
down. History, so far as I know, does not record
the words of the lady on whose head the pea-hail-
storm descended, nor what the butler said, in repri-
mand to the footman, afterwards. But I do not think
that that subaltern would have been much concerned
at his superior officer's rebuke. He had been honoured so very highly that the most acrid censure of
the most majestic butler would merely glide off him
without doing him scathe. It is a story that illustrates delightfully Mr. Gladstone's impulse to a
simple and natural act of kindness. He just did the
thing which his warm heart prompted without
thinking of such incidental circumstances as other

people's opinion of the act, or the destination of a dish of peas.

I need scarcely say that in these trifling reflections and details which I have here set down about this very great man I do not imagine that I am presenting anything approaching to a portrait of him. That was not my intention. He has been already sketched at full length again and again by many a limner many times more practised and expert. His greater qualities and his splendid services are common knowledge. I may perhaps add one testimony, rather striking, to his eloquence, by a witty Frenchman, and one who certainly had formed no preconceived notion in his favour. It was in the days, towards the end of the Eighties, if I remember right, when Mr. Gladstone first began to visit Biarritz. He used to delight in watching the giant waves of the Biscayan coast dash on that rock-bound shore—possibly the finest exhibition of ocean's fury and glory that the world has to show. This Frenchman, since deceased, had formed his opinion of the Liberal Prime Minister mainly from the conversation that he had overheard, or had taken part in, at the British Club, where used to gather a society of English visitors and residents who were for the most part of the class whose members take pride in describing themselves as " Conservatives and Sportsmen "—in other words, pleasant English gentlemen, of the Eton and Oxford type of education, who had never vexed the brain with great efforts of thought. The day of Mr. Gladstone's arrival happened nearly to coincide with that of the departure of one of the most prominent of the annual visitors to Biarritz at that time, Mr. Everard (since made Sir Everard, K.C.V.O.) Hambro, the English banker and financier. The Frenchman aforesaid, on the day of Mr. Gladstone's coming, and with his opinions formed by what he had

overheard of the English talk, observed that " Il y a
trois malheurs de Biarritz, le départ de M. Hambro,
l'arrivée de M. Gladstone, et le chapeau de Miss ——."
Charity requires that a blank shall be recorded for
the name of the English lady whose headgear so
poignantly offended the delicate æsthetic sense of
the Gaul.

I do not know that anything ever happened to
modify his vexation of spirit over the last of these
misfortunes of his native town, but in respect of the
second : " l'arrivée de M. Gladstone," it was but a day
or two later that I found him in a very changed and
chastened mood. In the interval Mr. Gladstone
had made a speech—I think at some luncheon or like
function at which he had been entertained. He had
spoken in French, although he was not at all fluent
in that language. My friend, the Frenchman of
" les trois malheurs," had been one of his audience : he
could not say enough in praise either of the speaker
or of his speech. And this is how he put it : " He "
(that is Mr. Gladstone) " could not speak French
—no. But if he had thought over each sentence for
a year, he could not have found better things to say."
That, as it strikes me, is a wonderful testimony.
A man who had the natural gift of oratory, as Mr.
Gladstone possessed it, could turn it to such admirable
account as this, even under the difficulties imposed
by a language in which he had very little ease of
speech !

A great many people remarked, in Biarritz, a fact
about Mr. Gladstone's appearance which was so
familiar to us in England that we had ceased to
remark on it, that although he was, in actual stature,
quite a small man, yet he never gave you the impression of smallness : you could not associate him with
any measure below the average. This was, surely,
because of the large capacity of the head ; and more

particularly, because of the eagle-like glance of his widely open eyes. As the head was large and striking in comparison with the whole figure, so the eyes were disproportionately large and effective in comparison with the whole face, and thus the total expression became one of force and massiveness rather than of anything on the small scale. It was very singular.

Mr. Gladstone's attitude towards Ireland occupied so much of the political stage in the middle Eighties that it is difficult to get away from that drama and from its actors. It is most natural to speak of those Liberals who did not follow him as seceders, but it has always to be remembered that it was really Mr. Gladstone himself who seceded, who departed from the recognised line. It was those others who were steadfast in the path which they had set out to travel under his guidance. It is but one testimony the more to his masterful dominance that we find it so easy to speak of them as the deflectors, the truants. The truth is, that, for many of them, Gladstone, the man, the leader, had come to stand almost in the place of principle. He *was* their principle, and when they abandoned him they all had a secret sense of guilt, as though they were being false to their convictions. Scarcely ever, in the whole course of history, has a leader conducted his followers into a dilemma of such difficulty. And the difficulty of the dilemma is really a measure and an acknowledgment of the extraordinary supremacy of the chief who led them within its jaws.

CHAPTER III

LORD HARTINGTON (LATER, DUKE OF DEVONSHIRE)

IT is a curious and significant thing, that when
Mr. Gladstone, in 1886, began to formulate
his new attitude towards Home Rule, there
was much speculation as to what this, that,
or the other of his followers might do, but there was
never any question at all about the position that Lord
Hartington would take up. Mr. Chamberlain men
were doubtful of. Sir Henry James, late Attorney-
General, who almost certainly might have been Lord
Chancellor had he continued faithful in the train of
the great Liberal chief, was not expected to be a
deserter ; but he sacrificed in some measure his
career for his convictions. He would have none of
Home Rule. Mr. (now Viscount) Morley was one of
those about whom there was little doubt. He would
not waver in fidelity ; and, moreover, the new policy
of his chief was perhaps an older policy with him.
But just as surely as Mr. Morley would go with Mr.
Gladstone for Home Rule, so surely, men thought,
Lord Hartington would not go with him ; and the
majority were quite right.

The opinion, thus proved correct by the event, was
confidently held not only by those who knew Lord
Hartington in any personal sense, but by thousands,
and perhaps by millions, who had never heard him,
had never seen him, and who, in the case of the large
majority, had probably never read a word of his
speeches. Just in what manner it is that the national

opinion of a public man is formed, whether by one passing on his own view, and another adopting it, and the mass thus growing snow-ball fashion, it would be very hard to say, but of the gradual infiltration into the bulk of the people of a tolerably definite estimate of the characters of their leading men there can be no question. The wonder is that it is so generally correct. The population of Great Britain is composed of so many millions, " mostly fools," as Carlyle genially tells us, and probably quite truly ; but out of this mass of individual foolishness it is marvellous how some collective sentiment and opinion is formed which on the whole is just and wise. Amongst the rest of the leading men of the Eighties, as, indeed, of every modern period, Lord Hartington came under the verdict of this national tribunal.

What the nation saw in him was a man slow to act, slow to think, yet a man who would never be hurried into action before the slow processes of his thought had shown him with tolerable clearness the goal towards which his act would tend. It saw him as a man who, once his mind was made up about the desirable end, would very hardly bend from it. They trusted him as absolutely honest, absolutely sure to be true to his convictions, having " no axe to grind," no ambition to gratify. The accident of his birth and heritage had put him far above the common temptations which might work upon men to whom less had been thus given. They liked him, moreover, as an owner of race-horses, showing what they would not at all admit to be their common " weakness " for a " bit of sport." They liked him none the less because they judged him slow of thought, for the majority of them were not very quick of brain themselves. Suspicion is deeply rooted in their nature. Englishmen have always been a little distrustful of brilliancy, because brilliancy implies a speed of brain-wave which few

LORD HARTINGTON (DUKE OF DEVONSHIRE) IN THE HOUSE.

of them can keep pace with and which they fear to follow, just because they cannot keep close enough to it to see towards what shore it is tending. They fear it may dash them upon some rock. They prefer the slower rate which permits them to see the haven towards which they hope to move.

All these attributes were summed up for them, though of course very few would formulate them to themselves in any conscious estimate, in the personality of Lord Hartington. I happened to say once to a politician of the other section of the Liberal Party—that section which had gone docilely with the great shepherd of the Home Rule flock—that the qualities of Lord Hartington, his cool, steady judgment, his reluctance to be hurried, his freedom from all emotional excitement and enthusiasm, were such as to be of great value at times of national crisis. I had forgotten, for the moment, the exact political hue of him to whom I spoke, or perhaps I might have said it otherwise. Be that how it may, his answer was : " Do you think his qualities would ever have brought him to the front if he had not been a marquis, and a duke's son ? "

I had to admit, at once, that they would not. But then, my friend—I do not know how consciously or intentionally—had diverted the issue. I had spoken merely of the intrinsic value of these qualities in a statesman already near the head of affairs. He had replied with a question as to their value in lifting him to that position from the starting ground of— shall we say ?—a commoner who enjoys no especial privilege from any achievements of his forebears. Evidently Lord Hartington's attributes were the very opposite of those which we may call " push-ful," the attributes that would impel a man from lowly place to high station. And that very fact, I ventured to contend—that very fact might be used as a most powerful argument in favour of hereditary rank, and against the theory that if all men are not, indeed, equal, they ought to start so. The contention of at least one large school of modern socialistic thought is that all men ought to commence life with equal opportunity. They may be right. I am not committing myself to one side or other in this debate. But I do maintain that if such qualities as those which Lord Hartington personified may be of value— and I have not the smallest doubt of their value— it is a value which cannot conceivably be brought into the scale in a society which has no members whom the accident of heredity places, without effort of their own, in high station. The effort to attain that station is just the kind of effort which does not belong to those who have the qualities characteristic of Lord Hartington.

A very brilliant sketch of Lord Hartington's slow moving mental processes has been traced in a very brilliant book, published a year or so ago under the title of *Eminent Victorians.* Mr. Strachey, the writer, brings it in, incidentally, in his chapter on General Gordon, showing how the gradual conviction forced itself on Lord Hartington's mind that Gordon could not, conceivably, be left to his fate in Khartoum without, at the least, an effort for his rescue. The result of that belated effort is another story, and one most painful to the national conscience, and so must ever remain ; but at all events it gave Lord Hartington the opportunity to show, what indeed none ever doubted of him, that he had the full courage of his opinion, once it was formed, and would carry it to its only logical conclusion. This, of course, was while he was still a member of Mr. Gladstone's Cabinet, and before the great secession.

It was a prominent feature of his strong character that he never shrank from an act which he believed to be his duty because of its unpleasant nature, and duties of the kind were, perhaps, more often than we have been allowed to know, delegated to him by his colleagues who were more acutely sensitive or less courageous. An amusing instance in point is the story, which I believe is quite truly narrated of him, about a certain Education Bill which Sir John Gorst had very much at heart, but which the Government found itself obliged to drop. They were all very sorry when the necessity arose, and there was much discussion as to the best and most kindly mode of conveying the decision to Sir John Gorst, so as to cause him as little pain as possible. There was a natural reluctance on the part of each of the members to be the bearer of such unwelcome tidings, and general relief when Lord Hartington offered to take the burden off their shoulders and be the herald of ill news. We may imagine them, as soon as he had started on his mission, wondering in what form of soft words he would wrap the message up so as to break its content gradually and tenderly to the hearer. And this is how he did it : He went into Sir John Gorst's room, took up his customary attitude with his back to the fireplace, and announced curtly, " Well, Gorst, your damned Bill's dead."

It is just possible that this method of inflicting the wound, short, sharp, and decisive, may have been really the most kindly and tactful that could be desired. I do not know. It is possible that the very extraordinary bluntness of its delivery in this form may have imparted into the unwelcome message some slight comic relief. Blunt, to comicality, in the narration it certainly sounds, but it does not appear that Sir John Gorst ever resented it at all, nor that any estrangement between the two followed on it. So all was for the best, and Lord Hartington's courage had saved his colleagues from a job which none of them relished. A more subtle diplomatist, trying a more delicate method, might in the end have given far more offence. No doubt Lord Hartington knew the man with whom he had to deal and judged rightly of the best mode of dealing with him.

The truth is that, although Lord Hartington was not at all a clever man, he was that which is far better than clever, he was wise. It is wonderful, looking through his long political career, how few instances, if any, we may find in which we may say, " Here he was wrong ; here he made a mistake." It may be that he avoided mistakes largely because he was so little adventurous. He did not take chances, in great affairs, although he did own race-horses and although he was fond of bridge at high points. His bridge-playing was done in his characteristic way—slowly, with much fumbling at his cards, many cogitating " hums " and " haws " ; but generally with the production of the right card at the end of these strange processes. If the people whom he played with found it a little trying, they had not the courage to tell him so, nor would he have minded in the least, nor have hurried himself at all the more, had they done so. He was so wise that he knew perfectly well that he was not clever. It was one of his complaints against his destiny that all through life it had brought him into the society of men, and compelled him to engage with them in big business, who were very much quicker in thought than himself. He realised it fully, and in that full realisation and in the undaunted facing of all its consequences, lay a great part of his strength. He was absolutely honest, even to that farthest and most difficult extreme of honesty which gives a man the rare faculty of being honest with himself. The honesty of absolute simplicity is a common character-istic of the Cavendishes. I remember Lady Frederick, who, of course, was not a Cavendish by birth, but had

married into the family, in course of telling a story
about some domestic happening, saying, in the most
casual and matter-of-fact manner, " No Cavendish
can tell a lie, so——" The story went on to the consequences of this inveterate truth-telling. It was
in a Cavendish house that she told the story, and in
large part with a Cavendish audience, and it was
remarkable that none of them made any comment on
this *obiter dictum.* It was just accepted as an obvious
matter-of-fact observation, much as if she had said,
" No Cavendish can jump six foot high." I am not
even quite sure whether she said it altogether as in
unqualified praise of their qualities. It had the air of
suggesting in them a lack of the requisite imagination
to invent the thing that is not. In any case, there
it was—this testimony thus lightly given to their
invincible honesty—and no one regarded it as remarkable in any way nor as open to the slightest
question.

Lord Hartington, in the power of this really rather
formidable honesty and simplicity of the Cavendishes,
often drove a far cleverer but more pretentious ad-
versary into a very nasty corner. His was all the
strength of a man who has the honesty and courage
to admit that he does not know, and it is a courage
which often turns a situation to the singular and even
ridiculous disadvantage of the man whose weakness
is the very common one of pretending, and very
likely of fancying, that he knows more than he does.
It never worried him to confess his own ignorance, and
he was never ashamed of asking questions, in order to
learn ; and in this way he no doubt arrived at acquir-
ing a great deal more knowledge than would be
gained by one who was afraid to ask because the asking would be a confession of ignorance. When one
who is thus pretending, or thus self-deceiving, is
asked by one who has none of these pretences, a

question of some simple kind and is unable to produce
a sufficient answer, the garment of pretence begins
very quickly to wear grievously thin and to reveal
a nakedness beneath which compels the wearer to a
blush.

One of the Cecils, of the generation now taking
active and distinguished part in public affairs, told
me a delightful tale of himself and Lord Hartington,
very characteristic of the latter. They were in the
smoking room at Hatfield. No one else was in the
room. They had sat for a long while in silence, the
young fellow, lately down from College, not caring
or daring to interrupt the soliloquy of the famous
politician whose mind, the young man doubted not,
was revolving great affairs of State. At length,
after all this rumination, the great man spoke, and
this is what he said : " I can never understand how
it is that hot water runs all over a house in the pipes
—it goes up to the top of a house—can you ? "
" Well, then," said this young Cecil, telling me the
story, " I began to tell him all that I remembered
about that sort of thing—what I'd heard at school,
how hot water was lighter than cold and so it rose
up in the pipes and went all over the house. He
listened very attentively all the time I was talking,
and I was rather pleased with myself. I thought
I did it all rather well. When I had done he did not
say anything for a minute or so. I was rather disappointed, expecting him to say how clearly I had
explained it ; and then at last he said, ' I don't
think that can be it ! ' "

That was all ; not another comment, good or bad ;
no praise to the young fellow for having at all events
done his best to give an explanation ; no alternative
suggestion offered to this one thus curtly rejected.
But it was an observation which had its reward,
for luckily the young fellow, shy though he was and

tremulously expectant of a word or two of commendation, was blessed with an acute sense of humour,
and has cherished the incident in inalienable possession ever since. There is not the slightest doubt
that it has afforded far more gratification in the end
than the highest laudation at the moment could
have given.

Of course Lord Hartington was, as usual, perfectly
correct in his judgment. The explanation proffered
by the young man was not " it," nor anything like
" it." The cause, as I take it, why water rises in
the hot-water pipes and flows all over the house is
the same as the cause why the cold water flows
upwards similarly ; namely, that the water in both
cases is brought from a higher source, and that the
weight from above forces the water in the pipes to
" seek its own level," as the common and not very
illuminating phrase has it. But that does not
matter : the story's the thing—the story and the
striking and humorous presentment of Lord Hartington's way of thought and singularly blunt way of
expression.

There was one side of his nature which was continually suppressed and hidden under his cold and
unsympathetic manner, and that is the artistic and
æsthetic side. Music and poetry, the latter especially,
had a great attraction for him. I do not know of
any verses of his composition, but I should not be
in the least surprised to hear that he had so written.
It is quite unlikely that a man so fond of reading
poetry would not have made some attempt at self-
expression by the same means, though it is perhaps
still more unlikely that a man of Lord Hartington's
reserved nature would have allowed any eye but his
own to read his poetic compositions. His skill in
putting words together was considerably greater
than might be gathered from listening to his speeches.

His delivery was not good; he hesitated and thought
long. But when you read the speech which had
sounded so poorly it was surprising how well the
periods flowed and how sequent and close was the
train of argument. All through the piece he was a
man whose outer aspects did but little justice to the
strength and balance of the qualities underlying them.

His statue in Whitehall is an admirably good likeness, giving just that impression of cold, proud aloof-
ness which his living presence was apt to convey.
That it is an impression which greatly belied the
really good and kind heart of its original, I have
just stated, but it is scarcely to be expected that the
marble shall reveal more of the truth than the living
flesh of which it is the copy. It gives us the impression, too, which is precisely just, of a man whose
sense of public duty was profound, and whom no
light consideration would divert from the line to
which he was convinced that duty pointed. If no
place is to be found in a pure democracy for statesmen
of Lord Hartington's peculiar gifts, it is very certain
that democracy will be by so much the poorer for
such purity.

CHAPTER IV

CHARLES STEWART PARNELL

THE most strange and remarkable character of all the men who figured largely in the Eighties was that of Charles Stewart Parnell. That is a statement which may be made with some confidence, and without any avowal of political bias. Whether we rate him hero, as did some, or villain, as did more, we may never doubt that his qualities were very different from those of our common humanity. It was a character, indeed, so strange as scarcely to appear quite human : more like some weird, rather diabolic freak ; rather diabolic, and yet with some qualities that came near the heroic. Quite an extraordinary man.

I was saying this, or something like this, to a friend —a statesman still living, and at that time in the Cabinet—who knew him rather intimately, which I did not. " Well," he said, " perhaps he is something of an enigma; but it is an enigma with a key. You most remember this : the master passion of Parnell's life was not love of Ireland, it was hate of England. If you will bear this in mind you will find that it explains very much."

That is a terrible indictment of a man, especially in the mouth of a friend. I do not think that the friend realised at all how terrible it was. It is at once giving over the man as entirely diabolic, with no heroic trait to redeem him ; for to take hate as the mainspring of life's action is to become very devil. But Parnell surely was something other and better than this. If it was no more than hate of England that he lived to gratify—well, he had his opportunities for this again and again, and he turned them to account. We must admit that ; but in fairness we must admit also that he always contrived to turn those same opportunities to the advantage of Ireland. It would be extravagant to say that he did, or tried to do, good to Ireland, merely because Ireland's good was England's wrong. He could have done his ill turns to England equally without the good turns to Ireland. He was not all hate.

But that he was very largely animated by hate we cannot doubt, and part of the wonder about him is that a sentiment so vivid, so deep, and so enduring, ever should have taken such entire possession of a man so cold, so hard, so unimpressionable. It seems to have been one of those cases, of which instances are not rare, of the invasion of a nature generally unresponsive by a single powerful sentiment. And it is just because it is single that it is powerful, having fewer rivals than those which meet and clash in the souls of men more easily and more often invaded and influenced.

Parnell, as everybody knows, this uncrowned King of Ireland, was purely English. It appears that he had not a drop of the Celt in him. His forebears came to Ireland from Cheshire : I think in the time of Charles Stewart's great-grandfather, or a generation earlier. This great-grandfather became Chancellor of the Irish Parliament, and gave up his office because he would not vote for the Act of Union. Irish nationalism, therefore, was at least two generations old in the blood of these quite English Parnells by the time that Charles Stewart came to the fore. His name Stewart he had from his mother, who was an American. A brother of the Chancellor's

C. S. PARNELL.

great-grandfather was a member of the English
Government, and it was he that brought the title of
Lord Congleton into the family. Somewhere back
among the branches of the genealogical tree roosted
Thomas Parnell, the poet. Thus the inheritance of
this Parnell of the Eighties was not without its
various distinction. It promised something, but
he would have been a gifted prophet who would have
foretold the nature of the product which the promise
bore.

When Charles was at Cambridge it seems that a
thing happened which had consequences quite dis-
proportionate with their cause. We may imagine him,
if we please, a shy, reserved youth, with feelings
sensitive and deep, which he hid under an affected
cynicism of manner. His biography has been
splendidly done in the two volumes by his friend,
Mr. Barry O'Brien. It is so well done, and the
subject is such an interesting one for study, that
after you have named Boswell's *Johnson*, and set
that on a shelf by itself as a thing apart from all
other biographies, you then have to put Barry
O'Brien's on the next shelf below, along with Lock-
hart's *Scott* and very few others. It is great biography.

I do not think that it contradicts such an impression
of the young man at Cambridge as I have tried to
give. But, however that be, it was while he was there
that he heard of an outrage, of what evidently struck
him as an intolerable and an unforgivable outrage,
inflicted on his mother in their Irish home in Wicklow.
She was an American, as aforesaid. She was suspected
of Fenian sympathies. Already, two generations back,
this English family had given cause to know that it
stood for " Ireland for the Irish," by the opposition
of the Non-juring Chancellor to the Act of Union.
While Charles Parnell was away at Cambridge there
had been some Fenian trouble in the neighbourhood

of his home. The Parnells were supposed either to
have concealed Fenians in their house, or documents
of a compromising kind, or weapons. At all events
a search party arrived, insisted on going through
the house, would not be denied entrance everywhere, actually would penetrate into Mrs. Parnell's
own bedroom and turn possible hiding-places upside
down there with sacrilegious hands.

That, at least, is how the young man at Cambridge
received it, when all was related to him. It was
rank sacrilege, and violation of what should have
been the sanctity of his mother's room. It appears
that the act, of no great importance in itself, sank
deep down into the soul of this proud, sensitive, aloof
young fellow. He brooded upon it, probably more
than a little morbidly. It grew to seem a monstrous
thing. Its memory and its infamy influenced his
whole nature. It turned him into a hater, a hater
of the England by whose order this thing had been
done. That, as it appears, has to be taken as in some
sort the key to the enigma of his very extraordinary
mentality and story. It is very strange, but it is
not unprecedented, that a root of bitterness springing
from such a source as this, and implanted in a sensitive
soul at its most impressionable age, should morbidly
affect a whole life. That there was a strain of mor-
bidity in Parnell's nature it is scarcely possible to
doubt. He showed, again and again, a ruthlessness,
not only towards England, but towards the people
of his own adopted, and, in spite of all, as I believe,
his beloved Ireland, which certainly was not normal.
They were traits of which he had already given
evidence in boyhood. He was a cricketer, apt to
assume all such captaincy as might be conceded to
him, for he was masterful and dogmatic. Also he
was litigious and pugnacious, exacting, like Sarah
Battle, the rigour of the game. If an incoming

batsman exceeded by a second the two minutes' interval allowed since the outgoing of his predecessor, he claimed the wicket at once, and with insistence.

In such sort the boy was father to the man. Then he was nervous and excitable. He was apt to sleep-walking. All this is evidence of a hyperæsthesia which may have taken on that cloak of cynical callousness in some measure as a protection.

The men of the search party that invaded his mother's bedroom do not seem to have found anything to incriminate any one, unless it were a sword belonging to Charles, which they took away with them. What he wanted with, or what right he had to, the sword I do not know, but probably the taking of it from him was as another coal laid on the fire of his wrath. And what finally kindled all into a white heat which never cooled during his life, was the treatment—namely, the death penalty—meted out to certain of the Fenians, whose only offence, a mere nothing in the eyes of Ireland, was that they had killed a sergeant of the Constabulary. A howl of execration rose up in all the South of Ireland, and translated itself into lurid words in the papers, at this perfectly just sentence, as I presume that it was. But, of course, what appealed to the young Parnell was the howl, and not the justice. After that, he determined that he would go into Parliament and would do—much as in fact he did, though, of course, he had not formed any detailed plan in his mind. He made plans slowly. He spoke with difficulty. One might draw a certain queer, but not inapt, comparison between him and Lord Hartington in their mental processes. Both were slow of thought and slow to act, preferring silence to speech; both exceedingly resolute, even to death, when their slow minds were resolved. Parnell, to be sure, gave the impression, and had the fame, of a far more clever man than Hartington, slow of thought though both men were ; but the difference was that Parnell, intently concentrated on the one great interest of his life, had always thought out beforehand any incident bearing on it. He was never caught unprepared. Hartington, on the other hand, with a far less absorbed interest in the political subjects in which his position and sense of duty obliged him to engage, began his study of each new incident or problem as and when it came into his purview for decision. It was thus a long while before he was prepared with his answer or scheme. Parnell, having foreseen each event, had his answer and scheme already thought out in all like cases.

I do not know about Parnell being honest, as Hartington was. He proved himself more than once perfectly capable of that of which the Cavendishes, as a family, were said to be incapable—telling a lie. But he was, I think, if we may say so, an honest liar. I do not believe that he would tell a lie on trivial occasions to deceive a friend, but I also believe that there is no lie that he would not tell, no promise that he would not break, either to friend or foe, if the occasion was the furtherance of a cause which he had at his heart. He would be quite unscrupulous then.

So he resolved to go into Parliament, with such a programme in his mind as all this suggests ; and after a rejection or two he was elected—in 1875. It is curious how everything worked to intensify Parnell's hate of England. He found himself, though pure English, looked down on as an Irishman at Cambridge ; he found the Irish Party looked down on ,as a thing of naught, in the English Parliament. What attracted the Fenians to this young outlander, shy, difficult of speech, and seemingly timid, was that he would stand up in the English Parliament and, firmly and coldly, though with stammering eloquence, maintain his equal right with the best English member, even of the Front Bench.

He spoke little and read little, and his thought did not travel a wide range ; but he thought a great deal for all that, and it was thought concentrated within a small circle, namely the best means of making the voice of Ireland heard in the English Parliament, the best way of embarrassing the English Parliament until it should listen to that voice, and also the best means to employ outside the House in order to achieve that liberty without which Ireland never could be free of the humiliation that England stamped upon her. Those were his aims and the objects of his thought—thought, cool, slow, wise, so far as means to obtain these ends were concerned—and the Irish Party in the House and the Fenians outside it very quickly perceived that they had in their midst one who was entirely unlike themselves, yet one who was devotedly attached to their own aims ; and they realised, too, that, largely on account of his unlikeness to the rest, and of the qualities in which his difference consisted, he was the man to lead them.

His own manner never gave the slightest reason to doubt but that he thought so, too. He treated them with a frank contempt which, while it galled them, yet disposed them to accord the superiority which he so obviously and even so offensively claimed. At least, they could say among themselves, he is no less offensively superior in his manner towards the Englishmen too, and that is how we like to see them treated. He treated the leader of his own Party. Mr. Butt, in just the same manner. Against all Butt's instructions and injunctions, he obstructed business in Parliament and incited others, especially Biggar, who could speak from dewy eve to early morn, if need were, to obstruct also. When Butt

3

publicly rebuked him, he kissed the rod smilingly, in the knowledge that Butt's rebuke in the English House, and the sympathy with which the House heard it, were the undoing of Butt in the eyes of Ireland.

All that, however, happened before the Eighties. By 1880 Butt was dead, Parnell was the acknowledged leader of the Irish Party ; he was also President of the Land League, and it was in this year that he went to America, making speeches and arousing much enthusiasm for Home Rule. He invented the ingenious, the devilish, and the effective device to which Captain Boycott, the agent of Lord Erne, had the unfortunate distinction of lending his name. In the following year the Government arrested him and threw him into Kilmainham gaol. With coercive measures in full force it is not very obvious what else they could have done. To imprison subordinates and leave him at large would not have been very logical. But it had the effect of increasing his influence with the more extreme of the Irishmen. They had complained of his " moderation," but the fact that the British Government proved its sense of his dangerous qualities by imprisoning him did not endorse the view of him as a " moderate " man. He came out of Kilmainham with his position greatly strengthened.

It was early in 1882 that the Government, despairing of the effects of their Coercion Act, released him, but there followed only a short interval before the passing of the Crimes Act, as a sequel to the tragedy, in Phœnix Park, when Lord Frederick Cavendish, the Chief Secretary, was murdered with Mr. Burke, the Under Secretary. It is said that the murderous attack was intended on the latter only, and that the former suffered purely from the unhappy accident of being in his company at the time.

There can be small doubt to-day that Parnell was terribly distressed. A little later, when he had to go through his famous trial, with the forged letters of the infamous Pigott as evidence of his active approval of outrageous crimes, there was a section of the British public prepared to deem him capable of the worst of them, and even to have known beforehand of the proposed attack on the Castle officials, and to have acquiesced in it. With the exposure of the forgeries in the letters and Parnell's inevitable acquittal, the weight of the worst suspicion was lifted. Burne-Jones, who went to see the trial, said that Parnell's face in aspect was Christlike ! But some portion of the suspicion, no doubt, continued to prevail. Persons who would not take the trouble of studying the most patent facts would still throw out dark hints. It was a case of some of the mud sticking. Forster, in the House, vehemently and acrimoniously accused him of implicity in crimes and outrage very soon after the Phœnix Park incident, and it took all the persuasions of his friends to induce Parnell to make any reply or reference at all to the accusation. When he did, at length, yield to those persuasions, the form of his reply was in effect a declaration of contemptuous indifference to a charge coming from such a source and brought before such a Court. He virtually denied the right of the English House of Commons to sit in judgment; said, roundly, that he did not care a scrap for their verdict, that it was to Ireland only that he looked for approval of his actions, and for Ireland's sake that all were done. He did just say that it was the merest moonshine to suppose that he could have any connection with the campaign of violence, or could imagine that Ireland's cause could be in any way helped by it ; but he said it in such a way as to convey the impression that it was a purely incidental statement, that he regarded it as hardly worth the making, and as so obvious that none but a fool could require it to be affirmed. Of course the whole scornful tone of the speech made the worst possible impression on the House. Equally of course, and just because of the bad impression which it made there, it created the strongest possible impression in Parnell's favour in Ireland—which is what he cared about. He was not, really, addressing himself to the English House of Commons in this so-called " defence " : his words were meant for the people of Ireland and for the Irish in America ; and by them they were welcomed and cherished. That was the right way to talk to the House of Commons—to show them that you did not care a pin for them or their opinion of your actions. Here was a man ready to do all and dare all for Ireland's sake. Parnell had foreseen it. He was an extraordinary Parliamentary tactician.

A little later we find almost all the leading English statesmen in turn coquetting with him, each trying whether the Irish leader could be brought to fall in with his own pet scheme of extension of local government for Ireland, or Home Rule in one or other of its more limited senses—Chamberlain, Bright, Randolph Churchill, Hartington a little, finally Mr. Gladstone going farther than all the rest¹ and at length producing something with which Parnell was graciously pleased to express himself moderately satisfied. It was a measure of satisfaction which would leave room for the entry of an Oliver Twist-like demand for more of the same kind very shortly. Meanwhile had taken place that short-lived alliance of Home Rulers with Tories, when Lord Carnarvon was Lord-Lieutenant, of which Mr. (now Lord) Morley spoke to a friend of mine as " an unholy alliance." Unholy or not, it was not of long duration. Mr.

Gladstone, with his proposals going so much farther towards meeting Irish demands, outbid all that the Tories dared offer, and the Home Rulers returned to stand by the Liberals again in a brotherhood to which Mr. Morley was able to give his unqualified blessing.

And all these wooers, no matter what success or ill-success they met with from the Great Coquette, for that is a title which Mr. Parnell thoroughly well deserves, came back with one single chief impression. " What chiefly struck you about Parnell ? " you asked. The answer of one and all was the same : " His silence."

It was quite a just answer. He had it—the gift of silence—almost beyond any other man who was in any degree intellectual. It was a great source of strength to him. Men always wonder and speculate, and fear a little, about the thoughts that are going on in the brain of a man who does not utter them, and generally, in all probability, they attribute to the unspoken thoughts a subtlety and depth which they might not be found to equal if they were brought to the utterance. Even with Mr. Gladstone, whom he came into more accord with than any of the others, his silence was remarkable. He was invited to Hawarden, and went there. I was given an account of what happened by a fellow-guest. " It was wonderful," said the raconteur, naturally falling into a cricketing metaphor ; " Mr. Gladstone kept bowling him half-volleys all the time, but Parnell never stepped out to one once. He hardly answered. He said hardly anything at all."

Nevertheless the visit was quite a success, in the sense that all were disposed to like him, although all felt that there was something a little uncanny and scarcely human about him and his reserve. There are two words, often coupled in our English

conversation, which certainly Parnell went through
life using less frequently than any other known
man who has possessed the gift of words so long.
Those two words were " Thank you." He had
a capacity, which amounted to genius, of refraining
from saying " Thank you." It had the effect of
making men feel, when they had done something
for him, or made some concession to him, that they
had not done enough, or, at least, not as much as
he had expected. It was irritating. It perhaps
irritated them to give him more in order to see
whether they could not wring a word of gratitude
out of this irresponsive being. But they could not.
Ingratitude is the independence of the heart. Parnell, intellectually a creature of strange independence,
was independent no less, or even more, on the senti-
mental side. Once he was in money difficulties.
Mortgagees were foreclosing on his patrimony. The
debt was some thirteen thousand pounds. He was
always careless of money, and probably most of the
debt was incurred through political ways of dis-
bursement. Be that how it may, his friends opened
a subscription to pay off the indebtedness and save
his estate. Enthusiastic admirers subscribed up
to something like forty thousand pounds, mostly
in small sums and from small people. " Parnell's
tribute," it was called. He was presented with the
cheque just before a great political meeting in the
Rotunda, so that he might have a convenient opportunity of giving thanks to the people for this wonderful offering. He stuck the cheque in his pocket ;
he addressed the people on the political situation ;
and he never said a word in reference to the cheque
at all, or showed the smallest sign of gratitude for it !
It might never have been given. Surely his was an
independent heart !
But if the many wooers got but little out of this

unpromising Penelope—after all, that most famous
classic instance has some right to contest with him
the title of the Great Coquette—no one can well
say how much he was getting from them the while.
There is not a doubt that he was learning, learning,
learning. He was a man who read little, but learnt,
as he silently listened, from the words of men, and
thought much on what he heard. He learnt how
to deal with men—not men only in their common
humanity, but with each man according to his individual difference. And he learnt just how far
each man and each party, and each little group within a party, was prepared to go in the direction of
giving to Ireland (for the sake of the peace which his
obstructive methods had made them yearn for as
men yearn only for that which they find to be very
hard to get) that which he deemed that she required.
It was knowledge which enabled him to take the
utmost advantage of every occasion as it arose, and
to judge to a nicety how far he might go, or might
permit others of his party to go, in way of insult
to the Mother of Parliaments before the spokesman
of the great mother would suspend them from further
present opportunity of insult.

We all know, of course, what the result was of
Mr. Gladstone's wooing. The Great Coquette dis-
missed all other wooers when he found that Gladstone
was ready to yield. The alliance was struck ; with
what result we are aware : the introduction of the
Home Rule Bill of 1886, the schism of the Liberal
Party, the formation of the Unionist Party, the re-
jection of the Bill, the General Election, and the
return to power—to overwhelming power—of the
Unionists. The figures read : " Unionists, with
Conservatives, 393 " ; " Gladstonian Liberals, with
Irish, 275." Just as Hartington had announced to
Gorst, " Well, Gorst, your damned Education Bill's

dead," so now the country said, with equal decision, to Mr. Gladstone, " Well, Gladstone, your damned Home Rule Bill's dead."

It was dead, and dead, too, therewith, all hopes in Parnell's mind—if ever he had hopes (which is most doubtful)—of Home Rule for Ireland passing the English Parliament. Obstruction had proved a useful weapon. It had achieved the end of compelling the House to turn its eyes attentively on the small group of Irishmen which it had theretofore been able to disregard. But really it had not been much more than an irritant. Some counter to it was sure to be raised, and was devised in the form of the " Closure." Hereafter neither Biggar nor Sexton, nor any of those extraordinary word-weavers, might weave interminably. In a House with a Unionist majority of 118 the little Irish group could carry no weight to tilt a scale. The situation had the air of *impasse*.

So Parnell seems to have felt it. He attempted a Land Bill, probably knowing it was doomed to failure. He prophesied, before its rejection, that if it did not pass violence and disorder would follow. It was thrown out, and, true to prophecy, the Plan of Campaign, and all that it involved, was the sequence. At this time Parnell, doubtless, was very weary of the struggle. Some tried to incriminate him as the originator of the deliberate series of outrages due to the Plan, and of its very organisation. As a matter of fact the truth appears to be that he was too ill a man and too harassed a man to have any fight or desire for fight left in him. Now and again the old fighting spirit would flare up and drive the worn machine, but it was rather a flickering and fitful business. He realised, too, that not only he, but his Ireland, needed above and before all else peace and rest. So to deem him the soul of the Plan of

Campaign was as absurd as to deem him the instigator
or accomplice of the Phœnix Park murders.   He
deplored these acts of violence, not on account of
their violence, but on account of their ill-advisedness
at the moment.

It was the moment when the *Times* published
those articles, " Parnellism and Crime," which led
to the appointment of the " Parnell Commission "—
Justices Hannen, Day, and A. L. Smith—to the
evident and incontrovertible proof of the forgery
of the published " facsimile " letter, to the suicide of
the forger Pigott, to the triumphant acquittal of
Parnell.

There followed a time, in the reaction, when he was
made a kind of pet in Liberal circles—a curious pet,
whom all petted and stroked, but who never gave
back a purr in response.   He was received with
heart-rending enthusiasm at a dinner of the Eighty
Club, such statesmen as Lord Spencer and Lord
Rosebery making very much of him.   There was
only one heart which did not seem moved by the
enthusiasm—Parnell's.   He was still frigid.

Then fell the bombshell of the O'Shea affair,
explosively.

Of course it was no new affair : it had been there,
a known fact to his friends, in the background of
Parnell's life, for years.   But suddenly it exploded.
No one did not know of it.   What should the Party
do ?

That was the question which was agitated in
Committee Room 15, Parnell himself in the chair,
conducting the case against himself in a position of
official impartiality, yet straining points to his advantage in all the spirit that he showed when captain
of a cricket eleven and claiming the wicket of the
opponent who did not come to the crease within the
statutory two minutes.   So the question was voted

on, and the decision was cast : the Party would be faithful ; they could not part from their old leader.

But they had reckoned, and had voted, without their great new ally, Gladstone, and his conscience. He and his conscience take counsel together : they call in Morley to their debates, and the result is a letter saying that Mr. Gladstone can no longer remain leader of the Liberal Party if Mr. Parnell remain leader of the Irish, that Party's ally.

Again there is debated the question in Committee Room 15. The old question is re-opened. And this time, in spite of the fighting of the leader, in spite of his influence and his ancient fame, the vote, taken anew, goes otherwise. A majority secede, scared by the Gladstone letter, which had found its way into the papers. Parnell, if a leader at all, leads only a minority. The Party—that is, the majority— is under McCarthy. It is the end, and a sad and rather squalid end, withal.

Politically speaking it is actually his death. He glimmered up again, with new-found energy, over the Kilkenny election. But what could it matter ? He was wearied to death, worn out with fighting, with illness of a rheumatic kind, with all the harassing and the *débacle* that the wretched O'Shea entanglement brought. He still kept the frigid, proud face to the world, but the man was done. At, or soon after, the Kilkenny election he caught a chill. Of course he took no care. He would not have been himself had he cared. He travelled with the chill on him. In time he sickened and died, a finished man, though not by any means an old man, in the autumn of 1891.

Certainly he allowed himself no chance. The cynic coldness which gave him that independence of heart, with all that it brought him of power, and the little that it brought him of love, he extended

even to himself. For himself he had as little tenderness as for another. One desperate human passion
we must admit that he had, and must wonder at
it and deplore it : wonder at it the more because of
the tragic cost at which he clung to it, wonder at its
white-hot intensity in a nature generally, or at
least apparently, so cold.

But there we touch perhaps the ultimate question
of the nature, of the personality. Was it a nature
really cold, or was it, as happens, a nature, on the
contrary, singularly sensitive and tender, which had
taken on, as a mask and a defence, the armour of
an affected callousness, firm-riveted with the strength
of an unusually determined will ?

I do not know the answer: I only suggest the question.
I incline to believe this to be the true key to that
very extraordinary character. There is some evidence
in its support ; for example, that morbid nervousness
indicated by his sleep-walking as a boy. Moreover,
he did retain a tenderness for one at least of his family
—his mother. He would telegraph to her, telling
her not to worry, saying that he was all right. A son
with no sympathetic feeling does not trouble to do
that. That he was a " good " man, in any conventional sense, most assuredly I am not claiming for
him. I have already recorded his cynicism in regard
to truth, where untruth would serve his ends. Before
the Parnell Commission he frankly and unblushingly
admitted that the reason why he had made a false
statement was that it might mislead the House of
Commons. The irony of that admission is that, in
point of fact, he was mistaken in giving that account
of it. The true fact had slipped his memory—namely
that he had made the statement in respect to certain
secret societies only, and not, as it was interpreted,
with the intention of its application to all like societies
in Ireland. But that is a detail of no moment : the

interesting point is his careless indifference to a trifle such as purposely and by false statement misleading the English Parliament.   It is highly characteristic.

Certainly, unless it were Mrs. O'Shea, Parnell had none, so far as one may discover, whom we may call, in any sense at all intimate, his friend ; none to whom he unbosomed his thoughts so that they might tell us what manner of man he really was.   To those closest about him he remained a sphinx.

A singular trait in his nature, as it appears on the surface, is his superstition.   Religion seems to have had no grip on him whatever, but he was genuinely gripped by superstitions, childish and Celtic, even if he had no other quality of the Celt.   When he was very ill he aroused himself hurriedly to blow out a third candle which one had lighted who was writing a political document at his bedside, just because three candles was the number that are lighted about the corpse laid out for a " wake."   The ill-luck that the triple illumination must bring he could not bear.   Similarly, he would have none of another document of like kind in which the clauses were thirteen.   It could have no fortune.   The clauses must be cut to twelve or stretched to fourteen.

It sounds scarcely credible, but his very faithful biographer, Mr. O'Brien, sets both instances down as indubitably true.   We cannot doubt them.   But may we not see in them again some witness to that view of his extraordinary character which I have suggested ?   I would not press them, but I think that they are not without significance.   That Charles Stewart Parnell was a good man, as I have said, few will claim ; that he had elements of greatness, very few, I think, can doubt

CHAPTER V

JOHN BRIGHT

THERE can be little question that of all those who deserted Mr. Gladstone's banner when he carried it into his Home Rule campaign in 1886, the squire whose loss was most grievous and most costly to him was Mr. Bright. Mr. Bright's, of course, was a name to conjure with in the Sixties and earlier—in the days of Cobden, the Manchester School, the Corn Laws, and so on. It really needed some such impetus as the leading of his chieftain into what he deemed the perilous country of Home Rule to make Mr. Bright reveal himself as still a great power, capable of influencing the thoughts and the votes of large numbers.

There has been some misunderstanding as to what Mr. Bright actually did at the time of the Home Rule schism. Very careless readers of events have assumed that he was a member of Mr. Gladstone's Government, and that he left it, to join the new Unionist Party, on account of irreconcilable difference of opinion about Irish matters, the actual fact being that he threw up his office some four years earlier, because he found himself utterly unable to approve of that " forward " policy in Egypt which led up to the bombardment of Alexandria in the days of Arabi Pasha. It was impossible for Mr. Bright, with his peace-loving character, to agree in any policy that could be termed forward, except under clear and stern necessity for its forwardness ; and it was equally

45

impossible for his truth-loving character to acquiesce, even tacitly, in any policy opposed to his principles of right and wrong. Therefore he resigned office, so as to express his disapproval of the Government's action and to play no part in it.

These being the facts of the case, it has happened that some readers of events, only one degree less careless than those who imagine that he left the Cabinet on the Home Rule question, have gone to the other extreme of error and, knowing that it was not in consequence of the Home Rule Bill that he left the Government, have assumed in their haste that he took no part at all in that debate and its immediate consequences, and that he counted for nothing in the result. Very far from that, he probably, though not in the Cabinet at the time of the bringing in of the Bill, counted far more than any other single man, not so much, perhaps, in its rejection, as in the ulti-mate sequence to that rejection—which was the appeal to the country, and the General Election which brought in the Unionists with preponderating power. Though Mr. Bright had quitted the Government on the Egyptian policy, he had not, on that account, gone out of politics nor out of Parliament. He was still a faithful follower of Mr. Gladstone, though not active as heretofore in the councils of the Govern-ment ; his fidelity was of long trial and was fully trusted ; it still remained to be shown that it had a breaking point beyond which it could not hold.

To many, as I have said already, fidelity to Mr. Gladstone—the personal fidelity—had come to take the place of fidelity to principles and convictions. Mr. Gladstone had become their principle. It never was so with Mr. Bright. No man had a more exalted opinion of Mr. Gladstone—and that is a very great deal to say—than he, and there was one respect in which he rated Mr. Gladstone higher than any other

(*From a photograph by Messrs. Elliott & Fry.*)

JOHN BRIGHT.

man in the country, as I imagine, rated him. For beautiful eloquence and power of oratory in its finest and widest sense, there was only one man, I believe, of all those who had heard both statesmen speak, and thus had the opportunity to judge of them, who rated Mr. Gladstone above Mr. Bright. All others arranged them in the opposite order of merit : Mr. Bright first, Mr. Gladstone second. The one exception, the one man who put Mr. Gladstone first, was Mr. Bright. I think it is Justin McCarthy who recorded that Bright waxed quite angry with him for suggesting that he, Bright, was a finer orator than Gladstone. He at once began quoting passages from Mr. Gladstone's speeches to prove the contrary. Most of us find it enough to say, in respectful admiration of the powers of both, that, other points of comparison apart, Bright had none of the verboseness which often impaired the grandeur of Mr. Gladstone's periods. By that alone Bright is at once established, where the competition might in other points be a close one, as the superior. One speaks, of course, of the comparative merits in set speech. In debate, strong and witty as Mr. Bright would be at times, Mr. Gladstone, immensely more experienced, was also immensely more powerful and trenchant.

In spite, however, of this lofty and in one regard at least exaggerated estimate of Mr. Gladstone's gifts and genius, Bright's character was too strong and too firm in its conviction ever to accept a personal fidelity in lieu of a principle for his guide. Where he could no longer agree, he had the courage and the independence instantly to assert a difference of opinion, and, faithful to that opinion, to part company. He had sat and voted as a Liberal in the years between the Alexandria business in 1882 and the Home Rule business in 1886. He had spoken seldom : he seldom did speak except on great issues. Little issues did

not appeal to his very practical turn of mind, neither
did eloquence for its own sake, though he was so great
a master of it, interest him at all. He never spoke
for speaking's sake, but always for the sake of the
cause he was pleading. All this was part of that
simple sincerity which he reverenced above all other
qualities in politics. It was part of the reason for his
profound reverence of the chief whom his convictions
drove him to desert, that Mr. Gladstone was so
deeply sincere and earnest.

Just because he had spoken little and had not
shown greatly in the forefront of the battle, people
in the country had ceased to think much of Bright :
he was fading out of the fickle mind of the multitude.
Then came the Home Rule challenge, as we may call
it, of the trusted chief. It was as a gage thrown down
by way of a test to faith. Who would accept it ?
How would it be taken ? There is little doubt that
Mr. Gladstone was sadly disappointed at its reception.
His personal influence was very powerful, but it
was not quite all that he had believed it to be. Perhaps that is hardly a fair statement of the case ;
perhaps we should say, rather, that he believed so
implicitly in the justice of the Home Rule cause,
once he had made it his own—it was his custom,
and a prime source of his ability to bend men to his
view, to deem thus of all causes which commended
themselves to his own conviction—that he could not
conceive it possible that others would not come to a
like opinion when he explained to them his grounds
for it. That probably, rather than any egotistic
idea of his personal power over them, persuaded him
that he would be followed faithfully. There were a
few, naturally, of whom there was doubt. No one
expected Hartington to come down any untried by-
ways at the bidding of any chief. But of Bright
there was some reason to think, questions of leadership

quite apart, that a Home Rule policy for Ireland would meet views to which he had already given expression. He was always the friend of the oppressed, always in favour of liberty. He had already shown himself sympathetic with the sufferings of Ireland and anxious to relieve them. All this, however, was before his leaving the Cabinet, and at least one significant incident had happened since which might have shown that Mr. Bright was not likely to support a measure calculated to throw power into the hands of men so likely to abuse it as the chief men of the Irish Party had proved themselves—even as far back as 1883. In the House of Commons he had spoken of them as " an Irish rebel party," and had taunted the Conservatives for seeking alliance with them. The taunt was fiercely resented. Sir Stafford Northcote moved a resolution declaring it to be a breach of privilege, and only failed in carrying it by a small balance of votes. All possible advertisement and publicity, therefore, had been given to Mr. Bright's probable attitude and action in view of the proposals of 1886 ; but still, in consequence of his earlier sympathies with Irish struggles, and even with some of the less dangerous of the Fenian activities, it seems to have been generally thought that he would be content to follow his old leader into the lobby on a division. Certainly, whatever doubt faithful Gladstonians may have felt as to his attitude, they had little anticipation of the energy of action into which he was quickly roused.

The truth is that while Mr. Bright was so ardent a lover of liberty, he was at least as warmly devoted to peace and order, and that devotion had been tried beyond the breaking point by the disorderly and lawless proceedings which the Irish Party did not trouble themselves to disavow. The violence, which they did not even attempt to control, in Ireland had

4

alienated him, had changed him from friend to foe,
and it was a costly loss to the cause of Irish independence. At several meetings in the country he employed all the force of his eloquence to plead the
maintenance of the Union under the old conditions,
and to oppose the solution suggested by Mr.Gladstone.
His eloquence alone might have accomplished much ;
his personality and the value which men placed on
his judgment achieved far more. Here was an
avowed lover of liberty in the abstract, and one who
had given much of his life to working for its sake—
one, too, who had proved himself Ireland's friend—
most strongly hostile to this measure to give Ireland
freedom. What was the obvious inference to be
drawn ? It was known that no consideration of
party or of profit could weigh with him. Only
one conclusion could be reached, that something
must be radically wrong with the measure itself,
the objections to it must be very grave, if a man of
Mr. Bright's character and disposition could find
nothing to recommend in it and very much to condemn. There is no doubt whatever that his attitude,
his speeches, and his writings, determined the attitude
of a great number of the electors, and largely helped
to bring in the Liberal-Unionist and Conservative
coalition on the flowing tide.

And whatever men thought of Mr. Bright's political
action at that time, whether it surprised them or
merely fulfilled their expectations, all were astonished
by the almost youthful fire and vehemence with which
he both voiced his views and uttered them in letters.
Those who remembered his eloquence in the troublous
days of the Corn Laws maintained that it had lost
little of its old quality, and were more than a little
superior. They were surprised, not because Mr.
Bright, in the Eighties, was a very old man—the
last year of the decade saw his death, and he was

born in the year 1811—but there was surprise, because his powers, when he did make a public appearance, had seemed to be failing, or at least to have no great driving force behind them. Dr. Dale has written of him, as recorded in the *Encyclopædia Britannica*, in reference to his speech when he took the Rectorship of Glasgow University, " It was not the old Bright "; and, Dr. Dale adds, Mr. Bright told him at the time, " I am weary of public speaking. My mind is almost a blank."

This was in 1882. Of course it gives an exaggerated account of his state of mental apathy, but constitutionally, in spite of all the great work that he did, he was accounted by his friends and co-workers as an indolent man. He had no personal ambition. No adequate driving force therefore, in these days, as age came upon him, was there to incite him. He did, in all probability, fall into a relative apathy. But then, of a sudden, he was like the old horse hearing the hunting horn once again—he saw a cause which called forth his enthusiasm, his mental energy and all his faculties, and he took all the fences with the zeal of a young one. And although all his eloquence and persuasion were thrown into the balance against the larger independence of Ireland, this was not because he loved Ireland less, but because he had regretfully come to the conclusion that the time for such relative independence was not yet, but that her freedom, as proposed by Mr. Gladstone, would be a menace both to herself and to the United Kingdom.

Yet it would not be fair comment to say, therefore, that he changed. Consistency is perhaps a doubtful virtue in a statesman : it is at least a doubtfully good master when it is allowed to take the mastery ; and the idea that it behoves him to be consistent at all costs has been the bane of many a man's true judgment. But Mr. Bright was absolutely consistent throughout his career. It would be difficult to name a man who changed less. Even in outward aspect, and even in the fashion of his garment, he changed very little. It was always something like the garb of the Nonconformist minister—frock-coat, little tie, and so on—at the farthest remove possible from that of the sportsman or the country gentleman, with the former of whom, at least, he had no sympathy whatever. He was a man of cities, and typical perhaps of the provincial cities rather than of the metropolis.

From all portraits and caricatures of him, which were many, and from all that his contemporaries tell us, he must have worn the look of a man of middle age while he was still young. His fashion of shaving the mouth and leaving a fringe of whiskers and beard framing the face made him look older than his years, and he maintained this style to the end. The fringe grew whiter, and perhaps he wore his hair rather longer, so that he came to seem somewhat like a venerable and benevolent old lion maned in grey; but it was the fashion to wear the hair rather long, even in his young days, so he did not alter much even in that regard.

And as he had the aspect of comparative age while yet a youth, so, certainly, he came early to the possession of wisdom and to the acceptance of the highest principles as the guide of his actions. By religious conviction he was, of course, nonconformist. His father, Jacob Bright, was a Quaker, a cotton-miller of Rochdale, and at sixteen years of age John was already in the business. All his early training was in the ways of sobriety, carefulness, and godliness, and he never departed from these paths throughout life. Literary and philosophic questions attracted him from the first, and it may be that but for Cobden's influence and invitation he would never have gone into public life at all. So soon, however, as the Anti-

Corn Law cause had once made its appeal to him he found it irresistible, and gave all his great gift of oratory to its service. From henceforth British politics demanded him, claimed him, and could not allow such power to go unused. This son of the Quaker, the sect of silent listeners, waiting for the inspiration, discovered himself the possessor of an oratory which England had long lost, and which, it may be said, she has not found again since his death. The appreciation of Lord Salisbury, not a man given to extravagant praise, has been often quoted, and it cannot well be bettered : " He was the greatest master of English oratory that his generation—I may say several generations—has seen. At a time when much speaking has depressed, has almost exterminated eloquence, he maintained that robust, powerful, and vigorous style in which he gave fitting expression to the burning and noble thoughts he desired to utter."

CHAPTER VI

MR. CHAMBERLAIN was one of those about whose probable action there was much speculation when Mr. Gladstone declared for the great adventure. On the one hand it was known that he had been not adverse to a liaison with the Political Penelope, provided always it could be on lines of his own dictation. That is to say, that he was in favour of according to Ireland a far more liberal measure of self-government than she enjoyed, but at the same time had never declared himself prepared to go the length proposed in 1886 by Mr. Gladstone. The Great Coquette had not repelled those half-hearted advances, no doubt rating them the while at their true value—and no higher. No liaison had been formed ; at the best it may be said to have been but a promising flirtation.

Nevertheless it sufficed to indicate the bent of Mr. Chamberlain's thought. Being willing, of his own initiative, to go thus far, might he not, under the impulse of the great leader's example, go with him to the end ? That was how the question was debated, until Mr. Chamberlain himself, at an early stage in the proposals, gave it a decisive answer. He resigned his office of President of the Board of Trade and withdrew from a Government of whose policy he could not approve. It was said that it was the specific proposals in regard to the Irish land,

(From a photograph by Messrs. Russell & Sons.)

JOSEPH CHAMBERLAIN.

rather than to the general government of that country, to which he took particular objection. Be that how it may, he did not hesitate. He seized the earliest opportunity afforded by the great debate initiated by Mr. Gladstone on April 8th, to make his intention clear, and therewith to make it clear that it was final.

The defection of Mr. Chamberlain was a blow nothing like so severe as that of Mr. Bright's hostility to the Home Rule measure, but it was grave, for he had already assured his position in the country. It was a position not quite like that of any other statesman. He was in no sense a democrat. Modern Socialistic theories would have dismayed him. But by one means or other, and chiefly perhaps by some masterful qualities of honesty, courage, and clear vision, he had impressed his personality on that great mass of common sense, so immensely wiser than we should expect from the folly of its individual factors, which we call British public opinion. He had attributes and gifts which his acute countenance, with its very obvious resemblance, in the rather aggressive nose and other facial angles, to Pitt, did not suggest, nor was there suggestion of great qualities in the inevitable eye-glass and the no less inevitable orchid. His qualities, however, are most justly to be called great, seeing that, over and above those already named, they included both sympathy and imagination.

It was not unnatural that when he first came into the House, " a Birmingham tradesman " as he was described—in point of fact, partner in a big industry in that town—the cynic prophecy should be made, " will turn Conservative and get a peerage." In part the prophecy was fulfilled, though he was perhaps rather pushed into the paths of the Tories than chose them of his own free will. On the defeat of the Home Rule Liberals a coalition between the seceders and the more advanced of the Conservatives almost necessarily followed. Mr. Chamberlain had his personal ambitions no doubt, but very early in his career he gave evidence of his sympathy with the working people, and he never lost that sympathy. With Abou ben Ahmed, you might write him as one who loved his fellow men.

Somehow, by virtue of that insight or that inspiration which is so inexplicable, yet so indubitable, a conviction of this characteristic of him had penetrated into the public opinion of the nation. The working man believed in this monocled and buttonholed gentleman with the sharp features as his friend, and a useful, valiant, and forceful friend withal. He was not long in the House before giving it cause to know the fine edge of his debating weapons. Within a short while the people supplemented the conviction of his sympathy with their cause by a further conviction of the rightness of his judgment. In a word, they believed in him.

I very well remember, a few years after the Home Rule split, dining at one of the big restaurants with a small party, among which was the wife of one of the Liberal Ministers. Though she was a firm and faithful lover of her party, she had an eye for humour, on whichever side it was to be found. We had just passed the throes of a General Election, and one or two were telling stories of election experiences. Then she came out with this : " I overheard two working men talking, when they didn't know I was listening. One asked the other whom he was going to vote for, and the other said, ' Well, I'm going to vote for —— old Chamberlain, 'cos he's pretty near always right.' " She gave us the adjective—which I have left decently blank—the most popular and variously used of all in the language, at the pitch of a fearless, clear-ringing voice, which made half the restaurant suddenly turn astonished eyes upon us and disposed me

to an inclination to crawl and hide under the table ;
but it was an admirable expression of the opinion
which the people in general had formed about Chamberlain.

When I told this story some while later to a
Gladstonian Liberal he was very ready to laugh at it ;
" but," he went on, rather petulantly, " it's very funny
that the people have that idea about him, because
as a matter of fact, if you look at his record, you'll
find that he's been pretty nearly always wrong.
There's hardly a measure that he's advocated that's
ever found its way on to the Statute Book."

Perhaps that may be, but even if so, as I might
have pointed out to my friend the Gladstonian who
made the comment, the writing of an Act on the
Statute Book is not a final test of its wisdom.   That
last is a proposition which all party politicians will
readily endorse in its application to the enactments
of their opponents.   Chamberlain, in his time, brought
forward and advocated many a measure and many a
principle which did not pass into our legislation ; but
they may have influenced national opinion and
affected later legislation which did not own its
connection with them, none the less.   George Russell
tells an amusing story of the " three-acres-and-a-
cow " project which Mr. Chamberlain, with Mr. Jesse
Collings, more or less propounded and abetted as
the solution of the agricultural problem.   Every
countryman was to possess his cow and his three acres
on which to feed it : that was the project, stated, or
almost caricatured, in its crudest form.   Of course,
so stated, it is not practical politics, and of course
Chamberlain, though knowing as little as was possible
about cows, and still more Jesse Collings, who was
perfectly intimate with them, knew that it was not ;
but it was taken as an indication of Mr. Chamberlain's
interest in the agricultural labourer, even if he did

not understand the labourer's difficulties. " Three
acres will no keep a coo " was the criticism of the
Scot, who sought to wring a living out of grudging
soil. Acres, as a means of livelihood for cows or
men, are not everywhere the same.

So the project was not practical, but the battle-cry
which it provided was a most useful one. It won
votes, and at a dinner party shortly after the election,
as Mr. Russell tells us, Chamberlain, seeing the figure
of a cow in silver among the ornaments of the table,
apostrophised it : " Oh, you precious animal ! Where
should we be without you ? "

The three acres and a cow were not to be the
salvation of agriculture, but they were the salvation
of the party. Thus Mr. Chamberlain got his roots
well down into the soil of the country and received
much support from it, although he understood it but
slightly, if at all. And long before this, before even
he came up to London and entered the House of
Commons, he had actively interested himself in the
betterment of the working people of Birmingham.
There he received, in return, the support of industry
which he thoroughly understood ; and we may begin
to realise how it was that he struck the popular
opinion in such manner as to receive, whether or
not he deserved, that encomium which the lady in
the restaurant recited in that gay, cheerful voice
which sent shivers down our backs. A little later
again, and he was Colonial Secretary, and in that office
he became identified with a policy which was likely
still more to commend him to the adventurous and
perhaps slightly acquisitive spirit which is one of
the normal characteristics of the Briton. He stood
for " Jingoism " and imperial strength and unity.
We live in a generation which has perhaps forgotten
the very origin of the term " Jingo." I do not refer
to its use as a form of asseveration which all true

lovers of their *Ingoldsby Legends* will trace back to
the shrine of the good " St. Genulphus." I mean
only its later political use as the label, usually affixed
by its opponents, of an aggressive national mood and
action in foreign affairs. It was actually taken, I
believe, from the words of a song sung at the music-
halls to a rather dismal but easily caught tune at
the time when Russia was feared as the great menace
to our power and to the peace both of Europe and of
Asia. So far as my memory serves it went thus :

> " We don't want to fight,
> But, by Jingo, if we do,
> We've got the ships, we've got the men,
> We've got the money, too.
> We've fought the bear before,
> And we'll fight the bear again,
> And the Russians shall not have Constantinople."

" Ople "—if you please—with a very long dwelling
on the " o." The Russians will not, as it appears,
have Constantinople : the gifted composer was correct
in that prophetic affirmation ; but it was not due to
our arms that that unfortunate bear did not get it.
His own claws were sufficiently effective weapons
for his destruction without our ships and men and
money. But this foolish chorus gives the explanation
of the manner in which that term " Jingo " came
into use to designate the kind of mood which Kipling
was to stigmatise a little later as the mood of the
" frantic boast." Chamberlain, identifying himself
with that Imperialism which would draw close the
bonds between mother country and colonies, Chamberlain, almost the only man of his day to try to put
himself into the place of the Colonials, so as to see both
Colonial and Imperial problems with the Colonial eye,
Chamberlain, in fact, as first to realise the enormous
and essential importance of the Colonies of the
British Empire if it was to do that task in the world

which appeared to be ordained for it, became the modern and living re-incarnation of St. Genulphus. For most men he was, in himself, " the living Jingo."

It was an estimate which, though none higher could possibly be conceived by those who formed it of him, did him nevertheless, as I am convinced, a great injustice. I do not believe for a moment that Chamberlain had any adventurous or acquisitive ideas or ideals. The notion that he would be in any real and effective sense at the back of that puerile attempt at brigandage called the "Jameson raid," is patently absurd, yet there was a considerable section that held it as an article of faith for months, if not for years. He was far too clear-sighted to desire for Great Britain that she should extend her burdens beyond those already imposed on her, even if the prospect of extension were a far more beguiling one than that abortive effort in the neighbourhood of Johannesburg. But he was earnest in his aspirations that she should at least receive some return from the burdens, that she should make them a source of strength, if possible, not of weakness ; and he saw that this could happen only on the condition that the links which should bind the children to the mother were real and of mutual advantage. He thrust the Colonial question into the forefront of the battle on every possible occasion, in pursuance of this end, endeavouring to obtain the best solution of it. Thus he became associated in men's minds with all that was most assertive and aggressive in foreign affairs, for he would stand no truck with a foreign power which seemed inclined to interfere with or to limit the Imperial unity. And truly he was assertive and aggressive enough in those conditions, but he cherished no ideas of " world dominion." He knew that Great Britain had fully enough of the world and of its " white man's burden " for her

share, but he desired that she should be free to deal
with her own in her own way.   He was ready to cry
" Hands off ! " to any that tried to meddle with her,
and ready to fight to the death if they would not
heed the cry.   And such a man, from Palmerston
onward—and backward too, for the matter of that—
has always appealed to the British spirit, were he
right or were he wrong.

So Chamberlain's was a name to raise a cheer in
any popular assembly, and none could say how far
he was likely to go.   Some measure of the expectations formed of him may be gathered from the success
of that caricature in which Arthur Balfour, his chief,
was represented in form of the dog at the mouth of
the gramophone listening to " his master's "—that
is, to Chamberlain's—" voice."   It was a very common belief that Arthur Balfour, of indolence and indifference rather than of any actual weakness, allowed
Chamberlain to call the tune, though sometimes
it did not accord with the nominal leader's idea of
harmony.   He was regarded as the " strong man."

And then, in a moment, a lamentable accident in,
or from, a hansom, robbed him of his effective strength.
By a curious chance I happened to be an eyewitness.
I was walking with my brother up Whitehall, and
just as we passed the Scotch Office a hansom overtook
us, and as it came abreast of us the horse fell, the
doors appeared to fly open and the occupant of the
hansom was forcibly shot forward over the horse's
loins and came head-foremost on the road.   There
were many passers-by, and even before we could
reach the fallen man and horse they were surrounded.
We were hurrying to keep an appointment, there were
more than enough willing hands to help, and we went
on.   Of course we had not had time nor a sufficient
clear view of the face to recognise the victim of the
accident.   It was only some hours later, when we

read the evening papers, that we understood that it
was Mr. Chamberlain whom we had seen thus
grievously projected into the roadway.   I remember
that there was a large triumphal arch, of corn sheaves
and the like, erected in the roadway as a triumphal
exhibition of Colonial produce, and it was suggested
that the horse, by shying at this edifice, had caused
the accident to the great Colonial Secretary.   Whether
that were so or not, it soon became apparent that
the shock suffered by Mr. Chamberlain was far more
severe than either he or any one else realised at the
time.   At first he treated it lightly, as a man of his
courage and resolution would.   He was cut about
the head, and it was thought that this was done by
the shutter falling on his head as the cab came down:
This was the driver's view of the cut, but it was pure
speculation.   When the horse was on the very point
of falling to its knees, the hansom driver on his high
perch would be otherwise engaged than in looking
down through his trap-door to see that all was well
with his " fare."   Those cuts and blows, as I rather
think, were inflicted by the stony roadway as the
unfortunate victim's head came forcibly against it.
There is no difficulty in accounting for them.

The accident did not immediately drive Mr.
Chamberlain from his activities.   All his life long he
had been something more than a passive resister
to the advice of his doctors.   His principal form of
exercise had been the puffing of big cigars.   Even now
he was very long in acquiescing in the conviction
that he could no longer take his place in the political
arena.   With unabated courage and cheerfulness he
faced the truth which he was gradually driven to
recognise as inevitable.   He still had many months
of life before him, but even before his comparatively
early death his name became an honoured memory
rather than a living force.

CHAPTER VII

SIR WILLIAM VERNON HARCOURT

WHEN Mr. Gladstone started on his adventure along the paths of Irish Home Rule, and thus tried beyond the breaking point the fidelity of so many of his followers, there were two, at least, of his chief lieutenants who remained staunch : Mr. Morley, now Viscount Morley, and Sir William Vernon Harcourt.

With Sir William Harcourt I had first made acquaintance at a most disrespectful distance in the very early days of the Eighties, when I was an Oxford undergraduate. Sir William was member for Oxford —for the Borough, not the University—and on appointment to the office of Home Secretary sought re-election. His opponent was Mr. Hall, the brewer. We—that is to say, myself and other voteless and graceless undergraduates—deemed it our bounden duty to attend Sir William's meetings. We styled ourselves in those days " Conservatives and sportsmen," and thought it only right to bear witness to the faith that was in us by interrupting the candidate at the least opportune moments of his speech by derisive howls and cheers. Owing in the main, as we doubted not, to these our statesman-like efforts, Sir William was rejected by Oxford town, and Mr. Hall was elected in his stead. In a short while, however, he was fitted with a seat where our influence could not prevail, and came into office as Home Secretary at the beginning of this period.

The contrast between the two faithful lieutenants was rather striking. Their fidelity to the great chieftain was the one and only characteristic which they seemed to have in common. It is not my business to attempt a sketch of Lord Morley, who is still with us, who did what I judge to be the best of his political work, in India, after this date, and perhaps, in the monumental life of Mr. Gladstone, his greatest literary work also. During the first half of the Eighties he did not hold office ; indeed, it was not until 1883 that he entered Parliament at all. And in the Parliament of 1886 he was appointed to the then especially important office of Chief Secretary for Ireland, only to be set down, together with all the rest of the Gladstonians, by the General Election following the rejection of the Home Rule Bill ; therefore it might seem as though he could scarcely count for much in these years. Yet, in point of fact, there is no doubt that he counted for a very great deal, and had so counted for some time before he appeared in person in the forefront of the battle.

Although there was one side, the religious, in which he stood as far apart as well could be from Mr. Gladstone, yet in all other respects—as in his firm adherence to principle, his earnestness of purpose, his democratic trend, and his love of the best in literature—his character and line of thought were very much in harmony with those of his leader, and exactly such as would commend themselves and their possessor to that leader's attention and respect. There can be no question about the respect and attention paid by Mr. Gladstone to Mr. Morley, and it is likely enough that his policy at that time was coloured more than he knew by Mr. Morley's influence. It is tolerably certain that although the " flying of the Home Rule kite," as it was called, took by surprise a large number of Mr. Gladstone's close friends, it

SIR W. V. HARCOURT.

came as no surprise to Mr. Morley. Indeed, it is more than hinted that the idea was introduced as a piece of, we will not say practical, but may at least say possible, politics to Mr. Gladstone by Mr. Morley. Conceivably it may have risen out of conversations between them, the one contributing perhaps even he himself hardly knew just what quickening impulse as interchange of ideas went on. This is the manner, at all events, in which many events, both in politics and other human affairs, come to the birth, with little clear knowledge on the part of the parents of their children.

And if Mr. Morley had this influence, which there is very much reason to think that he exercised, over Mr. Gladstone, there is at least equal reason to suppose that he influenced Sir William Harcourt as much, or more. That is why, though I abjured all intent of attempting a sketch of Mr. Morley, I have so far tried to shadow in what I believe to be his very considerable part in determining Mr. Gladstone in his attitude towards Home Rule. It is an influence which we are obliged to take into the reckoning, if we are to estimate aright Sir William Harcourt's attitude, not only to this but also to other problems, such as the Egyptian question, which came into prominence both while Mr. Gladstone was Prime Minister and also while he was in opposition.

Never, as aforesaid, save in respect of fidelity to the chief, could two lieutenants be less alike. Sir William Harcourt was of patrician race. He had the blood of kings mingling with the stock at some remote period, and a very innocent pride, which he is supposed to have assumed as a consequence of that tributary stream of purple, was made the target of some sly derision by his opponents—occasionally, also, by his friends.

And his opponents were many. This scion of high

5

race could, and did, personate to the full Rudyard
Kipling's ideal of " the first-rate fighting man."
He played the rôle of a civilised " Fuzzy Wuzzy " to
perfection. Not only was he in fact a fighting man,
but he also looked it. As he stood there, a tall,
full-bodied figure, with head thrown back and chest
well forward, he seemed to be saying to all and sundry,
" Come on, I'm ready for you." And he always was.
He was built on almost Herculean lines, and the
weapon that he wielded was something like an intellectual club of Hercules. It was a bludgeoning
instrument of force and weight, rather than any fine
rapier to be delivered with a mere wrist-turn. Sir
William Harcourt's were great body blows. But,
heavy as they were, he could deal them with a wonderful agility. He was a quick debater, and though his
retort would not be subtle it would be instantly
delivered. He gave the opponent no respite. He
had acquired and practised an incisive literary style
in articles contributed to the *Saturday Review*, and
later had written weightily and with large knowledge
in the *Times* over the signature of " Historicus."
So he had his vocabulary at command, although, to
say truth, his writing was always far more scholarly
and finished than his speech.

Thus he was a very able and forceful squire, and did
more than yeoman's service ; yet, at the same time,
his method had all the defects of its qualities. He
could knock down foes, but he was no adept in the
gentle, yet sometimes far more valuable, art of making
friends. He was in truth rather a dangerous ally,
although so powerful. He was, I believe, a very
kindly natured man, and yet he always seemed
singularly insensitive to the pain and offence that his
hard words could not fail to give. It appeared to
come quite as a surprise to him, and as yet further
incentive to wrathful indignation, that people should

be pained and offended by anything that he might say. And this was the more curious because he himself was very far from callous to the pin-pricks of criticism. A pin-prick gave far more offence to his own sensitive pride than any offence that it seemed to him at all reasonable for one of the victims of his own attack to feel under a hurricane of his cudgel-blows. He would rage away at others, and expect them to accept it all in very good part and be all the better for it, but could not endure with any equanimity one tithe of the like chastening from the rod which he deemed that they ought to kiss with gladness.

Somewhere, in spite of his great courage and intellectual gifts far above the common, there seemed to be in him—was it a lack of sympathy?—at all events it was an almost absolute lack of ability to look at a question from any other point of view than his own, or to realise that there could be another point of view which a rational man might hold. When a man did put forward an opinion differing from his, it never seems to have occurred to him to weigh that opinion and see whether, by any possibility, it could have validity. What he did was to scold at the man and to treat him as an unreasonable and a naughty child for the criminal folly of holding a view which was not exactly that of Sir William Vernon Harcourt.

In the circumstances of the Liberal Party at that moment—by which I mean the moment of Mr. Gladstone's divergence from the recognised highway and plunge into the debatable country of Home Rule—it has always seemed to me a little doubtful whether Sir William's championship was really of more service or dis-service to the cause. He was a most valuable man, of course, for demolishing the argument of an opponent. That was his great asset. He knew no fear ; and not only were some opponents' arguments bludgeoned out of being, but many an opponent refrained, in fear of the prospective bludgeoning, from bringing his argument to the birth at all. In such service as this no other man could be of equal use, perhaps, with Sir William. But then, just at this anxious and doubtful moment, neither the merits nor the probable issues of the political conflict were obvious to men's eyes ; there was no clear and clean-cut division between those who were for the great ohieftain, Home Rule and all, and those who felt constrained, not without pain and grief, to break their unspoken vows of homage if the maintenance of those vows had to involve them in support of the new policy. Thus there were many standing at the parting of the ways, anxiously debating which of the paths they should take. A relatively small weight thrown into the balance on this side or that is enough to decide the minds of men so hesitating.

When you have a person standing thus at the cross-roads, and you desire to have him follow you down one of them, it is really not the best possible means of persuasion to scold him violently for being such a donkey as to hesitate at all. The result of that is rather apt to be his bolting at full gallop down the other road.

Yet this, or something very like it, is the means that Sir William Harcourt was rather disposed to adopt with any waverers. He could not understand how they could waver, and he told them so, very clearly indeed : more clearly and forcibly perhaps than he realised, certainly more forcibly than they were likely to relish. The consequence was that many a waverer went over, " stock, lock, and barrel," to the enemy's ranks, whom a more gentle and conciliatory wooing might have rallied to Sir William's and his chief's support. But the practice of any arts of conciliation was apparently impossible to him. He behaved as if scarcely realising that such arts existed,

or had any value. Thus it was that he was so useful
a fighting man in face of an avowed foe, but of no use
whatever, and perhaps somewhat worse than useless,
for the at least equally valuable purpose of gaining
friends. It is probable that he went through life in
perfect unconsciousness of this disability. It is
probable that it was the chief reason why, after the
passing from the scene of the great chief, the mantle
of leadership fell not upon his shoulders but on those
of Lord Rosebery, preferred before him. It is certain
that he was both vexed and genuinely surprised at
this preference. He would not have been thus
surprised, though he might have been no less vexed,
had he only had a little clearer insight into his own
qualities, and into the effect that they had in their
forceful but unsympathetic reaction on other men.
He did not seem at all able to appreciate why his
influence was not greater ; for while he was fully able
to realise his force, he failed to realise his lack of those
persuasions which may often achieve more than
force. The result, when Lord Rosebery was made
Premier, was not a little pathetic. Sir William had
given far more service to the party, yet the party
overlooked his claim and chose another as its leader.

Nobody whose judgment was worth considering
ever doubted for a moment Sir William's essential
honesty in political life ; at the same time no one
could ever claim for him convictions and purpose of
a temperature at all approaching that of the burning
earnestness which fired Mr. Gladstone. For all the
energy of his speech, political and moral questions
did not present themselves to Sir William's mind as
being of that supreme and all-engrossing importance
which they assumed with Mr. Gladstone. Mr. Morley,
in his own way, which gave less impression of the glowing warmth that the eloquence of the great leader could
not fail to kindle, nevertheless convinced men of his

seriousness of purpose as Sir William, who protested so much more vehemently, never could convince them.

The " full-dress " history of those times remains to be written, in spite of the eminent contributions already made towards it by such volumes as Mr. McCarthy's *History of our own Times* and Mr. Morley's own *Life of Gladstone*. But as those contributions fall in, they supply a growing mass of testimony to the immense influence of Mr. Morley on the views both of Mr. Gladstone and of Sir William Harcourt. It is testimony which is received with some surprise ; it is an influence which was not appreciated by politicians generally at the time that it was being exerted ; it is very likely that it was not at all fully recognised by those who benefited by it (or suffered under it, as you prefer) ; that is to say, by Mr. Gladstone or Sir William Harcourt themselves. It is possible that one man only, Mr. Morley, quite realised it.

That he would be fully conscious of his share there can, as I think, be little question. He was (happily, we may say he is) a very clear-sighted man. He was very sensitive, to the point of nervousness, in public, and it was therefore difficult for him to make a forcible impression on a large audience. But in spite of that difficulty and that nervousness he was not at all disposed to underrate his abilities nor to doubt his judgment and the accuracy of his opinions. Although he was such a delightful and even brilliant writer, with so copious a vocabulary ready to his hand, yet his nervousness and ill-delivery made his speeches sound as though they could scarcely be the product of the same fine brain as that which had created some of the passages in his books. It is true that the speeches " read better than they sounded," to use the commonplace, but still they did not read like his writings. Nevertheless, in spite of his disability

to give forceful utterance to his views in public, he
was never in any such difficulty in private conversation. There he could be incisive, clear, and very
insistent. He could be the more insistent just because
he was so very quiet. A man of noisier speech could
not have penetrated your mind by reiteration, under
different forms and from different points of attack,
of the same argument. A noisier man would have
aroused irritation at the reiteration, and would
very soon have been unbearable. But it was part
of Mr. Morley's strength to be so quiet that he could
say the same thing again and again, dressing it up
in different verbal raiment, so that you did not
recognise it too immediately and so grow surfeited
with it. And by this reiteration the argument gained,
in time, perhaps without the full consciousness of
those who came under its power, a singular effect.
It was a process of peaceful penetration. If we
regard carefully the mind of Mr. Gladstone in its
changing points of view towards the Egyptian
question, towards Home Rule, and towards several
other salient political problems of the time, we may
see, as I believe, that it was gradually turned and
influenced by Mr. Morley : turned towards the opinions
which were constant and native to Mr. Morley's mind,
so that in some degree it is true to say that he was
the leader of his chief. When I write of Mr. Gladstone
changing his point of view I am not venturing on an
unfavourable criticism. The mind that is incapable
of change on political questions is far more open to
blame. It was part of the reason why Mr. Gladstone
kept both the youthful vigour of his mind and also
his firm hold on his party, so very long and under
such hard stress, that it was a mind which did not
grow rigid with age, but remained ever open to new
ideas.

And as we may see Mr. Gladstone gradually penetrated by the unobtrusive, unhurrying, but unresting influence of Mr. Morley, so too we see Sir William. We find him, an heir to great aristocratic traditions, gradually absorbing and assimilating views about the democracy at home, and also about foreign peoples, which were imbued with colours that his own mind never would have given them. He presents, in fact, a very curious figure, and a figure, as I have hinted, that, for all its pugnacity, was not without its pathos. For undoubtedly he was in the end, to himself, something of a disappointment and a failure ; something of a puzzle, too, because he could not understand why it was that his party did not either esteem him more highly or love him better. Really, as we have to suppose, it was their affection far more than their esteem that he had failed to gain. And yet he had qualities to merit affection equally with esteem. It was his misfortune that he failed, owing to a defect of insight and sympathy far more than to any lack of kindliness, in earning his due credit for them. It was that which made the failure pathetic—that it was the failure to win hearts of a man kindly enough at heart himself to wish to win them, and genuinely puzzled, as well as sharply disappointed, by the failure.

CHAPTER VIII

THE MEMBERS FOR NORTHAMPTON

I SCARCELY know another man whose physiognomy was so distinctly and so queerly expressive of a distinct and queer personality as Henry Labouchere's. He must have been a very dull and uninterested student of human faces who would not say to himself, looking for the first time at Labouchere, " I wonder ! " If he did not know the man, his wonder would be " who that man is ?—what his face means ? " If he did know the man, and thousands who had not seen his face knew him in the wider sense of reading him and reading of him, then perhaps he would be yet more interested, saying to himself, " That face reveals the man." And so it did. It was a perfectly honest face, so far. But did it reveal a perfectly honest man ? That was the question which a great many were constantly asking. I do not mean that there was any possible question of honesty (or should we say of dishonesty ?) in the petty, pocket-picking, financial sense. That was quite out of the question. But what was very much in the question, and of its very essence and point, was whether one could trust the man politically. And that was a question which those enigmatic features of his certainly did not help to answer. It was a baffling countenance to him who would study it and try to read the soul behind it. It was a question which his record did not answer, neither did you find any solution in his writings, his speeches, nor in his vivid but not revealing conversation. And I think that the truth of the matter, the root of the riddle, is that in reality Labouchere did not know, and therefore could not really trust, himself. I never knew a man who seemed to have so little principle to guide him. You may say of him that he went through life without a guiding principle at all. We have met many who seem to take a foolish pride in professing a cynic absence of principle, but in Labouchere's case I believe that it was perfectly sincere. It had been left out of him. He was a singularly " a-moral " man. *Mores*, custom, opinion of his fellow-men, had as little influence over him as any guiding principle of a higher kind such as most men seek and find and accept with conscious gratitude.

All this reads, I know, like the portraiture of an unpleasant, perhaps of an evil person ; but Labouchere was in reality a particularly agreeable person, his conversation was never dull and had often a really witty turn ; and not only did his lack of principle not lead him into ways of evil, but there are very few men who have done so much active good in their generation.

" Labby," as all the world called him, whether they knew him or not, was the Labby who was the terror of one or two Ministries. They never knew what to do with him, nor what he would do and say next. As early as Mr. Gladstone's administration of 1886 he was mentioned as a possible member of the Government, and in 1892, Mr. Gladstone's last term of office, the question of his inclusion became acute. He was likely to be a thorn in the side of any Ministry which he entered. But on the other hand, would he not give even more mischievous and Puckish prods as a free-lance from without the pale if he were excluded ? That was the problem, finally answered

HENRY LABOUCHERE.

by his rejection. Inevitably he took his revenge in the form of an article in *Truth*, criticising the qualities of the Cabinet in a manner which certainly did not err on the side of reticence; but after this outburst, with a respect, quite out of keeping with his usual character, for the courage of Mr. Gladstone thus taking office at such an advanced age, he behaved himself quite decently and stung certainly not at all more fiercely and persistently than was to be expected of him. But besides this Parliamentary Labby, who was perhaps the Labby best and most generally known, we must never forget that he was " Labby of *Truth* " also.

I cannot think that people did, or ever have done, " Labby of *Truth* " adequate justice. When the paper first came out it was thought to be a most impertinent paper. So it was. Henry Labouchere, its editor, its owner, and its financier, was a most impertinent man. He was far past praying for on that account. There was no man who liked better to go prying into other men's affairs, or cared less or was more unabashed when he was found out. It was impossible to abash him : that was one of his qualities, and almost his most striking. So when *Truth* came out with its impertinences and personalities, which were new features in journalism at that time, we all said what a horrid paper it was. Of course those personalities would be nothing accounted of now, when everybody seems to like reading of their most intimate doings and mis-doings blazoned on the front page of some daily paper. There was already one paper which had launched out a little way into that kind of brackish water : that was the *World*, with Edmund Yates at its helm. Labby went one, or more than one, better than Yates, pushed farther out, into brinier seas, was a little more impertinent and personal. We had all liked the personal and impertinent *World*, though we had all said it was " a horrid paper." So when there came this yet more personal and yet more impertinent *Truth* we liked that even better than the *World*, saying that it was " even horrider." Of course Yates, in the old *World*, had protesting digs at the impertinences of its new rival *Truth*, and of course Labby, in *Truth*, dug back. It was said that the paper took for its motto, " I am Truth, and I am come to give the World the lie." It did give the *World* the lie, and the *World* gave it back again, and the readers of both were amused and neither was one penny the worse.

So that was all right, and did not matter one way or the other, but what did matter, and what is to be accounted to Henry Labouchere as a very large measure of righteousness, is that so soon as he had established his paper firmly on its feet by these rather dubious methods he set out to kick from that basis, so established, and kick he did, furiously and most effectively, at all sorts and conditions of wickedness in places both high and low. When one sees him at these virtuous activities, I think that we must pause again and take a glimpse of the man as a whole or we shall have his personality posing before us in a false and side-illumined light. I hardly believe, knowing the man he was, that it was for virtue's sacred sake that he kicked with this fury at all wickedness : I believe it was far more for the very fun of kicking. From his heart he enjoyed a fight. I believe that he would sooner fight a bad man, so as to try to make him better, than a good man ; but he would sooner fight a good man than not fight at all. And then he had a heart. If he had not a principle, he had a heart, and that is perhaps a better thing ; and into this kind heart of him it pierced poignantly that such things could be allowed to go on as the robbing of the widow, the orphan, the poor clergyman, or the guileless retired

officer, for the benefit of the iniquitous Company
promoter. It is the great and redeeming merit of
Truth, a merit that never, in my humble judgment,
has been credited to it at anything approaching a
right estimate, that no sooner did it hear of any
swindle of the kind than forthwith it " went for it "
with an unrelenting and vituperative attack which
seldom failed to scotch the snake if it did not kill
him outright. And of course it was Labby really,
as we all knew, who was the St. George of these
dragon - slaying ventures. They demanded, not
merely for their success, but even for their initial
undertaking, a perfect fearlessness and a deep purse.
Labouchere had the first by nature and the second by
ironical fate, which made him heir to the rich and
crustedly Conservative Lord Taunton. It was a
special source of amused gratification to the inheritor
that his reversion should have been in the temporary
keeping of a peer of such respectability whom he had
loved to shock by his Radical vagaries. I suppose
that if a phrenologist had examined the skull of
Labouchere he would have found a profound pit in
the place where the bump of veneration is due on the
normal head, and a similarly deep cavity should have
been observed on the cranium of that other statesman,
his contemporary and in some mental aspects so like
him, Lord Randolph Churchill. At least, if that
science could not discover such depressions, it must
stand discredited by the very failure. From the first
Labouchere was incorrigible. When sent, in his early
days, to Italy with important dispatches of State,
he did not arrive at his destination : no news could
be heard of him, nor of his dispatches. At last, after
a week's interval, his address was discovered—Monte
Carlo ! The tables had every attraction for his
sportive temperament. Recrimination and expostu-
lation, in the most severe language known to

diplomatic courtesy, were sent after him ; to which he replied, by telegram, that he much regretted the delay in delivering the dispatches, but that the pay of a Queen's Messenger was so very meagre that he had been obliged to walk all the way, and Monte Carlo was as far as he had been able to get in the time.

This is a digression—as Labouchere himself digressed from the straight road to Rome—but once he got on the trail of one of the Company promoting swindlers he never digressed from that path of vengeance. He must have been a real terror to those gentry. He himself had a good knowledge of Company business to start with—that was a useful asset in dealing with the people who were financially queer. I remember that at one time he was Chairman of the Westminster Aquarium Board, which was not managed to the satisfaction of the shareholders, and they elected another very singular, though much less known man, Captain Molesworth, R.N., to its Chair in Labouchere's stead. Labouchere knew the ways of the tricksters ; he could perfectly well afford the costs of a libel action, if they had the courage or the character to bring one against him, and of an adverse verdict, if they should happen to obtain one. But in point of fact he knew his quarry too well to be often in danger of any reprisal. Seldom had they either courage, character, or money to come into Court. Also, even an adverse verdict did not mean a total loss to *Truth*, because of the value of the advertisement given the paper by the action. I think that he rather liked being in the Courts. Certainly it never troubled him a whit. It is difficult to imagine any situation which would. He carried *insouciance* to a fine art. In one of the many legal actions in which he was engaged occasion arose to say something about his banking account, and then it came out that he had left his pass-book lying at his bank, without taking the trouble to inquire how his account stood, for something like five years—a model client for any banking establishment ! A man so indifferent to the money issue as this heedlessness indicates, so indifferent, also, to any threat or abuse or opinion by his fellow man, must have been a dreadful lion in the path of the promoting hyena. We know, or at least by looking up the record of past years of *Truth* we might discover, how many insanitary swindles he brought to the purifying light of day. But we should make a very great mistake and a very insufficient calculation if we were to take that as the measure of the frauds that he was useful in suppressing. To that positive number we must add all that x—the unknown quantity—of similar frauds which died still-born, which did not dare to come to the birth, just because their would-be perpetrators knew that this lion was here, couchant, ready to spring if they should show themselves out of the dark places in which they concocted their schemes. We must add the two together, the known with the very much larger number of the unknown, in order to estimate at all truly the swindles that " Labby of *Truth* " was the means of preventing, or of checking, and the numbers of unfortunate poor and guileless people whom he thereby saved from very dire straits. Never, as I think, has nearly enough honour been done Henry Labouchere for his good work in this respect. It is easy to say that it was done in the first place in the interests of his paper. Very likely. But at all events, whatever the immediate motive, done it was, and it was work well worth the doing, for which many, without in the least suspecting it, have cause for gratitude. If there were more papers of the fearlessness in exposure of financial scandals and frauds which was the characteristic of " Labby's *Truth*," the world would be financially cleaner than it is.

Labouchere can very well afford to rest his claim
to fair fame—not that it was a claim he would ever
have urged—on that. He had no great legislative
measure to his credit, long as he was in Parliament.
On the whole we may certainly say that he was on
the side of the angels; that is, of the Radicals, for
we are fallen on days when all that is Radical is rated
angelic, and *vice versa*. He was one of those who
helped to set the train running along democratic
lines which have led to a station, by no means yet a
terminus, such as few of the initiators of the movement imagined, and fewer still would have desired.
For such legislative progress as he set his hand to,
the democratic powers of to-day may thank him.
He was also one of those Englishmen, partly by reason
of his Gallic extraction, who helped to make possible
that Anglo-French *entente* which has saved the world
to-day, for he was at home in Paris as few Englishmen
are or can be, and helped to show Frenchmen that the
differences of the nations which the Channel divided
were not beyond reconcilement. Thus do men now
and then build better than they know. Among his
contemporaries Labouchere was most appreciated,
as many have told me, in the House of Commons
smoking-room, when one never knew with what quip
or unexpected turn he might brighten up the talk.
"What, another Bung got a Beerage," was his
comment when a good brewer was awarded ·a title
worthy alike of his excellent work for his party and
of his ale. That is only a sample. No doubt a
Parliamentarian of his time and party could give us
many much better, but it is fairly typical of the
quaint, humorous, school-boyish, irreverent whimsies
which he would flash out with a grim smile, concealed
under the beard but revealed by a queer lift of the
corners of the eyes under the shaggy brows.

The actual value of the work that he did as a

legislator was probably as nothing in comparison
with his yeoman service as a swindler-hunter in the
pages of his paper ; still it had points on which another
man might very well hang himself little votive offer-
ings for his own fame. He had already been twice
in Parliament for short periods, when he was returned
at the General Election of 1880, but had made no
name, had taken no prominent line. And at this
General Election he found himself as one of the two
members for Northampton, in double harness with
a queerer colleague, in the opinion of the majority
of the House, even than himself, to wit Mr. Bradlaugh.
Labouchere came to Westminster with the views—
so far as he held, and averred himself as the holder of,
settled views at all—of an advanced Radical : advanced, and Radical, be it understood, according
to the standard of the day. These standards change.
It was just about this time that the popular novelist,
Miss Broughton, wittily expressed herself in respect
to the change of view which the passage of years had
brought towards her own books. There was a day
when she had been regarded as somewhat daring,
when there was question whether the Victorian young
person ought to read her, but now—— ! " When
I began to write," she said, " I was regarded as a
Zola : now I am looked on as a Charlotte M.
Yonge." I think she rather regretted her lost claim
to shock.

Similarly, Labouchere, were he living, might well
say of himself, and possibly might so speak of his
yoke-fellow of Northampton, Bradlaugh, also : " We
used to be regarded as Lenin and Trotsky ; now we
are looked upon as Lord Selborne and Walter
Long."

Though they thus came in together, representing
the same constituency and to some extent the same
ostensible shade of political opinion, and though

6

they had this, at least, in common, that neither cared greatly for the opinion of the respectable citizen, still no two men could well be much farther apart in their mental character. Bradlaugh—I must speak of the man only as I had very small opportunities of judging of him—was full of honest convictions, very much in earnest. The last thing of which Labouchere realised the importance was " the importance of being earnest." That admirable comedy was already, in all probability, on the stocks, or at all events simmering in the greatly gifted brain of the writer, but Labouchere had not yet the opportunity of learning its moral, if it had any to convey. Bradlaugh shocked the House far more severely than Labouchere; he even animated the usually decorous proceedings by physical violence in resisting his removal from those high portals. He declined, in the first instance, to " kiss the book." And I believe that he did it all from conviction that it was a duty, a duty owed to truth and honesty, which he put far above any owed to decency or decorum. These last were gods to whom Labouchere likewise was quite indifferent, but, unlike Bradlaugh, he was indifferent to those other gods also—*parcus deorum cultor*, no matter what the attributes of the divinities. Bradlaugh endured a great deal of personal physical inconvenience, rather than acquiesce in what he thought wrong. Labouchere had no such decided views of right or wrong as to deem the suffering of inconvenience for their sake to be worth while. So, at least, I judge of the two.

Many people were deceived, as I am obliged to think, in this respect, about Labouchere. They would say: " Oh, it is all put on, this cynicism, this indifference. It must be so. Underneath it all he is very much in earnest. Unless he were in earnest he would not run such risks as he does in his attacks on the Company promoters and the like. He con-

CHARLES BRADLAUGH.

tinually stands to lose money by the libel suits they bring ; and of course he gets nothing if he wins."

But, thus arguing, they were surely judging Labouchere by themselves ; and surely Labouchere was, just in this, different from them and not to be judged by the common standard. He had more money than he needed, and he was sufficiently capable of detachment from the folly common to most men of regarding money as an end in itself, instead of as a means. Therefore the fact that he must stand to be shot at, financially, in consequence of his fearless exposures of frauds, left him quite unaffected. He could not conceivably be mulcted in a penalty so heavy as to compel him to any change in his comfortable way of life. Moreover, the libel suits, as I have noted, were by no means likely to be a clear loss, even if they went against him. There was always the compensating value of the advertisement for his paper which the lawsuit brought, to set in the other side of the balance. One would have to be very conversant with journalistic finance to make anything like a just estimate of that value, but surely it must be considerable.

So we cannot accept his action in this regard as much evidence of earnest purpose. Had it entailed on him any personal inconvenience it would be evidence far more to the point, but there is no evidence to show that he recognised any purpose in life which would be worth a sacrifice. Bradlaugh, his colleague, was cast in very different mould. The story of his entry into Parliament, in this very first Ministry of the Eighties, will not be forgotten. He presented himself at the Bar of the House and demanded, quoting ancient statute to support his claim, to be allowed to " affirm " his allegiance, since the form of oath contained words meaningless and even offensive to him.

Bradlaugh, it should be noted, did not belong to that large class of unbelievers in Christian doctrine who subscribe themselves " agnostic." There was nothing of this pale, negative complexion about him. He was nothing if not positive, aggressive, assertive. He called himself, frankly, an atheist, and an addition to that libel might well be made and he be called a dogmatic atheist. Atheism is itself a negation which hardly seems worth fighting for ; but that was not Bradlaugh's view at all. He had fought for atheism, he had lectured for atheism, he had made himself the leader and spokesman of a group who followed him along the paths of atheism—to no particular goal that the ordinary man was able to recognise. It was to most people a wonder that they should be in so great earnest over a no-creed of the kind ; but Bradlaugh himself would have said that it was not the negative principle of atheism for which he contended, but that his contention was against the positive principle of falsity which was contained in all religions. Thus he would have claimed to justify himself.

But when he came to the Bar, and demanded to affirm, he put the whole House in a quandary. Speaker Brand, like Lord Hampden, did not know what to do. He referred the matter to the House. The House did not know what to do. It referred the matter to a Committee. The Committee, after examination of the statute on which Mr. Bradlaugh rested his claim, said (by a majority of one vote, as was stated) that he could not affirm. Meantime, having paid his respect to all the gods of atheism by the protest which he had made, Bradlaugh wrote to the papers saying that he was now prepared to take the oath, though it would mean no more to him than a mere affirmation, and following this announcement he came up to the Bar again, a day or two later, and demanded to be sworn. Whereupon Sir Henry

Drummond Wolff, on the look out for trouble—
that is to say, for any trouble which he, as a member
of the band of guerilla warriors then known as the
" Fourth Party," could cause the Government—
jumped up and objected to the swearing, under these
circumstances, of the new member.

From this arose argument and counter-argument ;
the original question became tangled up in devious
threads of subsidiary problems : Could an atheist
be allowed to take the oath? Could a man who had
refused to take the oath once be allowed to swallow
it at a second venture? Could a man be allowed to
affirm if he refused the oath?   It was ostensibly
to discuss this last problem that a Select Committee
was at length appointed, on Mr. Gladstone's motion.
The Committee found that Mr. Bradlaugh could not
take the oath, but that he might affirm, if he cared
to do so on the understanding that the Committee's
finding did not hold him scatheless of any penalties
which might be imposed on him if any member brought
against him a successful suit for taking his seat and
voting in the House when he had no right so to do.

So, that recommendation coming before the House,
it was promptly rejected by a sufficient majority,
who probably voted, as usually happens, on a question
considerably wider than that which was actually
submitted to them. The vote, in Parliament and
out, is not strictly logical. Any question of law raised
by the Bradlaugh case had probably become merged,
in the minds of most of the members, in the more
general question which they would be subconsciously
putting to themselves in some such form as " Is a
fellow like this Bradlaugh fit to be a member of our so
honourable House ? " and, voting accordingly, they
decided on his exclusion.

It was easy to vote, but they found it not quite so
easy to exclude. Perhaps Bradlaugh conducted

himself with no great dignity, but certainly he succeeded in making the proceedings in Parliament appear highly undignified. He kept trying to make a bolt for the Bar in order to snatch the Testament and swear. Constables, like " full backs " guarding a Rugby football goal, collared him as he ran in and dragged him out again. An order was passed expelling him from the very precincts. Violence, and much of it, to the measure of ten strong policemen, was needed to enforce it. Bradlaugh was a man of gigantic strength and frame. He was self-educated, had begun work as office-boy, proceeded to be a common soldier, had some training in a lawyer's office ; that is to say that he learnt self-reliance and something of law and something of the use of very unusual thews and sinews. He exercised the latter at the expense of the ten policemen, but they were too many for him. When he resigned himself, dishevelled, torn, and bleeding, to their hands, he was quite friendly with them, and the friendliness was mutual.

But he had already gained a hearing in the House. After the vote excluding him, he was permitted to state his case from the Bar, and stated it well, in a powerful, far-carrying voice. The impression he made on members was good, perhaps better than they wished. They could not dislike the enormous man, with his capacious brainy head and extraordinarily long upper lip, who seemed like a Titan challenging the worst that men or gods could do him. He was a pathetic, at the same time as a tremendous figure. His very vesture had a pathetic aspect, for this most militant atheist was always garbed in the style of dress and necktie that is generally worn by a Nonconformist divine. But if members were thus attracted, despite themselves, by his personality, they were firm for his exclusion, none the less.

His constituents, of course, by reason of this

exclusion, were the more determined that he should represent them. He resigned his seat more than once, but only to be re-elected. For the first six years of the Eighties the Bradlaugh trouble was " something chronic," as is said in the vulgar tongue. After the General Election of 1885, the House met under Speaker Peel, succeeding Speaker Brand, who had retired to the Upper House, and Bradlaugh took the oath which had no meaning for him without opposition. Doubtless he was not the only member who attached small importance to it, but none other had cared to avow so aggressively their view of its insignificance.

Once they had admitted the dangerous lion into their midst, the House did not find him roaring so very furiously after all. He was a valuable, hardworking member. His oratory gained the commendation of such a master of the art as Mr. Gladstone himself. The measure which he was most directly responsible for passing, though I do not think it was brought forward in his name, was that which now permits any member who objects to take the oath to make affirmation in its stead. Any affirming member may now feel that he owes to Mr. Bradlaugh that he is able to enter the House without making a more or less painful compromise with his conscience.

Bradlaugh's Parliamentary activities almost exactly fill the decade, for he died at the beginning of 1891. He was not sixty years of age, but his life had been very hard and full of stress, and in spite of his great physique it had worn him to pieces. Labouchere, on the other hand, to whom life was by no means so strenuous a business, went on into the twentieth century. It was perhaps in Mr. Gladstone's brief but stormy last administration in 1892 that he was most often in the forefront of the battle. He was a member of the Parliamentary Committee appointed in 1897 so inquire into the unfortunate " Jameson Raid," as it was called. He was member for Northampton for twenty-six years, from 1880 right on to 1906, but in his later age his enjoyment of a fight grew less keen and he took a smaller share in party politics.

CHAPTER IX

GENERAL GORDON

SINCE the execution of Charles I, the fate of no one Briton has so profoundly stirred the heart of the nation as the death of Gordon at Khartoum. Nay, more ; while there was a certain division of opinion about the former, a section of the nation deeming it, if not an act of justice, at least an act of necessity, there was no such divided view about the latter, except it be that while all saw it in the light of a disgraceful error, to some it appeared a hideous crime.

Gordon, as circumstances have since made clear, was sent to Khartoum at a time when it was morally certain that, save for some special interposition of Providence, he would not come back alive. The circumstances, to us who read the records, have only become clear since the event, but the Government of the day had the most full opportunity of knowing the circumstances : there can be no doubt that it did know them. Yet it sent Gordon out. It is not at all impossible, Gordon being the man that he was, that he, who as we must think also knew the circumstances, believed that the miraculous would happen, believed that a special intervention of Providence would occur, believed that he had been divinely appointed as the instrument for relieving the troops in Khartoum and would receive divine help in achieving the task. It is quite possible that he may have believed that. It is quite impossible,

however, to think that the British Government
believed it ; nevertheless, it sent him out.

It sent him out partly, no doubt, because the nation
was clamorous that he should be sent. They were
clamorous that something should be done to relieve
a situation that was unbearable to the national pride
and to the national sense of humanity. Therefore
they clamoured for Gordon. They did not know,
they had not the means of knowing, that the situation had become worse than unbearable, that it was
already desperate, that sending any single man,
Gordon or another, to retrieve it was sending another
living man to join the number of those already lost.
The Government knew it ; but the Government
had not the courage to tell the nation how desperate
the situation was. They were in the dilemma of
being obliged either to tell the truth or to yield to the
clamour. They had not the courage to do the former,
therefore they had, perforce, to do the latter. They
sent out Gordon.

It is hardly the place here to dwell on the story of the
days that followed, the hopes, the fears, the expedition of Lord Wolseley, hurriedly despatched, carried
through by that very masterful and accomplished
soldier with a success, a speed, and a punctuality
that were marvellous in face of all the difficulties,
but arriving " just too late." " Just too late,"
as we were told ; but it is always open to more
than doubt whether they would have been in time
had they arrived days or even weeks earlier ; whether
the Mahdi had not the whole situation in hand
whenever he chose to stretch out the hand and grip
it ; whether he had not for weeks been playing the
game of cat and mouse—himself cat, Gordon mouse.
It looks much like it. A few weeks earlier might
have been " just too late " still. In any case, it
was soon realised that it was a failure that never had

GENERAL GORDON

a chance of success, and the failure was not allowed
to stand between Lord Wolseley and the full recognition of the ability with which the expedition was
planned and executed. I am quite aware that this
is a statement of the case which cannot go un-
challenged. It is a matter of common knowledge
that General Stephenson, then in military command
in Egypt, was not in favour of the " all-river route,"
but of the overland way across the desert by Suakin
and Berber. Wolseley insisted on getting over the
habitants, whom he had proved so well in Canada,
and going all the way by the Nile. As the event
turned out it appears likely that time might have
been saved had the desert short-cut been taken.
That enough time could have been saved to save the
situation, even had the force been able to arrive in
full strength by the possibly earlier date, is scarcely
credible in view of the numbers that the Mahdi had
at his disposal. But whether Wolseley were right
or wrong in his choice of plan, none, I think, have
ventured to criticise the almost perfect execution
of the plan once chosen, and the full recognition of
the extraordinary ability with which the expedition
was planned and executed. The whole story is
poignantly alive still in the hearts of all of us who
knew it and who knew Gordon in the Eighties, when
it was enacted. It hardly enters, strictly speaking,
into the portraiture of Gordon, because we knew
him, for such as he was, more than ready to go
fearlessly to meet any fate which duty seemed to
point out to him, long before he proved it in this
final test. What does enter essentially into his
portraiture, and in itself virtually amounts to the
very sketching of the portrait, is the explanation of
the reason of the people's clamour, and their belief
that he was the man, and the one man, who could
do what we now know to have been the impossible.

What is very extraordinary is this kind of implicit belief in him, which was not restricted to the British race. Whenever any Government or Potentate was in trouble with their people, or with an alien people, it was their impulse to send for Gordon. Thus, the Emperor of China sent for him to put down the Taiping rebellion. This was the affair of the " ever-Victorious Army," as it was called. Gordon did not call it so, and the high-sounding name was not quite earned. But he and that army gained victories enough, at all costs, to achieve their end. The rebellion was put down. The Emperor offered him " up to half his kingdom " in the Oriental form of statement, but Gordon would take nothing. The Khedive was in trouble ; he invited Gordon into his service. Gordon went. Then he returned home, and desired to leave that service, but the Khedive reminded him of his promise, and Gordon went back again to the Egyptian business, but only on the understanding that his own conditions were granted, namely that he should be appointed Governor-General over all the Soudan. He had to go to South Africa, because there was trouble with the natives and Boers there. Just at the beginning of the Eighties, Leopold, King of the Belgians, was very anxious to get him to go out to allay discontent among the natives in the Congo, but for some reason Gordon did not consent to that mission. In brief, wherever trouble arose in any part of the world in which white men were dealing with men of colour, Gordon was sent for, or entreated ; and, more wonderful still, this white man was summoned again and again, as at the behest of the Emperor of China, and again at the call of the Khedive, to help even where it was coloured man against coloured man. The record is quite amazing.

From the record we turn naturally to the reason,

and that reason must be discoverable, if at all, in
the character of the man. Its statement must be
his portrait. Perhaps, by way of outline, I may be
allowed to quote briefly from an article of my own
concerning Gordon, contributed to the *Cornhill
Magazine* of February 1917 :

" There was about him a boyish, almost a childish,
simplicity and directness which gave him the power
of appealing very intimately to a boy's mind and
heart." (Let me say, in parenthesis, that in this
simplicity and directness lay much of his power of
appeal to the minds of those people, rather more
primitive than the Western Europeans, whom the
Chinese Emperor or the ruler of Egypt might call
him in to help. They are perhaps on rather the same
plane as the boy of Western Europe.) " To me,
hardly more than a child, he would talk even then of
God and of Jesus Christ as if they were personal
friends whom we knew in common. He never had
the least sense of embarrassment in speaking of his
religion, and this perfect absence of self-consciousness
freed him from that very British shyness which makes
so many of us ashamed of exhibiting what is really
the finest in our thoughts and feelings. And by
virtue of this freedom from all self-consciousness
on his own part he was able to help others to throw
off their own reserves and to show forth the best that
they had in them. It was all, of course, but one
aspect of his utter fearlessness, demonstrating itself
thus on the moral side, as often, in other crises of his
strenuous life, in the face of physical peril—a very
great soldier and hero.

" It is wholly unnecessary—it would be little short
of an impertinence—for me to insist on that greatness
and heroism. The very name of Gordon can hardly
fail to suggest an incarnation of heroic virtues.

" There is, however, one side of his extraordinarily complex character to which I would invite attention, because I think that it has often been overlooked, obscured by the more striking qualities—his hard-headedness. He was R.E.—a sapper—primarily a scientific soldier. Thereto he added, as he gave frequent proof, a remarkable faculty of organisation and administration, as well as a marvellous aptitude for the leadership of men. With these intellectual and moral gifts he was, withal, mystic and fighter— a threefold combination very rare."

Elsewhere, in the same article, I wrote :

" Of his reason for doing this, or for not doing that, he would say quite simply, ' God would wish it,' or ' God would not wish it.' It is a reason which any one of us might confess to himself, intimately, but it is a reason which we are shy—more's the pity !— of admitting even to a friend. Far less would we state it to the man in the street.   But Gordon would ; and in his absolute simplicity he could not see why he should not."

And again :

" The most remarkable feature of Gordon's religious belief is, I think, his intense faith in the personal indwelling of God's spirit in the human soul. It is the quality of faith commonly ascribed to the mystic ; and to the mystic we commonly ascribe, as a usual condition of his creed, the contemplative life. Here and there, very exceptionally, in history we find such faith in the soul of the man (or woman) of action. And therewith, in their union, we have the hero-saint.

" Of this high company was Gordon—by virtue of heroism and saintliness united, an inspired leader of men. He could bend men to his will, and make

them follow him, as very few have been able to influence and guide them.   But again, as just said,
he had, to complete an extraordinary personality,
the quality of penetrating scientific intellect.   That
trinity of rare and precious gifts made him a man
perhaps unique in human story.   I, at least, am at
a loss, turning its pages, to find one just like him—
his equal in gifts so various and so rich."

So I wrote of him, and in what degree a reader
may find this at all explanatory of his character
I hardly know.   It is a character extremely hard of
understanding by us who are ordinary men, because
he was such an extraordinary man.   The ordinary
epithets cease to have their meaning when we try
to fit them to him.   Thus it appears meaningless
to say of Gordon that he was " courageous," or
" brave," for courage and bravery assume something
fearful which is faced by the resolution of the will
of the brave man.   But Gordon had no need of
courage, because for him the fearful thing did not
exist.   He was fearless ; and when we say " without
fear," we say at the same time " without the occasion
for courage."   I do not think that I exaggerate his
psychic outlook on things terrible to most men when
I affirm that he knew no fear of them.   His life
was a strenuous one, indeed, yet he says again and
again in his letters how greatly he would prefer death ;
and although this is a statement which is rather
to be suspected on the lips of another, there is no
doubt, as I think, that it represented the truth that was
in Gordon's mind.   He feared the possibility of long
drawn-out suffering, as who that is human and
sentient would not fear it ?   In one of his letters he
writes : " I do not look on death as anything but
joy, and that intense joy ; but long and continued
bodily suffering is appalling.   To die is only a

moment's agony, but a long weary life subdues us. The sacrifice of a life is nothing, but the sacrifice of a life's duration is that which we withdraw from." In another letter he writes : " The archers wound me sorely at times, and the infirmities of the flesh make me desire death that I may be dissolved and at rest. Life is no light penance, and yet we so often cling to it ! "

It is tolerably apparent that for a man who could write like this and voice the very truth of his convictions in such words, the " King of Terrors " must be not only no more formidable than a bogey, but actually the supreme benefactor. Armed with such conviction he could not fear. To live, appeared to him to need courage ; not to die.

Nor is it illogical, on these premises, that he should not care at all for another man's opinion of him. The conventions had no claim on him. It is recorded of him, and I believe the story is quite true, that once when he was in London the then Prince of Wales, who was afterwards King Edward VII, " commanded " him, as it is called, to dinner. To which command Gordon sent back answer to the Equerry that he hoped His Royal Highness would excuse him, as he never dined out and always went to bed at nine o'clock. After he had put down, or had wielded the main hand in putting down, the Taiping rebellion, the Emperor of China, after making him all those offers of remuneration which he refused, finally sent him a large gold medal. Gordon, because he was afraid that looking at it might incite in him sentiments of pride in the achievement, broke it up and distributed the pieces among his men.

If it be possible at all to realise such a man, a man prompted by such motives, let us try to realise him next on the way to Khartoum, sent out to perform his impossible task ; sent out under the direction of Sir Evelyn Baring, who became Lord Cromer later.

(From a photograph by Dittrich, Cairo.)

LORD CROMER.

Baring was a splendid official, administrator, and organiser. What he did for Egypt seems impossible to overrate. But he was an official all the while, accustomed to say to this man " Go, and he goeth " ; and the man to whom he had now to say " Go ; go along the official rut as I have gone and as I order you to go," was Gordon, a man such as I have feebly tried to sketch him. And the last time Gordon had gone to the Soudan he had gone as Governor-General !

I do not suppose there can be a doubt that Gordon was not quite in a normal condition at the time. Perhaps a man so extraordinary never could have such an epithet as normal given him. Throughout life he had believed himself directly and supernaturally guided, as Socrates and many others have believed. With such a belief, and with every disposition to follow the supernatural rather than any official guidance, it is ever a wonder to me how Gordon remained a soldier. Probably he would not have so remained in ordinary regimental work, but his record shows him to have been free-lancing in some strange quarter of the globe almost continuously after his Crimean service. Sir Evelyn found him quite impossible either to control or to comprehend. All the way to Khartoum he kept sending telegrams, of which the tenor of one would often contradict another. Sir Evelyn more than hinted that he was drinking : that alcohol was the disturbing cause. I do not think there is a doubt that at this time Gordon was taking a drug, but I question whether it was alcohol. That matters little, however. Two more incompatible men to work together could not easily be found ; and they did not work together. Had they been ever so harmonious, however, the result would have been the same. The task of rescue of the garrison was, humanly speaking, impossible, save by some such expedition as that which the Govern-

7

ment sent out ultimately for Gordon's rescue. Had
that expedition started when Gordon started, with,
or instead of, Gordon, the situation and Gordon would
have been saved. But the sending of such an expedition then would not have pleased the British
nation, and the Government was bent on pleasing the
nation. Instead of an equipped force it sent Gordon.

I have tried—I have found it very difficult—to
give some idea of the man who was Charles Gordon.
What I am totally unable to offer any explanation of,
or even to give any account of to myself, is the secret
of his influence over Oriental and African peoples.
When he was at home, stationed at Gravesend to
look after the forts along the Thames, he spent most
of his spare time visiting the poor, forming a boys'
club which was the beginning of the Gordon Boys'
Home, and so on. His influence over these people
was only a little less remarkable than over the
Easterns. One part of the secret of it, no doubt,
was, as I have said, his simple directness of speech
and act. He had a simple direct look in his eyes, too,
which spoke tacitly in the same sense.

And part of the secret, which the British Government would be wise to realise, since it has to bear
so large a share of the White Man's Burden, in
dealing with those who are not white, is that his
influence was due very largely to what is commonly
called prestige. Prestige, before it can be of use,
has first to be acquired, and Gordon's acquirement of
it was in China. He acquired it, perhaps, by his
direct methods, honesty, justice, and fearlessness.
Maybe we have had many political Gordons on the
way to acquire something like the same prestige,
but not living to take full value for it. Bullets used
to whistle around Gordon, but did not find him.
An ounce of lead six inches this way or that of the
course which it took, and all would have been finished ;

but that fatal six inches of aberration from its path of destiny was not allowed. So we may ascribe this ascendancy to what we please in the way of such humdrum qualities as I have suggested above ; we may say, at all events, that wi⁺hout such qualities that ascendancy could not have been all it was ; but when we have affirmed so much, we still have to confess that the solution of the secret is not there. It has escaped us. Others have dealt justly, honestly, directly, and so forth with the nations under our rule, and they have had their due reward ; but they were not Gordons, and they have not had Gordon's reward. Something there was at the back of all these which Gordon had uniquely, and which we cannot catch in any mesh of words. We may suggest some hint of it perhaps when we say " personality." That may serve as a suggestion : I am not professing it an explanation.

So Gordon went out, and he suffered the inevitable. He suffered the fate which the British Government should have known to be inevitable when they sent him. Their sending him was a folly, and perhaps a crime. But of almost all the ventures which Gordon undertook and which, up to this last, he carried to a successful issue, nearly the same might have been said. In each instance it looked as if only by some special Providence success could be wrought, and on each occasion as if some special dispensation had been vouchsafed. After all it is not wholly impossible that there were those in the Cabinet who believed that Gordon might be granted a peculiar portion of the divine help.

We all know the tragic end ; but what all do not realise is what that end has meant for our country. It is generally amusing, as it is generally futile, to speculate how the future would have gone had this or that event happened otherwise. We may speculate, if we please, on the fate of Egypt and of the Soudan, and of Gordon, had Lord Wolseley's admirably planned and executed expedition arrived just in time instead of just too late.   But, whatever the outcome of that speculation be, no matter how glorious the merit that we ascribe to Gordon and how prosperous the conditions that we imagine in those countries of the Nile, we still can scarcely find in all this a value to counterbalance the value of Gordon's death happening as and when it did.   We saw him as a beacon : sorrowing, maybe, for the succour which did not come, so that he might finish the work to which he had set his hand (his attitude of thoughtful sorrow is admirably expressed in Thornycroft's statue of him in Trafalgar Square); we saw him as a man of sorrow and disappointment, yet still saw him as a beacon light, still heard him as a trumpet call, to show and to sound the way of duty and self-sacrifice. Under no other circumstance could the light have shone so bright or the call have sounded so clear. He filled the eye of a grieving and indignant people. His example shone forth to us from the ramparts of Khartoum, where we imagined him gazing, gazing, weekly, daily, hourly, down the course of the ancient river up which he vainly hoped to see the boats ascending to his help.   For thousands of people of the English race that has been the vision glorious which has inspired them, if not indeed to be Gordons, to be, at least, their own best selves.   We cannot conceive that either longer life or another death could have left him quite so glorious, quite so conspicuous, quite so helpful to inspire us with something of his own fearlessness of all the little terrors which men have invented for their own undoing.   For my own part I often think, grievous as the pain of his loss was, that I would not have it changed.   Valuable above the life of other men though his life might be,

I cannot conceive it more valuable than his death, nor even conceive for him any other way of death in which its value would have been the same.

He was a man of great friendships, and his loss was widely as well as profoundly felt. But he was never a social man in the sense of going to places where society resorted. He would not dine out, and the *convenances* would have bored him hugely, had he allowed them the opportunity. But he did better than that, for he never went where there was this risk. His figure was no way remarkable, nor were his features arresting : you would pass him in a crowd and not notice him. Only when you had looked at him more than once, the look that he would return on you would remain with you. It was very direct and searching, out of friendly but very shrewd eyes of light grey iris. It was a good face, and a good-looking face and a strong face, as you found when you began to take stock of it ; but long before you had done all this you were likely to be feeling rather conscious that those eyes had already taken their full account of your face and of much that lay behind it. There was a hint of mesmerism about his power. He did not say the pleasant things that would make you happy, if he did not think them true. As I say, he did not respect the *convenances*. Somehow he gave out the idea of a rather terrible honesty and sincerity ; terrible because it was almost a rebuke to those whose sincerity was of the kind that serves well enough in the world and is taken for what it is worth. His sincerity was of quite a different standard, and you felt it to be so.

History may give us men as great and as good as Gordon ; possibly greater and better ; but this we may say with confidence, that she does not give us another man at all like Gordon. He was cast in a new mould, and no second copy has been issued from it since.

CHAPTER X

THE brilliant soldier who had failed to relieve and to retrieve Gordon received a Viscounty for his failure. He was already a Baron.

It is to the credit of the Government and of the nation that they could pass and approve this grant of honour. The way of the world is too often to judge every attempt by its failure or its success, and to condemn or praise in accordance with the issue. In this instance it showed exceptional clear sight and liberality of judgment, for though this was an attempt that failed, the world perceived that the failure was due to the impossibility of the end proposed. The expedition itself was perfectly planned, perfectly executed ; its commander and organiser really deserved only the larger meed of honour from the nation because he gained none of the honour which would certainly have been his had the end been a possible one with the means, and with the time, at his disposal.

I think it was the one failure, if it is so to be cited, in the whole long course of Lord Wolseley's career. All his other expeditions were triumphant successes, for their aim, though often difficult, was at least possible of achievement. The record is a very remarkable one.

Even in the very early days of his soldiering it looks as if Wolseley had shown uncommon qualities.

This was in the Crimea. He had gone out as an infantry soldier ; he was soon selected to serve as assistant in the work of the Royal Engineers.

The soldier who could think and who would apply his brains to his profession was more rare in those days than he is now. Wolseley gave such evidence of this ability that he was immediately appointed to a post connected with the transport and the disembarkation of troops.

If a young soldier was to learn something of transport and commissariat it is likely that there could not be a much better, a much harder or a much more painful school for him than he would find in that Crimean campaign. Perhaps it is not for us, who have perpetrated our own Mesopotamian campaign (in its early stages) to say too much about the Staff work, and especially about the commissariat and the medical departments, in the Crimea, but it is quite certain that young Wolseley must have had many an object lesson there in what it was advisable to avoid ; and it appears that he took the lessons to heart and assimilated them.

He was naturally quick to learn. One could not look at his alert, eager face and the open intelligent eye and doubt it. He had some likeness to Charles Wyndham, the actor, in the Eighties, though perhaps it was due as much to his manner of wearing his greyish hair, falling a little over the forehead, as to any real resemblance of feature. But the aspect of vivacity and of readiness to receive and respond to an impression was common to the two men. They were alike, too, in slight, active figure and in medium height.

After the Crimea it appears that Wolseley was already a marked man. Wherever there was work to do which required special organisation, and it is seldom that this is not called for in the thousand

and one odd jobs around the ragged corners and edges
of our Empire, the authorities sent Wolseley to do it.
One of his qualities seems to have been a ready
confidence in his own ability to carry things through.
He was Irish born and bred, which may account for
some of that quality. In any case, an unbroken series
of surprising successes was soon to give it full warranty.
It was necessary, of course, that he must have further
years of qualifying experience first, before command-
ing. He was at the relief of Lucknow ; and after
the Mutiny took part in many small campaigns in
India, and later in one of greater note in China, where
he was with the force that entered Peking in 1860.
Already he had begun writing on military subjects,
and it was in 1869, when he was still only thirty-six
years of age, that be brought out the *Soldier's Pocket
Book* (*The Soldier's Pocket Book for Field Service* was
its full-dress title), which was a text-book for many
years to follow.

That publication put the hall-mark on his reputation. Very shortly he was in command of the Red
River expedition, as it was called, in Canada, to
suppress the revolt inaugurated by Louis Riel. After
a complete and quick success in this command he
came back to the post of Assistant Adjutant-General
at the War Office. The next little expedition that
he took in charge was the Ashanti War, with the
march to Coomassie and final capture of the capital.

All this was before the Eighties. Just at the
beginning of the decade he was in South Africa,
" winding up the clew," in Homeric phrase, of the
Zulu War, but returned in 1880 to take up the appointment of Quartermaster-General, and two years
later that of Adjutant-General to the Forces.

He had scarcely entered on this new post before he
was summoned to Egypt to put his hand to check
the trouble which Arabi Pasha was creating (or with

which, at least, Arabi's name was most prominently
associated).   As with every military venture to which
he committed himself, the result was a brilliant
and a brilliantly rapid success.   I have mentioned
these few of the leading points in Lord Wolseley's
career in order to make clear how uninterrupted
was the series of his victories.   They were achieved
in little campaigns ; we may perhaps say, they were
short campaigns.   That is perfectly true, but at
the same time that we make this admission we may
well speculate how much larger and longer they might
have grown had it not been for the masterful dis-
positions of Wolseley in planning out the details
beforehand, so that, once started, the mechanism all
moved smoothly through, without a stop or hitch, to
its appointed end.   Wolseley did not live, unhappily,
to be a spectator even of the Great War, still less a
participator in it.   Born in 1833, he lived the full
average span of human years without seeing Britain's
fight for life.   In the relatively slight peril of the
Empire in the Boer War, his organisation as Commander-in-Chief was a chief means of giving her the
force, large beyond the expectation of almost all who
were best qualified to form a useful opinion on the
figure, which she needed to gain the victory.   But
the qualities which Lord Wolseley possessed in uncommon richness were just those of which our poor
country found herself in sore need in the later days
of her worst trial.

He was a scientific soldier, as I have said, at a time
when the numbers of scientific soldiers were very
few, when it was scarcely realised that such an
attribute as science of any kind could be required of
a soldier—especially of a soldier in a marching
regiment.   Wolseley's brain was too active to let
him bow assent to that easy and lazy creed.   He
must be at work on something.   Even in his older

days I have seen him in the train, on the way down to his home in Sussex, with desk and papers littering half the carriage, and writing an article or a paper or a memorandum as eagerly as if his life depended on it all through the journey. Needless to say, in the course of this career of which I have shortly jotted down a few chief stages, he was culling honours, medals, bars, letters of distinction after his name, occasionally a more materially useful grant of money, and so on. We knew him as Sir Garnet Wolseley at the beginning of the Eighties. It was for the Tel-el-Kebir victory over Arabi that he was made a peer. Then, from baron he was raised to viscount for the expedition that reached Khartoum too late.

He was a scientific soldier, and he was a fighting soldier, too. He was more than a scientific soldier, because he was a soldier of sympathy and imagination. He realised the needs of his men. He understood their wants. He knew that they could not fight unless they were fed, and even appreciated that besides their bodily food they needed that their hearts should be fed and filled with the confidence in their own power to achieve success. He managed to instil this influence into them by his own bearing and by his personality—especially, perhaps, by his own success : he was a " lucky " leader, a " mascot," at the same time as his great experience, his keen capacity for detail and his power of planning, organised for them the fullest supply of such comforts as are at all possible in a campaign. He knew both how to plan victory when the battle was set in array and also how to put in motion the mechanism required for bringing his battalions in good order to the field. He was an earnest student of the campaigns of great soldiers of the past. He produced books on Napoleon and Marlborough. His latest publication in book form was, I think, the autobiographical *Story of a Soldier's*

Life. But his pen had very little rest after he had put the sword finally into the scabbard. It was a militant pen, too, that he could wield, and after leaving the War Office he wrote of some of its shortcomings in terms that bit.

We have to estimate his value to his country not only by the achievements, though they in themselves are notable enough, that history has to put to his credit, but further, by the worth of the rather new idea of the British soldier which he imparted to the military profession. He demonstrated by example, as well as inculcated by precept, that it was a profession to be studied, not merely a happy-go-lucky affair to be " muddled through " somehow, with the British bull-dog pluck as its only asset.

Lord Wolseley was the first of the Commanders-in-Chief to be appointed on the five years' term of office, after the death of the Duke of Cambridge. His successor, in the middle of the Eighties, was a soldier only second in eminence, even at that time, to himself, and in later years second to none in all the Empire—Lord Roberts. He was Sir Frederick Roberts then. We knew a good deal about him in England, but the only reason why we did not know a great deal more and why we did not estimate him very much more highly than we did, was that almost all of his invaluable service had been done, thus far, in India, and that it is the besetting imperial sin of the ordinary Briton at home to pay criminally little attention to what is being done for him in Greater Britain. His autobiography, published in 1897, had for its very appropriate title *Forty-One Years in India.* It is possible that when Lord Roberts wrote this volume he looked upon his active career as a soldier almost in the light of history. He had done enough for most men. Yet he was still to see the country through its most critical moment in the Boer War. He went to South Africa, and, taking hold of the campaign with a comprehensive grasp which none of the generals had shown before he went there, carried it through a series of victories to a triumphant close. What later he did must be in the memory of all men : how he dinned into deaf ears the necessity of conscription, under the better title of National Service ; and how he died, as he had lived, in camp, while visiting our lines in France during the Great War.

It was both before and after, rather than during, the period of the Eighties that Lord Roberts was making his history—both his own and that of the Empire. He had already endeared himself to the Army under the title of " Little Bobs." With his little stature, for he was indeed a tiny man, he had done the deeds of heroes. In the Indian Mutiny he had " gone for " a standard held by two Sepoys ; had killed both standard bearers single-handed, and brought back their colours. He was V.C., and had all kinds of honour. But it was as the scourge of Afghan treachery that Sir Frederick Roberts, as he then was, was known in Great Britain at the beginning of the Eighties. It was in 1879 that the mission under Major Cavagnari had been massacred in Cabul. Sir Frederick was then at Simla, whence he hurried to Kurram and took command of that expedition which avenged Cavagnari and his companions and captured the city of Cabul. Here he was occupied in subduing the surrounding districts to something like obedience until the following summer, and was just about to withdraw his force within the Indian boundaries when he had information of the disaster of Maiwand, where a whole British brigade was totally defeated, and of the siege of General Primrose in Kandahar. Roberts was more

LORD ROBERTS.

than three hundred miles distant, with a country of desperate difficulty intervening ; Primrose and his force were in urgent stress ; there was no other British force within even this considerable range. Roberts' march to Kandahar is one of the monuments in military history. In that rugged district and amidst hostile tribes he marched over three hundred miles— 313 is the official figure—in twenty-two days, fought the battle of Kandahar the very day following, and was triumphantly victorious. It is a record which does marvellous credit both to the commander and to his troops. Probably no commander, not even Roberts, could have performed it with any other troops in all the world ; probably even those troops could not have achieved it under any other leader than that little man in whom they believed as if he were a god.

Already then, in the minds of all who knew anything of the story—and all England rang with the names of Cavagnari and of Maiwand—he was of " Kandahar." That title was linked to him by glorious bonds. He was made Baronet and G.C.B., and advanced to the command of the army in Madras.

Always it seems to have been his rôle to repair disaster. So we find it at Cabul, so at Kandahar ; and now, coming home on leave before taking up his Madras command, he was claimed for a like purpose in South Africa. There the Majuba Hill calamity had just occurred. Sir Frederick Roberts must go out to set it right. So he went, but on arrival found terms of peace already agreed. He came back to England and then returned to India. He became Commander-in-Chief in succession to Sir Donald Stewart in 1885. He came home in 1893 with the title, bestowed the year before, of Lord Roberts of Kandahar and Waterford ; and in 1895 was made Field-Marshal.

It is said that there was one thing and one alone of which Lord Roberts was afraid—a cat. I have been told that he was one of those people of ultra-feline sensitiveness who know when a cat is in the room although it be invisible. It is always a pleasant trait of weakness which makes a hero seem akin to our common humanity. Besides courage of the ordinary physical kind, Lord Roberts had his full meed of that higher sort which fears neither responsibility nor reproach. His National Service campaign was never popular, yet he never faltered in it ; and the Great War came to prove all his contentions right. And he must have had a great head, as well as a great heart, belonging to that little body. He planned every one of his campaigns, both the small and the large, with a skill which made all their mechanism go like clockwork ; and he seems to have been an exact judge of the force required for each task that he called on it to do, and also of the limits of what it could do. And he had that infectious power, magnetism, or call it what you will, which enabled him to get from his men the very best that they had to give—a born leader, a greatly loved man !

CHAPTER XI

IT is an exceedingly valuable asset for the Church to number among her hierarchs some who are distinguished in other sciences than those associated with theology or ecclesiology —and especially valuable if those other sciences be of the kind that are commonly named " exact." Whether rightly or wrongly, it is apt to appear to the ordinary man that these are the sciences which require a peculiar hardness of brain and incision of judgment. He has a particular respect for the intellect which is thus equipped : it is the practical, not the poetical ; it is not at all likely to be imposed upon.

Thus, the ordinary man, from his ordinary point of view. And when he finds a scientist of this brain equipment a devoted and convinced Christian, his own weak, hesitating faith receives immense comfort and reinforcement. If this man, he argues, with his intellect so severe and searching and exact, can accept these mysteries with such conviction, then they must surely be very truth. Who, at least, am I to doubt when such a mind is satisfied ?

Bishop, and later Archbishop, Temple was able to render this particular kind of service to his Church in quite uncommon measure. I wish it had been my privilege to know him better than I did, but though my personal acquaintance with him was very slight, and no more than such as a middle-aged and highly distinguished man might accord to a boy, I used to hear a great deal about him in Devonshire all through my school and undergraduate days. He was then Bishop of Exeter ; and he was a bishop of whom you would be sure to hear a great deal in his diocese, and, maybe, beyond its borders. His was a light which would not be hid under any sort of diocesan bushel ; in the first place, because of the kind of man that he was. He was always stirring, active, a tremendous worker, and disposed to get a full day's work out of others. Essentially a strong man in all senses of the term—mental, moral, physical—you could not tire him ; and he was something of a pugnacious man too, very ready to fight for that which his powerful judgment affirmed to be the right.

It was this militancy for the right which supplied the second reason why he was a bishop whose light would shine into all corners of the diocese, and farther. I was of such age at the time of his appointment to the bishopric as to be able to recall now some of the echoes of the storm of discussion which it raised. It was a Gladstonian appointment. He was a faithful follower of Mr. Gladstone and a resolute advocate of the disestablishment of the Irish Church. I am writing of the year 1869, *et circa*, when Dr. Temple, who had been for some ten years Headmaster of Rugby School, was brought to Exeter, in his native county. His own school had been the famous Blundell's at Tiverton, the nursery of very many of the Devon worthies. Thence he had gone to Balliol, had taken his degree with a double first, had been made a fellow, and a lecturer on mathematics and logic. Thus was the hall-mark of hard-headedness, so valued by the " man in the street," indelibly engraven by his University. Then, either while at Rugby or before, he had contributed an article entitled " The Education of the World " to a volume which caused terrific con-

(*From a photograph by Russell & Sons.*)

ARCHBISHOP OF CANTERBURY, DR. TEMPLE.

troversy in high places, *Essays and Reviews*. If any
of a younger generation read those essays to-day he
may very well wonder what all the pother was about.
They will appear to him as most unlikely to inspire
controversial heat. But the controversial question
of to-day is often the accepted verdict of the morrow.
These essays discussed such problems as those which
Dr. Temple was to deal with later, as Bampton
Lecturer, under the title of *The Relations between
Religion and Science*, with a liberality of outlook
and a candour quite unusual in a Churchman of that
time. It was not so many years since the publication
of that book which really did create an epoch, *The
Origin of Species*. Christianity was still reeling a
little under the blow, which many deemed to be
mortal, delivered by Darwin. Her own particular
version of the genesis of the world was discredited
by the witness of the rocks and strata. The eyes of
the mathematical lecturer, stout Churchman though
he was, refused to accept the blinkers assumed by
many of his day to enable them to pass by without
seeing the array of irrefutable witness. He wrote freely
what he felt to be the truth, and he had his reward.

This frank utterance of his thought was typical.
Throughout his life he gave himself far less to the
gentle art of making friends than to the ungentle
art of telling truth. Notoriously this truth-telling is
not a practice tending to easy popularity. It tends
to something that is a great deal better. Besides
the intrinsic value of that true word which the man
may have to tell, his candour and courage in its
telling ensure him eventual appreciation by the more
discriminating minds, and a respect which is not often
accorded to those who gain facile friendships. He
was recognised as genuine, a very dependable man,
a little rugged of surface, maybe, but of pure diamond
at the core.

8

Such a man as this it was whom Mr. Gladstone advanced to the See of Exeter. This, be it remembered, was at the very end of the Sixties. By a score of years earlier even than the Eighties, the man who dared to publish anything like advanced views on such a problem as the relations of religion and science was anywhere regarded with suspicion of heterodoxy, if not worse. But the reason why Dr. Temple was thus looked upon askance by some on his first coming to his Devon see was not thus chronological, solely. It was geographical, as well; for we of Devon, I fear, lived rather too far towards the sunset to catch any of the earlier beams of the dawn of progress. There was considerable outcry, protest, dismay at the appointment; but Dr. Temple was quite fearless. He had no idea of apologising for any of his acts or views. He was perfectly just, no respecter of persons; and a man of this character was absolutely certain to make himself appreciated and understood in the long run among the Devonians, for these are just the qualities which they admire. His clergy soon came to know that they could rely on him absolutely. So at Exeter he remained for more than fifteen years, and was sincerely regretted when he went, in the middle of the Eighties, to be Bishop of London.

By that time men knew him for what he was, a strong, just, broad-minded man, of great zeal for what he deemed the right and an amazing power of work. Thirteen and fourteen hours were spoken of as his normal working day.

Towards the end he had to suffer the penalty of this tremendous energy: his eyes failed. When he was raised in 1897 to the highest dignity in the Church, the Archbishopric of Canterbury, the prodigious working power was spent. His death came five years later.

Archdeacon Farrar, later Dean of Canterbury

Perhaps the value of a preacher's sermons is not very precisely measured by the numbers of the congregation that he attracts, but it is at all events a popular and a convenient standard ; and, thus estimated, few stood higher than Archdeacon Farrar. He became Archdeacon of Westminster in 1883, and had been Rector of St. Margaret's since 1876. His previous career had been one of much distinction. He had taken a first in " Greats," and I rather think that he won the " Newdigate." He became a schoolmaster and set himself to write books, in the form of novels, on school-boy life. In the intervals, by way of relaxation, he would now and then throw off a work dealing with Greek Syntax or the like.

It is a difficult art, that of writing of school life. There is but one who has made a real success in that art, and he was a man of but one book—to count. That was Thomas Hughes, of course, with his *Tom Brown* at Rugby. Farrar had been at some school in the Isle of Man and the school scenes in his *Eric, or Little by Little*, which was the first and best of his school-boy books, were based on that experience. He handicapped himself by the didactic moral purpose which is always obvious. They are not real, in comparison with the vividness of *Tom Brown*. But they achieved a certain popularity.

But the book by which he was best known, as it was also his best book, was the *Life of Christ*. He had all the possible qualities for so great and grave a task : knowledge, devotion, earnest piety, graceful phrase, and rather exceptionally first-hand acquaintance with that Palestine in which Christ's life was passed, and which probably has not very largely changed in the nearly two thousand years which have since lapsed. Farrar's *Life of Christ* is one of the relatively few books which are not likely to die.

Then, just after he had given up the Headmastership of Marlborough to come to St. Margaret's, he published a book of which the boldness took most people by surprise. Hitherto I do not think that they had associated him with strength ; or would it be more right to say that they deemed his strength to be rather in his gentleness ? Exactly how his ecclesaistical attitude should be defined I do not know. Assuredly he was not a High Churchman. His leaning was rather in the other direction and to the avoidance of ritual ceremony. Yet to speak of him as Evangelical would be to suggest an idea of narrowness which certainly was not part of his outlook. His position is indicated, in some measure, by the fact of his inaugurating the Anglican Brotherhood.

The book which surprised us then would, of course, surprise no one now, even from the pen of a divine of far less breadth of view than Farrar. Its title was *Eternal Hope*, and much of its purpose was to contest the doctrine, then held orthodox, of the sinner's eternal hopelessness, of his unending torture in the fire that is never quenched. It is singular, and a fact which throws curiously illuminating lights on that very curious product of evolution which we call the human mind, that gentle Christian men and women found it extremely hard to persuade themselves to part with a doctrine which implied a delight in cruelty enjoyed by their Christian God infinitely far surpassing the worst that the most savage imagination has ever attributed to the most hideous and bloodthirsty devil of its invention. They clung to their fiery and eternal hell. It appeared to many as if Farrar had committed an act of sacrilege, of blasphemy, in arguing for the rejection of this awful abomination. Had he done no other act of value in the course of his long and energetic life of usefulness, he would have justified himself more than enough by this single book alone, by its quenching of these eternal and infernal flames, and by the better hope—the " Eternal Hope," as its joyful title said—which it held before the eyes of men whose own imagination had conjured to them a future of eternal desperation. In that book alone was cause sufficient why London went in its legions to hear Farrar at St. Margaret's.

He was an easy and fluent preacher, a little florid, fond of the picturesque phrase. In any sermon by Farrar you were disappointed if you did not at least once have mention of " the mother-of-pearl-coloured ocean." Some of the more fastidious professed to find the ocean, thus beautiful of surface hue, a little lacking in depth. But of his popularity there could be no question. It was, moreover, a personal equally as a professional popularity. He had a great social charm, a fine presence, a gentle, welcoming smile. On this social side he was ably abetted by Mrs. Farrar and their family. His, I think, was always a happy, peaceful outlook, inspired by the *Eternal Hope*, and unvexed by those temporal worries which beset, and upset, so many ; not at all because they are intrinsically formidable, but merely because the vexed spirit is too sensitive to their troubling.

Farrar was in London throughout the Eighties, and went as Dean to Canterbury in 1895, where he died in harness.

There were many other divines of eminence in these years whose portraits should be given if space permitted. Liddon, delighting great congregations at St. Paul's with his perfect diction, his rich eloquence, and his refined and beautiful face, has been very ably sketched by Mr. Russell. Ainger was at the Temple, as yet but Reader, soon to be exalted to the dignity of Master. " The Most Valiant the Master of the Temple " is, I believe, the full ceremonial title of that mastership, and it provokes a smile when associated with the aspect of Ainger, whom all that knew him loved, but in whom none could see a terrific or very militant figure. He was small, thin, wizened, with a narrow face and the whitest possible hair. Give George Grossmith a snowy head and you would have had a very good imitation of Ainger. He was a notable preacher, but his gifts were really literary rather than rhetorical. He was a great lover of Charles Lamb, whose *Life* he wrote, and I always used to think of his as a very kindred spirit to Lamb's, in its rare unity of gentleness and brightness. I could sympathise with him less in his admiration of Crabbe, whose *Life* also he wrote. He was, I believe, a very excellent amateur actor, though I never saw him on the boards ; but I have heard him recite to admiration. His reading of *The Ancient Mariner* made your flesh creep and haunted you for days. And when he recited the verses of his favourite Crabbe he did seem to get some life and spirit in them, which I never am able to awaken by my own reading. Doubtless Ainger was right, and mine the faulty taste.

Another who had not yet come to his own was Scott Holland, known at that time chiefly at Oxford, where he was a " Senior Student," as it is called, at Christ Church. London had not in those years its opportunity to realise that splendid eloquence which took it captive a little later.

In 1883 the Archbishopric of Canterbury passed at Dr. Tait's death to Dr. Benson, highly distinguished father of distinguished sons. It is a singular coincidence that at school with him, at King Edward VI's School at Birmingham, were both Lightfoot and Westcott. All three went on to Trinity, Cambridge, and Westcott succeeded Lightfoot, on the

(From a photograph by Elliott & Fry.)

ARCHBISHOP OF CANTERBURY, DR. BENSON.

latter's death, in 1889, in the Bishopric of Durham.
Later, Westcott was at Cambridge as Professor of
Divinity, where Lightfoot was Hulsean Lecturer.
About the time that Benson was consecrated Archbishop, Westcott became a Canon of Westminster,
and Benson almost immediately made him his exam-
ining chaplain.   So singularly intertwined were the
lives of the three school-fellows.   Westcott's name
is perhaps particularly remembered in connection
with the Revised Version of the New Testament, to
which he gave his devoted attention while he was at
Cambridge.   I imagine, though I speak with no
authority whatever for expressing an opinion, that
Lightfoot was really the most deeply learned of the
three.   Westcott was a man of wider interests : his
outlook embraced art, music, literature.   If the
Archbishop were to be described in a phrase, one
would say, I imagine, that he was a great ecclesiastical
statesman.   The better government of the Church
within its own walls, and the better relations of Church
and State, occupied his mind and were the objects
of his constant endeavour.   He was active on Parliamentary Commissions dealing with Church matters
and in the promotion of Bills affecting the Church—
in a word, he fulfilled to admirable perfection the
functions of this highest spiritual office.

The strong figure of Creighton had scarcely come
on the stage in any important rôle during the Eighties.
He was at Cambridge at that time, already hard at
his great work, *The History of the Papacy*.   He soon
became recognised as one of the leading men in the
Church, with a profound knowledge of ecclesiastical
history.   It was not until the appointment of Temple,
in 1897, to the Archbishopric that he was much in
London.   In succession to Temple he was made
Bishop of London, and from that time till his death,
in 1901, he was always in the forefront in his diocese

Dean Church, as he was always designated, was at
St. Paul's during all this decade, as he had been
almost all through the Seventies. He was appointed
to the deanery in 1871, and held it till his death at
the end of 1890. It was a long-held office, which
gave him a considerable leisure for literary work.
He wrote on Bacon and on Spenser, as well as on
many ecclesiastical questions, in a rather pure, dry,
and unimpressioned style. It would not be as untrue
as it often is to say that in this case the style was
the man—the natural expression of his own nature.
A pathetic interest attaches to his last appearance
at any public function. This was the funeral of
Liddon. His own health was very indifferent at the
time, and he died in the same year.

CHAPTER XII

HUXLEY AND THE EVOLUTIONISTS

THAT is a tremendously impressive face that looks down on you, in marble, on your right-hand side, as you enter the Natural History Museum, in the Cromwell Road. On the pedestal of the figure you will read Thomas Henry Huxley. Born May 4th, 1825. Died June 29th, 1895. It is an exceedingly well-graven image, showing much of the very nature of the great man and profound thinker who was its original, though the sculptor never had the advantage of seeing that original in life. Those who knew the living face best, and loved it most, find the lines which the photograph has shown the sculptor to be rather over-emphasised, so that the kindlier look which the face wore in life is lost. The statue, moreover, has the disadvantage that it is not placed in the position for which it was intended, so that the light does not fall on it as its creator had proposed. But the living face itself was tremendous, just because of those forceful and deep lines of thought and feeling which lend themselves to expression by the maker of images. There are faces which are as masks, hiding the character of the man behind them. This face is of quite another kind. It seems as if it must tell the true story of the man. And it does.

What is very singular about this quite remarkable face of Huxley's is, that its characteristic lines were graven, plainly legible on it, at an age when most faces still keep much of the smoothness of youth. It was not so with him. In the Eighties he was between sixty and seventy years old ; he had long ago made his name, had thought those thoughts which had so impressed themselves on his features, had done much of the writing which we still read with delight in the clear, trenchant style, though the science may to-day be as rungs of a ladder which others, climbing by their aid, have left below them. But they are rungs which those others have been able to leave, just because Huxley himself took a master-hand in fixing them in place ; and when he so fixed them they were the rungs at the very top. It must ever be so unless science itself ceases to mount higher.

Huxley, of course, builded largely on Darwin, as who did not that builded at all solidly at that time ? No doubt some of the earlier Darwinians deceived themselves more than a little, in the enthusiasm kindled by that new light which evolution shed, believing that the edifice based thereon was more immovable, more complete, and more heaven-scaling than further examination has proved it. Huxley, to whom scepticism appealed as a quite positive intellectual and moral virtue, was cautious. " Scepticism," he writes, in *Method and Results*, " is the highest of duties ; blind faith the one unpardonable sin." Yet for all his scepticism—he used to say of himself that he was rightly named Thomas, after the doubting apostle—he did not escape some share in the deception. At the same time he maintained his characteristic attitude so far that he always made one important reservation in his acceptance of the Darwinian view of the way in which new species are produced. And besides this reservation to his faith in the solution of biological puzzles by natural selection, he saw quite clearly that there always must remain one puzzle which evolution is perfectly

THOMAS HENRY HUXLEY.

inadequate to solve—itself. Given evolution, he might have believed that all terrestrial progress could be explained—I hope and believe that I state his position rightly in thus writing of it—but whence the gift was derived, from what hand it came, he deemed beyond all human knowledge. Hence, and so far, he was agnostic—a term still rather novel in the Eighties, and of Huxley's own adoption. It was a view of life, as I have tried to sketch it, which seemed as though it must bring with it most profound and tragic sadness. Could it well be otherwise? Listen to what he found when he cast up the account of evolution. This is how he reckoned the net result : " I know of no study which is so unutterably sad as that of the evolution of humanity as it is set forth in the annals of history. Out of the darkness of prehistoric ages man emerges with the marks of his lowly origin strong upon him. He is a brute, only more intelligent than other brutes ; a blind prey to impulses which as often as not lead him to destruction ; a victim to endless illusions which make his mental existence a terror and a burthen, and fill his physical life with barren toil and battle. He attains a certain degree of comfort, and develops a more or less workable theory of life in such favourable situations as the plains of Mesopotamia or of Egypt, and then for thousands and thousands of years struggles with varying fortunes, attended by infinite wickedness, bloodshed, and misery, to maintain himself at this point against the greed and the ambition of his fellow-men. He makes a point of killing and other- wise persecuting all those who first try to get him to move on ; and when he has moved a step farther foolishly confers post-mortem deification on his victims. He exactly repeats the process with all who want to move a step yet farther." (*Nineteenth Century*, February 1889.)

We hardly may expect a man with this desperate record of human misery at his heart to wear a smiling face to the world. He wore what had the aspect of a profoundly sad face ; though the aspect of an unflinchingly brave face, nevertheless. But those who knew him best, those of his own household who have the best and almost the only right to speak with authority on such a point, have affirmed him " the least sad man in the world." Could this be possible had he not some brighter hope for the world's future than this which his appeal to the historical record seems to forecast ? That he had this better hope, however, is testified by many of those pithy *Aphorisms and Reflections*, collected by Mrs. Huxley and published under that title in Macmillan's Golden Treasury Series. We have the key to it suggested in No. CXIX, for instance : " My belief is that no human being, and no society composed of human beings, ever did, or ever will, come to much, unless their conduct was governed and guided by the love of some ethical ideal." Much more fully and succinctly the faith here indicated is set out in No. CCLII :

" The theory of evolution encourages no millennial anticipations. If, for millions of years, our globe has taken the upward road, yet, some time, the summit will be reached and the downward route will be commenced. The most daring imagination will hardly venture upon the suggestion that the power and the intelligence of man can ever arrest the procession of the great year.

" Moreover, the cosmic nature born with us and, to a large extent, necessary for our maintenance, is the outcome of millions of years of severe training, and it would be folly to imagine that a few centuries will suffice to subdue its masterfulness to purely ethical ends. Ethical nature may count upon having to reckon with a tenacious and powerful enemy as

long as the world lasts. But, on the other hand, I see
no limit to the extent to which intelligence and will,
guided by sound principles of investigation, and
organised in common effort, may modify the conditions of existence, for a period longer than that now
covered by history. And much may be done to
change the nature of man himself. The intelligence
which has converted the brother of the wolf into
the faithful guardian of the flock ought to be able
to do something towards curbing the instincts of
savagery in civilised men.

" But if we may permit ourselves a larger hope of
abatement of the essential evil of the world than
was possible to those who, in the infancy of exact
knowledge, faced the problem of existence more
than a score of centuries ago, I deem it an essential
condition of the realisation of that hope that we should
cast aside the notion that the escape from pain and
sorrow is the proper object of life."

It was possible for him, therefore, with this ethical
aim in view, to possess his soul not cheerfully but with
a brave patience, in a tempered optimism. As he
writes elsewhere, " The conclusion of the whole matter
seems to be that if Ormuzd has not had his way in
this world, neither has Ahriman. Pessimism is as
little consonant with the fact of sentient existence as
optimism."

At that rather poor best he felt compelled to leave
the riddle. The two gods of Huxley's conscious
worship were knowledge and truth. He would have
said, in fact, that they were but one, since, for him,
although he had a keen appreciation of artistic beauty,
all truth must have a large element of the intellectual.
At the very moment when death cut his still keen
energies short he was engaged in a critique of Arthur
Balfour's *Foundations of Belief*, which had attributed
to the agnostics certain views which Huxley did not

admit to be an accurate account of their position.
I mention this controversy just at this point, because
the question in what degree truth is purely intellectual
is so closely involved in the question of the foundations
of our beliefs.   Huxley's criticism was intended to
be made in two halves, in shape of two articles in the
Nineteenth Century.   One was published, but the other
not—because death had in the meantime arrested
the trenchant pen of the writer.   I have always
thought the loss of that second article a very great
loss, because it was the second article in which, as
was sufficiently evident from the first, the writer
intended to concentrate the pith of his argument.
In the first he wrote with the velvet glove, in appreciation of all the brilliant merit of this contribution
to philosophy by one who was by profession a statesman, but under that soft glove one might feel, even
in these very phrases of laudation, that the hand
beneath was iron, and that iron, cold iron, would be
brought down with its full weight and sternness in
the concluding section.   But the iron never fell.

One need not be a scientific person in order to
appreciate the extraordinary clarity and the penetrating edge of Huxley's thought.   It is not a common
characteristic of men of science to take wide views.
Usually their range is restricted.   But Huxley's
range was exceptionally wide, and his essays on social
subjects are vital still.   We may read to-day that
essay on " The Struggle for Existence in Human
Society," in the volume called *Evolution and Ethics*,
and find that it is not only of living interest, but has
argument so in advance of the date (1891) of its
writing, that it has not yet been overtaken by
humanity's progressive thought.   It still points ahead.

Huxley devotedly worshipped truth, as he saw it,
and worshipped it quite regardless of the cost.   Even
if it led him right up to such a painful recital of the

world's story as I have quoted from his pen, he would not recoil from it, turn aside, nor strive to blur its poignant outlines under any veil.

Few people perhaps remember that in early life he had been in the Navy, as a surgeon. It is remarkable that a like early destiny was in some part the means of making the names of Darwin and also that of Hooker, the great botanist, and Huxley's life-long friend. What the *Voyage of the Beagle* was to Darwin, the voyage of the *Rattlesnake* was to Huxley. The *Rattlesnake* went out, on survey work, to Torres Strait, and in the southern and tropical seas Huxley found a wealth of animal life for his study. It was wealth which had not been very seriously raided before. He brought home new facts, new specimens, new deductions ; and the deductions were of such value that he came to his own, straightway, and obtained his due recognition from the biologists of the Royal Society. Darwin, Hooker, and Huxley all owed much of their opportunities to the spacious leisure which ship life in the old sailing days gave to all, and especially to those who were not actively concerned with the navigation. They had " all the time there was " in which to think, and the teeming life of the warm seas gave them plenty about which to occupy their thoughts. The mental apparatus which each of the three brought to bear on these problems was far above the normal standard. The outcome could scarcely fail to be remarkable. Like the others, however, Huxley did not long " follow the sea," and certainly there was little in his later appearance of the bluff sailorman ; save that he kept his face close-shaven except for some side-whiskers, there was nothing. His aspect revealed the man of thought, the student, in the tall, spare, but wide-shouldered figure, the splendid, forceful yet tragic features, the heavy shock of iron-

grey hair worn rather long.   No one who did not know
him was likely to pass him without asking of another
who might be better informed, " Who's that ? "
His was a face that arrested the eyes in a crowd.

There was a third god whom Huxley worshipped
with a less conscious cult than he paid to truth and
knowledge—kindliness. Just where he found room
for that saving grace in his despairing summary of
our fate I do not well know, but he was himself an
object lesson that the world has a better hope than he
perceived in it. To his own family circle, to his
friends and to humanity in its widest distribution,
a kind man, and a welcome and much sought guest
in all circles where his trenchant talk was appreciated.
To some who knew him little he might appear a stern
man, but, beneath the rind, he was not only warm of
heart, but even soft—soft, that is, to everything that
did not offend the great god Truth. That offence
was always, for him, the deadly sin. All the seven
deadlies of the Christian were summed up for him in
that. I write, at least, of the opinion which I, on
a very slight acquaintance which I much wish had
been closer, formed of him. And I do not think that
his *Life*, as admirably presented to us by his son,
gainsays that view. There was not kindliness only,
but humour withal, in the glint of the keen eyes that
were set in so deep under the shaggy eyebrows. It
was more often by the appreciative look than by the
spoken word that he showed his response to humorous
suggestion. His was the quiet, " pawky " humour
of the Scot rather than the more expansive and less
subtle English mirth, though I do not know that he
had a single vein of Scottish blood. It is true that he
was for two University sessions in Edinburgh, but
scarcely long enough to have assimilated its atmosphere. What he did most fully appreciate was the
tonic truculence of its climate. He often referred

to it with a most profound respect; and as for North
Berwick and its breezes, straight off the eastern sea,
he used to speak of it with an almost awful admiration as " a place to which people go, *from Edinburgh*,
to be braced ! "

Just what the value to science of Huxley's life and
work was, I suppose one would need to be a scientist,
and a scientist in his own line, which was biology, to
know; but if science had not claimed so much of his
thought he might have been a most effective statesman, public servant, or man of business. So at least
I have been told by some of those who sat on Royal
Commissions with him. There is no doubt that he
did much very useful public work on these Commissions, in spite of his engrossment in his profession
as a biologist. Indeed it was for this service perhaps,
even more than for his contributions to science, that
he was made a Privy Councillor. It is as biologist,
as thinker, and as writer however, that his name will
be remembered, and will go down to historical fame.

As we enter that fine central hall of the Natural
History Museum, we meet the large figure in marble
of Darwin, seated, facing us, and looking down upon
us from the first landing of the stairs. On the right
hand Huxley, also seated, and beside us, as we stand
regarding, Owen. These three, like three great gods
of Science, share the Pantheon between them. For
the rest it is filled with the stuffed animals and the
show-cases, from the huge elephant to the pigmy
shrew among the mammals, various insect demons
magnified to a terrific size, illustrations of colour
protection, all and sundry " exhibits." They form a
singular trio. Darwin and Huxley may be said to
stand solidly together for the new theories of evolution. Owen, on the other hand, although he lived
right through the Eighties, dying only in 1892, still
held, as fast as it was at all possible that a man of

9

science could hold such a faith, by the older scientific theories, though not perhaps to the exact letter of the Book of Genesis. If orthodoxy compelled belief in the literal reading of the Biblical account of the genesis of life in the world, it is plain that orthodoxy and evolution were incompatible. Hence arose bitter controversy, not always kept quite within the pale of courtesy and due reverence to a belief which, however the new scientists might be convinced of its proved falsity, was still sacred to very many. Bishop Wilberforce's attack, and Huxley's counter-attack— to write of it merely as a defence were to take all the edge off the weapons which he wielded with a terrible deftness—give good examples of the debate. But, in truth, all the weapons were with Huxley, in addition to a full measure of ability to turn them to account. Those who maintained the literal version of the Book of Genesis, declining to see in it a specimen of folk-lore common in its main features to very many races of mankind in very different parts of the globe, whenever man reached the stage of meditating on the creation of the life by which he saw himself to be surrounded and to be a part, had in the long run to confess defeat. The verdict of the rocks and strata of the earth, first called into court by the great geologist Charles Lyell, was even more decisively fatal to their case than the researches of Darwin or of Wallace. Gradually the Christian Church began to learn that it could concede all the most essential points claimed by the evolutionists, while still re-taining the most essential points of its own ancient faith. Professor Drummond indeed was soon to claim evolution itself as religion's ally, with his *Natural Law in the Spiritual World.* But for the moment faith in all Bible teaching had received a staggering blow ; and in their consequent discomfiture its adherents said many hard and bitter things of the great intellects and noble men who had brought it all upon them. No one can possibly read the life of Charles Darwin, as it is finely told by his son, and fail to realise that this was a man as great and good of heart as of brain, devoted to the service of his fellows and serving them with an unswerving eye to truth. A more perfect Christian in his character and in his dealings with his fellow men it were impossible either to name or to imagine. The wonderful modesty of the man and the tentative humility with which he advanced his great discoveries and theories were beyond all praise and most worthy of all men's imitation. But yet, most naturally, stinging things were said of him, of him and of Huxley also, by those with whose cherished views the new science came into opposition.

It aroused in its turn some bitterness of spirit in its opponents, but less perhaps in the great men themselves than in some of their disciples, possibly for the very reason that they were not quite so great and could not so generously forgive. Professor Owen, although at the outset fiercely opposing Darwin's theory of the Origin of Species, nevertheless seems to have regarded himself as in some sort anticipating Darwin himself in its discovery, so that his attitude is difficult to understand, and some of his writings are difficult to reconcile with each other. It was this, most likely, which gave such bitterness to their controversy. Moreover, Owen's concern with the affair was really very direct, and on this account also Darwin may have resented it the more. He was primarily an osteologist, a student of bones, whence it was said of him, with not more than tolerable accuracy perhaps, that from a fossil thigh he could reconstruct the complete prehistoric animal.

Punch, so far back as 1861, had a poem signed Gorilla," with a picture of the great ape and the

question under : " Am I a Man and a Brother ? "
of which one verse went—

> " Next Huxley replies
> That Owen, he lies,
> And garbles his Latin quotation ;
> That his facts are not new,
> His mistakes not a few,
> Detrimental to his reputation."

The controversy waxed fierce, far beyond the
bounds of merely scientific circles.   There is frequent
reference to it in the general writings of the day.
As Leonard Huxley reminds us, in the *Life and Letters*
of his father, " echoes of the great Hippocampus
question linger in the delightful pages of *The Water-
Babies.*"

It is all a debate which has no living place in the
thought of the twentieth century.   Here and there
you may still chance on some dear old lady who will
say with a pained look, when you speak of " the *great*
Darwin," or " the *great* Huxley," as the case may be :
" Ah, what I should call ' the wicked Darwin,' or
' the wicked Huxley.' "   It is all really dead matter
of ancient history, for it was in the Sixties that the
storm arose.   But it still raged furiously and vitally
in the Eighties.

CHAPTER XIII

SIR JOHN LUBBOCK (LATER, LORD AVEBURY)

WHEN you mention the name of any man or woman of note you commonly feel that you know with tolerable accuracy the idea that the name is likely to conjure in the mind of the person you are talking to. Of Lloyd George, let us say, or Foch, or Beatty, you know fairly well what their immediate thought will be, and what attributes will be associated with the names before their mental eye, as soon as one or other is mentioned. That was just as true in the Eighties of the eminent men of that day as it is now. But there was one man, exceptionally, at that time of whom you could not be in the least degree confident what kind of idea you would summon in the mind of a friend when you spoke his name. That man was Sir John Lubbock, who was afterwards created Lord Avebury.

If your friend was a Parliament man it is likely that Proportional Representation is the matter which Lubbock's name would immediately bring to his thoughts, for Lord Avebury never failed in his zeal in advocating this measure, conjointly with his friend Mr. Leonard Courtney, afterwards Lord Courtney of Penwith. If it were a City man that you were talking to, the name would at once suggest banking. Sir John's firm was Robarts, Lubbock & Co., and he was a leader in all financial movements in the City. If you spoke of him to a countryman, with an ordinary intelligent interest in the animal life that he saw about him in the fields and woodlands, he would at once say,

" Oh, yes—Sir John Lubbock—that's the ant man."
If you mentioned him within the learned precincts
of the Athenæum Club, there were still two lines of
thought that you might evoke; if you were speaking to
an antiquarian, the name of Lubbock would have
associations for him with the history of early civilisa-
tions; if a biologist, he would at once recall some
valuable original research work done by Lubbock in
the very early years of his career. And now, if you
went out into Pall Mall or Regent Street and said
" Lubbock " to " the man in the street," the answer
you would unfailingly get would be, " Sir John
Lubbock ! Why, yes ; that's the fellow what gave
us the Bank 'Oliday."

The extraordinary thing is that there was no
illusion nor mistake about any one of these varied
images that the one name might conjure up. All
were real presentments of a man of an extraordinary
number of interests and activities. It was a marvellous versatility, and of course it gave opportunity to
persons who were perhaps a little jealous for cheap
jibes. A much quoted jibe was that " the men of
science thought he was a great banker, and the
bankers thought he was a great man of science."
If any one will take the trouble to look at his *Life and
Letters*, which it was my own privilege to be allowed
to write and to edit, they will very quickly see that
this estimate is as unjust as it is illiberal. It was
really the scientists who credited him with very real
and original contributions to science ; and this, at
an uncommonly early age. They expressed heartfelt
disappointment when he forsook, or partially forsook,
the paths of science to wander in the wilderness of
political life. A little banking they could permit
him : it was at a very early age that he went from
Eton into the firm, and he found time for much
scientific work in the intervals of office hours.

SIR JOHN LUBBOCK (LORD AVEBURY).

It was marvellous how he found the time. All through life his economy of time was something approaching a miracle. He was full of small time economies. I remember staying with him once and hearing in the morning next to my dressing-room his voice as it were in recitation. I had an idea he might be saying his prayers aloud. The fact, as I afterwards learnt, was that he was opening his morning's letters, one by one, as he dressed, and dictating the answers to each, as soon as read, into a dictaphone. Thence the replies would be read off later, usually by the girls' governess acting as secretary, typed, and brought to him to sign. Thus, by the hour that he came down to breakfast, the bulk of his correspondence, which was vast, would have been dealt with and very few minutes wasted in it. He got through more work in the day than any other man I ever knew, yet he never seemed to be at all strained or overworked : the secret of which I presume to be that though he never left a minute idle he never hurried.

A very great deal of what Lord Avebury did, and also of what he was, is to be attributed beyond all doubt to the happy chance that as a boy he had the great Darwin as his near neighbour. Darwin lived at Downe, close to the family home of John Lubbock's father and his numerous brothers at Orpington. Evidently the great man became attracted by the boy. He advised him as to courses of study ; he infected him with his own zeal ; he taught him how to observe, what questions to put to Nature ; he taught him, too, the wise use of time, and both by example and by precept inspired in him the conviction of the value to a man's usefulness and happiness of patience and control over self. It is impossible to read Charles Darwin's *Life*, written with equal ability and affection by his son, now Sir Francis, and doubt that he was one of the very best of men, one of the noblest characters, as well as the man who has perhaps done more service to mankind than any other by his studies. Of like nobility, patience, and self-control became John Lubbock, very largely, as he himself was the first to say, through Darwin's influence. Even in his own home he was not without the incentive of example in scientific study, for his father was a great astronomer and mathematician. Both by heritage and environment he was well placed.

At the beginning of the Eighties Sir John, who had sat in the Commons for ten years for Maidstone, in his native county, was unseated, but he was immediately elected for a constituency which probably pleased him better—London University. It is a testimony to his quick grasp of Parliamentary procedure that though he first came into the House early in 1870 it was in 1871 that he succeeded in passing that Bank Holiday Act which made his name immediately known all over England. The first Monday in August was sometimes called the Feast of St. Lubbock by grateful holiday makers. He was successful in passing many other Bills while he was a member of the Lower House ; indeed the only measure, as I think, in which he was closely interested, which has not yet been put on record in the Statute Book is that Proportional Representation to which I have already referred. But, as we all know, that is far from a dead project even to-day, and maybe it will yet survive to be an accomplished fact to justify his work for it.

As almost always, there are two points of view from which this nearly unbroken success may be regarded, and it has been open to some who looked on it with a rather grudging eye to suggest that it was achieved mainly because the measures for which he fought were those only which he thought he might carry. Maybe. We may accept that criticism and yet ask

whether in thus limiting himself Sir John Lubbock
did not show the highest wisdom. Assuredly he had
sufficient occupation for his time : none are likely to
deny that ; and surely it was a sign of a good judgment to devote himself to those projects which he saw
a good chance of bringing to a useful issue, rather
than spend himself in vain efforts for causes which
he could not hope to win. As a matter of fact,
however, that first and most popular measure, the
Bank Holiday Bill, looked so unlikely to pass that
one so well versed in all the ways and wiles of Parliament as Disraeli himself, told Sir John that it was no
good his bringing it in : it could not succeed. But
bring it in he did, nevertheless, and pass it did.

He was a man of exceedingly quiet, one would say
of exceedingly modest, manner. He was perfectly
charming in the way that he would ask the opinion,
with an apparent deference, of persons, even of children, who could hardly conceivably have an opinion
worth listening to, on the subject of discussion, in
comparison with his own. Yet he did not think so ;
he was always anxious to hear a new view, never
knowing what new light it might throw. He had a
mind singularly open ; and yet, though open, it
was very carefully selective. He would take a word
of wisdom out of the mouth of a babe, but he would
not take a word that was not wise, even though
it fell from the mouth of one famed as a very fount
of wisdom. It is not at all surprising, nor contrary
to character, that he should neglect the advice of
Disraeli on a Parliamentary point, even on his first
crossing the Westminster threshold. Under that very
quiet manner he had a will of strong determination,
and, besides, a perseverance that one might almost
imagine he had acquired in imitation of those ants
that he was so fond of studying. One who had
worked with him in some political scheme told me that

his industry in writing notes with a view to getting support for his scheme was amazing : he neglected no possible chance ; and what was ant-like about him is that when he was foiled and worsted in one channel of attack he never wasted any time in repining, but immediately set to work to renew the attack by some other channel. Thus he was very difficult to defeat.

A great City magnate, who was a friend of his, gave me an account of a meeting of Foreign Bond-holders at which Sir John had to preside. It had to deal with affairs of South American Republics, and there was a strong revolutionary element, rather in keeping with the usual lurid temperature of those picturesque regions, resolved to assert itself at the meeting. His friend had rather feared for him, that he might not be able to rule the storm, " but," as he told me afterwards, " it was wonderful how that man, with his quiet voice, by just coming back and back to his point again after each outburst was over, and never losing his temper or his head, at length brought the whole meeting round to his own way of thinking and gained his end."

There was one quality at least for which even his detractors were bound to give him credit—his character, his absolute honesty of purpose ; and in every British gathering, at all events, that is an asset that counts for a great deal. I do not believe that he had enemies : he was so kind that it was hardly conceivable he could arouse enmity ; but he had detractors : men who were a little envious, because they could not imagine how it was that he, with such apparent ease, achieved successes denied to their more strenuous effort. And his ability was so little of the self-assertive kind that people were apt to underrate it. He wrote some of the most popular books in the world. I believe that with the single exception of *Jessica's First Prayer*, a small book for children of which probably few of the present generation have so much as heard, his *Pleasures of Life* has been translated into more languages than any other work ever written in English. His manner of reading was typical of his time-saving methods. He had a number of slips of paper, large enough for the taking of notes, always ready to hand, and as he read he used one of these slips as marker, to keep the place, and jotted down on it reflections and references to quotations, which quotations his secretary—usually, as before, the children's governess—typed off for him. In this way, with scarcely any trouble, he collected a great mass of extracts which he used voluminously in his own books. Call it " book-making," call it what you will—the result delighted millions.

And he wrote on a vast variety of subjects—those books of popular reflections, *Ants*, *Bees*, and *Wasps*, and all that series embodying his study of the ways of these insects and other animals, the *Origin of Civilisation* and the like antiquarian works, besides volumes on Proportional Representation, on financial subjects and so on, representing a vast industry and a wide grasp. They were all concerned with practical affairs. Pure literature, literature as an art—did not interest him, but his style was always easy and agreeable, never forced.

I do not think that it would be correct to say that he had a profound or a philosophical mind. Had it possessed profundity, as well as its wonderful versatility and lucidity, it would have been a super-human mind, transcending the natural limit. But its lucidity, within the wide circle of its range, was remarkable, and the ease with which he could switch it off from the discussion of scientific subjects to, say, the case of the Peruvian bondholders, was a wonderful testimony to the ease with which it worked.

It hardly needs to be said that a more delightful

companion for a country ramble could not possibly
be imagined. What struck me even more than his
facility in answering any question that it might occur
to one to put to him about any of the common objects
of Nature, was his ability to ask himself questions
about what Nature showed him. " Has it ever
occurred to you to wonder," he asked me once, " why
it is that some leaves are so very much more indented
than others—those of the oak than those of the beech
for instance ? "   And when I had to confess no, that
I had never thought of it, he said, " I think it must
be because the oak leaf has to be packed up so close,
in such a round bud : the beech leaf's bud is long, so
that it does not require so much folding. If an oak
leaf had no more indentations than a beech leaf,
I do not think that it could possibly unfold without
tearing."

Of course it is a very simple instance, and perhaps
a very obvious explanation, but it seems worth noting
as an example of the way in which Nature was constantly suggesting questions to him ; and I believe
that this power of setting themselves questions out
of the commonest natural objects must have been a
secret of much of the success both of him and of his
great master, Darwin. He always had a magnifying
lens in his pocket, ready for all occasions, and in
another pocket a book which he would bring out at
odd moments in course of going to and from his
business in the City, and so on. He was a great
believer in the value of turning the odd minutes to
account.

Just here it seems to me that I ought to put in a
word of caution, by way of corrective to the impression
which I fear I may be giving of Sir John's character
and of the man generally. I am conscious that I have
been drawing something like the portrait of the ideal
" good boy " of *Sandford and Merton,* or of some Sun-

day-school chronicle. Sir John Lubbock was a good, an extraordinarily good man, but he would not have been allowed to grow up among that athletic sport-loving brotherhood of the Lubbocks, although he was the eldest of them, and still be " soft " and a mere book-worm. He was quite a good cricketer : if he had remained a year or two longer at Eton and had not been taken away very early to go into the bank, he would almost certainly have been in the Eleven ; and he was, I am told, one of the best fives-players ever seen. It is even questioned whether he would not have been better than his brother Alfred, who was Eton's particular glory as a fives-player. The Lubbock boys had all sorts of sports in and about the family house of High Elms. There was a race-course among other " amenities." There were pheasants in the woods and legions of rabbits. Sir John was once commissioned by the brothers to buy some ferrets in London and bring them down to assist in dealing with the rabbits. He brought them accordingly, and put them into a Gladstone bag, which he pushed under the seat in the railway carriage and, absorbed in his book, had forgotten all about them until the peace of the journey was suddenly broken by a wild scream from a lady passenger. The ferrets had gnawed their way out of the bag and were all over the carriage. The exercise of Sir John's utmost suavity and tact, to say nothing of much active and agitated hunting in all corners and crevices, were required to allay the storm of terror and indignation.

On another occasion, when he was a good deal older than the age at which he had been employed as ferret-purveyor, he had set down his hand-bag for a moment in the station, and when he came back it had dis-appeared. He complained to the station-master of his loss. " Ah," said the official, " I am afraid you will not recover it. There are always rascals about waiting for just such an opportunity as you gave. But what was in the bag, sir ? " " There was nothing of really great value," Sir John answered ; " there was a German treatise on the Hittite inscriptions " (I will not be certain that this, precisely, was the subject of the book, but I know that it was in German and that its theme was an abstruse one), " and a paper bag containing some live bumble-bees." " Oh, in that case," said the station-master, " I think you may very likely get it back." And, sure enough, within a very short time a benevolent-looking old gentleman came into the station carrying the bag, which he handed to Sir John Lubbock, on the sugges- tion of the station-master, with profuse apologies, saying that he had taken it in mistake for his own.

Bumble-bees and Hittite inscriptions were pre- sumably not subjects of interest to the benevolent- looking old gentleman, but the story of the bees, and of how Sir John came to be thus conveying them about is rather interesting. It was winter, and he wanted some of the bumbles for certain experiments that he was making. Without great hopes of success, he put an advertisement in *Nature*, saying that he was prepared to give any reasonable sum for a few of them. To his surprise it was quickly answered by a man who offered to supply them at eighteen-pence apiece : to which Sir John agreed, and the bees in the bag aforesaid were the result of the transaction. But when the deal was concluded, Sir John wrote to the man who had sold him the bees and said, " Now I have got all I want, and I should be much obliged if you would tell me, for curiosity's sake, how it is that you manage to get the bees, now, in the winter." To which the man replied, " No ; I think I had rather keep the thing to myself. If the bees are worth eighteen-pence to you I may be able to do a good business in them with somebody else ; so, if you do not mind, we will leave it as it is." And to the day of his death Sir John was puzzled as to the means by which this secretive gentleman had been able to get his bumble-bees at that season of the year.

Sir John Lubbock's slight figure and rather delicate appearance did not suggest his possession of such untiring energy as his various activities witnessed. At the beginning of the Eighties, that is to say in 1881, he was President of the British Association, and in the same year was elected President of the Linnæan Society, which chair he occupied till 1886. All this while he was in Parliament, was engaged in his studies of the insects, was attending to the business of the bank, and, besides, was exceedingly hospitable and sociable. He was one of the latest survivors of the breakfast-giving habit, and all sorts of distinguished people used to find themselves, to their surprise, gathered round his table at the early hour when most of us feel least disposed to scintillate in conversation. But the hour of day never seemed to affect Sir John : he appeared to be at his equable best at all hours, indifferently.

His first wife was a Miss Hordern, but she had died just before the Eighties, and in 1884 Sir John had married Miss Alice Fox-Pitt, a daughter of General Pitt-Rivers, who had the famous museum of antiquities at Rushmore, the family home in Wiltshire. The antiquities had led Sir John to pay Rushmore a first visit, but it was an entirely different attraction that induced him to repeat it. The marriage brought most perfect happiness to both, though Lady Lubbock's genius was manifested rather in her wonderful gift for the decoration of modern houses than in connection with any one or other of the various studies that occupied her husband's attention. Her taste in the selection of colour-schemes and furniture really did amount to genius, and she had more than common opportunities for its exercise in the family house of High Elms, in the Kingsgate Castle on the Kent coast which Sir John bought and rebuilt especially for her, and in at least three London houses which they occupied successively.

One of his secrets for getting through so much work was his ability to delegate to others all that they were capable of doing for him. They would gladly accept these tasks, because of the interest which he knew how to arouse in them. His own interest and zeal were always infectious. Thus he set his daughters and their governess to visit the ants, and to write notes of their doings at fixed hours while he was away in the City. No single man could possibly have acted watch-dog for so long, unaided.

He changed very little in appearance from the Eighties and earlier till his death. As a young man he had ever looked older than his age, partly because he wore a beard; but as an old man his slight active figure gave him the aspect of being many years younger than he really was. In heart and mind he actually did remain young and eager till the end, always taking a pleasure in showing people the beauties that his microscope revealed, delighting to answer questions on scientific subjects; and within a month or two of his death he was still able to play his round of golf.

CHAPTER XIV

SIR THOMAS BRASSEY (LATER, EARL BRASSEY)

THE late Lord Brassey, shortly before his death, published his autobiography. But he did not call it by any such title, nor did his name appear at all on the cover except as author. He called the book *Sunbeam, R.Y.S.*, and to those that knew him this meant that it was his own story that it told.

Many men in history have been much identified with ships in which they have won fame, yet none of them, were it Nelson with his *Victory*, Drake with *The Golden Hind*, Sir Richard Grenville with the *Revenge*, so closely and so inevitably as Lord Brassey with his world-famous yacht. His name suggests the *Sunbeam* almost as certainly as the name of the patriarch of the Deluge suggests his Ark.

The *Sunbeam* was, of course, the love of Lord Brassey's life among yachts ; but it was not his first love. That first love was given to the *Eothen*, and I rather think there was another. But the *Sunbeam* was put into commission first in 1872, and scarcely ever went out of it. She did duty in the later years of the war as a hospital ship in India, and is now serving as a training ship at Pangbourne.

The autobiography does not concern itself with events in the author's life previous to his becoming yacht-owner. It is rather as though he thought that then only did he begin really to live, or, at least, to live a life worth writing about. It is not for me to supply the omission, because, of course, it is all a story much older than the Eighties ; but still there is one incident of some importance in his boyhood which I must relate, if only because it illustrates so well Lord Brassey's humorous outlook and whimsical way of relating events, especially those in which he was the chief adventurer. I would premise that though he told this tale with a perfect gravity,.it is not necessary on that account that it should be accepted as very truth to the foot of the letter, for you never quite knew how far he was serious and how far he was laughing in his sleeve and making sly trial of your perspicacity in detecting this intention. It was in the *Sunbeam's* cabin that he told us :

" When I was about nine—I forget exactly—my father said to my mother one day, ' My dear, Tom's getting a big boy ; it's time he went to school.'

" ' Yes, dear,' said my mother.

" ' Where shall we send him to school ? ' my father asked. ' I should like it to be a school near London, so that we could go down and see him every now and then.'

" ' Yes, dear,' said my mother again. So their inquiries were made, and it was found that the nearest school was Harrow.

" ' We will take him there to-morrow,' said my father. ' Order the coach to be ready directly after breakfast and we will drive out.'

" So the next morning the coach came round and off we went, my father and my mother and myself, and we drove up to Harrow School and my father got down and asked to see the Headmaster, and said, ' I've come down with my boy Tom, and I want to put him to school with you at Harrow.'

" The Headmaster said he was very sorry, but the school was full.

LORD BRASSEY.

"'Dear me,' said my father, 'I'm sorry to hear that. Could you tell me what the next school is, along this road ? We'll drive on to that.'

"'The next school going north ?' said the Head-master; 'that would be Rugby.'

"So my father came back to the coach again and said to my mother, 'My dear, this school is full. We must try the next. We must go on to Rugby.' So we drove on to Rugby and found that there was room there, and that's how it was I went to Rugby."

It is a curious way of selecting the place of a boy's education, even if we do allow for a little work of the imagination in its recital, but it seems as if a better choice could not have been made. Unquestionably it made a man of Tom Brassey, and that, above all, is what Rugby education set itself to do. It aimed at character rather than at very finished scholarship. I believe that the future Lord Brassey was not kept very closely at his studies, either at school or at Oxford, where he was at University College. His father was abroad a good deal at the time of what should have been his college days, engaged on big contracts for the railways in the northern parts of France, and I think I remember Lord Brassey's saying that he was much with his father at the time. Perhaps the father, whose views of education appear to have been unconventional, thought that the boy would learn as much of things useful knocking about and meeting all and sundry and seeing foreign life in France as he would in the faithful following of the Rugby curriculum. Perhaps he was quite right. It must have been due to this experience that Lord Brassey always maintained a fluency in the French language, whether for speech or writing.

He was fond of reading all through his life, and was methodical in making copious extracts from the books which appealed to him. His taste was sound, and

he always liked the best. The consequence is that
he accumulated many volumes of what he called
" Gleanings," several of which have been printed
for private circulation and one published, under the
title of *Warriors and Statesmen*. He had the extracts
collected and arranged according to their theme, under
headings of which the above is typical. He loved
poetry, and of course he was of the time to fall under
the spell of Tennyson. Tennyson, moreover, was a
personal friend and on at least one occasion Lord
Brassey lent him the *Sunbeam* for a holiday trip—
which did not turn out an unqualified success.

It is singular how intimately the value to the
nation and to the Empire of Lord Brassey's life and
work, and it is a value which it would be hard to
over-estimate, is associated with the gallant sailing
yacht that he loved. It was out of his love for her
and his sailing in her that the work sprang and grew.
He himself has told us of that birth and growth.
When he was cruising round the coasts of England
and Scotland he was struck by the fearless seaman-
ship of the fishermen everywhere. He had an obser-
vant eye and a mind which thought much on what the
eye showed him, and very seldom made a wrong
deduction. Thus considering the fishermen, he reckoned that in them the nation had a potential asset
that might be made invaluable, if rightly organised,
for manning our Navy in the event of war coming
with a heavy demand on our man power. Naval
Reserves already existed—I hope and think that I
am correct in this distinction—but their membership
was restricted to time-expired men of the Royal Navy.
What Mr. Brassey desired—he was not then Sir
Thomas, and it was not till a far later year that he
acquired a peerage—was to bring in these men who
had never been in the Navy, and train them so that
if and when a sudden call came a little more training

would suffice to polish them up to the mark of tolerably able seamen. It was thus that the Naval Volunteers came into existence, mainly by Brassey's exertion both in and out of the House of Commons— he was at this time member for Hastings—and also, incidentally, by his expenditure of a good deal of money in organisation and in circulating appeals to the men.

Fortunately he was a very rich man. He was the eldest son of the great railway contractor, who had contracted with great profit both to the railway promoters and to himself, while the whole establishment of the railway lines had increased the wealth and general prospects of the country almost beyond the most sanguine hopes of its originators. One may fairly write that this was a fortune fortunately inherited, by reason of the excellent use to which Lord Brassey put his money throughout his life.

He was a man of great simplicity, though on many sides very able, and by virtue of this simplicity he seemed able to get into friendship with fishermen or any whom he met. That " terrible gift of familiarity," first ascribed, I think, to Mirabeau, and quoted a thousand times in a wholly unintelligent manner, was his in large measure. There was nothing terrible about it in his connection. He was the personal friend of all his sailors on the *Sunbeam*; he knew their stories, would ask after their wives and families, and made himself one of them by sharing in all their work, pulling at a rope, taking a hand at an oar, and going aloft into the rigging. He continued this last athletic practice even in old age.

So when he set his heart on getting together the nucleus of his Royal Naval Volunteers, he had quite uncommonly good gifts for bringing those ends to pass. He succeeded in winning Government recognition for them : they had a uniform assigned to them.

He himself took his own share with them in a six weeks' drill. They had a great review at Windsor.

And then—they were disbanded ! All his work seemed to be brought to naught—and why ? For the reason, which seemed borrowed out of some Gilbertian opera, that the uniform was so like that of the naval officers that these last were much incensed about it all. In reality, no doubt, they were stupid people, without the foresight and imagination of Brassey. They thought the whole thing was moonshine and foolery. They did not believe in the volunteers being a source of strength in time of need.

So they were disbanded. In 1883, in a change of mood not at all unusual to the British Government, they were called into being again, and re-established ; and Brassey was made a K.C.B. in 1886 for his work in connection with their establishment. His own account of it says that all he did for the K.C.B. was the six weeks' drill which every other member of the force had taken part in equally, but of course he had really been the inspiring soul of the whole movement. Without him and his energy and his organisation and his liberality, it is likely that we should have had a great deal farther to seek when we came to man our largely increased Navy in the Great War. How much, in that regard, the nation owes the late Lord Brassey cannot be reckoned with any precision, but beyond all question the debt is heavy.

And then we owe him the *Naval Annual*. Exactly what the value may be of that yearly publication, again I do not know, but I do know that it is highly thought of. Its main purpose is the tabulation, in form convenient for comparison, of the navies of different countries. The late Lord Brassey started it, was its owner and editor for many years. There was a time when he was rather discouraged by finding that the Germans were bringing out a similar annual,

in their own language and for their own use, and had
made improvement, as he thought, on his model.
But that mood of discouragement passed : he applied
himself as keenly as ever to the work, stimulated to
make it better, and so again to lead the world, as he
deemed, in all naval matters, Great Britain should
lead. For many years the second Lord Brassey
edited the annual. His tragic and premature death
leaves its fate uncertain.

I have dwelt for a page or two on these two great
services that the first Lord Brassey did the nation in
the establishment of the Naval Volunteers—for they
were really due to him—and of the *Naval Annual,*
because I do not think that they have been recognised
as fully as they deserve. The principal part of the
rest of his life-work, and most valuable it was as well
as of supreme delight to him, was in the sailing of the
Sunbeam to all parts of the globe, and much of this
side of the story has been told very delightfully by
the first Lady Brassey in that book, *The Voyage of the
Sunbeam,* which won instant popularity and made the
name of the yacht what is commonly called " a household word." The English speaking world knows all
about this : it has a clear vision of the owner-
captain, a sailor-like figure on the bridge, at one time
or other bringing in his little craft through *Trades
and Tropics and Roaring Forties* to nearly every
important harbour in the Seven Seas. He stood, and
his ship sailed, for the unity of the Empire and for
Britain's mastery of the waves. She was but of
550 tons, with a draught of 13½ feet, and auxiliary
steam which would propel her at the moderate rate
of some eight knots. But her owner abhorred to
be driven to steam. He loved the sailing, and I
believe the happiest moments of his life were those
in which he could stand at the wheel of that good little
ship and see her responsive, with all sails set, to a fair

sailing breeze. He was a very bold seaman : he would not take in a reef till he was fairly compelled to. I remember very vividly his taking us out in the very teeth of a gale from Reykjavik in Iceland *en route* for St. John's, Newfoundland, with never a harbour or land of any kind to put in to, unless it were some ice-bound uncharted place in Greenland, in all the nine days (as it fortunately turned out) of our transit. Fortunately, too, the gale and the big seas proved to be the tail end of a just-passed storm, but they might equally well have been the head of a coming storm. As it was, that first night was a terror of rolling and tossing, for the *Sunbeam*, though a very admirable sea-boat, was a very lively one, with a great weight of lead on her keel which made her come back off her roll with a quick recovery most upsetting. And there was a lady passenger on board —my own wife—whom Lord Brassey promoted on the spot to the title of " the heroine."

He knew his business perfectly, however, as a navigator, though he was bold, and it is wonderful how seldom we hear of that gallant little ship in real trouble. She was busy in many voyages during the Eighties, while her owner was a Lord of the Admiralty. In the winter of 1880-81 she was in the Mediterranean, and in the autumn of the latter year cruising round the British coast ; in 1883 she went to the West Indies ; in 1885 she was in and out of the Norwegian fiords, with Mr. Gladstone as a passenger ; in November 1886 she sailed for Australia, and was there till December of the following year, Sir Thomas Brassey, as he then was, being Governor of Victoria.

I should imagine that Lord Brassey went through his long and strenuous life without creating for himself an enemy. I, at least, never heard man or woman mention him except with a smile and a word that welcomed the reminiscence. He was the kindliest of men, kindliest to all ages, to both sexes, and to all classes. He was a very true and large-hearted lover of his kind, and exceedingly generous with his wealth. He was not in the least like too many rich men whose generous impulses seem to have been soured by the many attempts to pick their pockets in the cause of this or the other charity, whether deserving or the contrary. He must have been defrauded again and again in the course of so many years of liberal giving, yet he remained to the end ready to believe the best, rather than the worst, of any suppliant.

Yet he had abundant shrewdness. He was really a little deceptive in respect to this quality, for in his speech he was always hesitating, with a good deal of " hum " and " er " between the words and phrases, so that the listener was apt to grow inattentive and let his thoughts wander. Subconsciously, too, it created in the listener's mind the idea that what was being said was not very clear in the mind of the speaker himself, who seemed to give out these signals of indecision. Lord Brassey was perfectly alert to detect this attitude of mind coming over his listener, and would suddenly, without any of the " hums " and " ers," shoot out a question which at once recalled the attention of the auditor, and put him at some pains to find an answer. After this reminder he would follow the rest of the harangue far more closely.

And, so following it, he would find himself repaid. Lord Brassey's manner and delivery in ordinary conversation did really intolerable injustice to the substance of what he had to say. The substance never failed to be of interest. He was a man who had seen very much of the world : he had begun to see it very young, with his father in France ; he had continued to see it in all quarters as he went voyaging in his yacht. He was a veritable Ulysses of experience; he knew all sorts and conditions of men and women, and could converse with them all with perfect and equal ease. And he was naturally gifted with a judicial mind, capable and apt to weigh these impressions and draw interesting and just deductions.

Thus the stuff of his talk was always very good, but you had to listen attentively to appreciate it, owing to the hesitating way in which it was given out to you. Most people do not take the trouble to give such close attention, and therefore, with the majority, he did not have the credit for anything like the acumen which he possessed.

There was none of this hesitation about his set speeches. He always prepared these with much care, and delivered them with a dramatic verve which enhanced the value of their points. There was no doubt of his ability or of his clear vision then. He was fond of reading aloud, whether prose or verse, and declaimed both well. On board the *Sunbeam*, when at sea, he read the prayers, and sometimes gave the crew a short address of his own preparation—all admirably and effectively done, with deep reverence. He would take his turn on deck, on a dark, cold, stormy night, with the hardiest of them. Then he would deliver them a homily which they listened to with a reverence equal to his own, because he had shown himself able and willing to take an equal share in their toil.

He had the figure of a seaman, not too tall, but square and sufficiently stout, with a round bluff face, fringed, in the Eighties and later, with some side-whiskers, which were only slightly pruned when these trimmings went quite out of vogue.

He liked his fellow men, and he wished that they should like him. It was a wish to which they fully responded. Although towards the end—he died in the midst of the worst days of the Great War—his

outlook was most pessimistic, he was, on the whole,
a man of happy nature. He had very much to make
him happy in the circumstances of his life, though
naturally he did not escape trials and sorrows such
as are the common human lot. The war tried him
cruelly, the more so that he had been an ardent
admirer of the German power of organisation and a
personal friend of the Kaiser. I almost believe that
he would have had us keep out of the war, consenting
to " join a German Zollverein rather than rely on that
broken reed France." This was his quotation of
words that the Kaiser had said to him. " It has
always been John Bull's way, whenever he saw a
fellow getting too big," Lord Brassey added, " to try
to give him a kick. So he is giving Germany a kick
now, and he's got himself into rather a nasty corner."

This was quite at the beginning of the war, when we
were taking Red Cross stores out to Rouen in the
Sunbeam in the autumn of 1914. " Yes," I assented
rather grudgingly, for I did not like to admit even
the most distant prospect of defeat, " I suppose he is
in rather a nasty corner for the moment. He's
got to hold on for a bit till Russia's ready ; then I
think it'll be all right."

" Ah," said Lord Brassey drily. " You believe in
the Russ ! "

That was all he said. I was rather indignant at
the doubt cast on " the Russ," in whom I did then,
in common with most British ignoramuses, believe
implicitly. But I have been struck more than once
since by the memory of Lord Brassey's pithy comment, for we were all just beginning, then, to talk
of Russia as " the steam roller."

How nasty that corner was in which John Bull
was to find himself, I certainly had not appreciated
then, and bitter disillusionment about Russia followed
for me and very many others. But for Lord Brassey

the disillusionment was no less bitter about Germany. As the months passed, and as it became more and more evident that she was waging war with a worse than Hun-like ferocity, that neither the laws of man nor of God commanded any of her respect, that " beasts they were and beasts they always will be," as so unimpassioned a critic as Mr. Arthur Balfour was soon to pronounce them—as all this was made manifest of the nation to which Lord Brassey had given his almost affectionate admiration, I think that his heart failed him, his hope of the world grew sick, and it was this mental disappointment as much as any physical trouble that hastened his end.

His passing came at a moment when death was very busy among us, but it may well be questioned whether the Reaper claimed another victim whose loss was deplored by as many friends as was Lord Brassey's. In 1890 Lord Brassey married Lady Sybil Capel, his first wife, who was a Miss Allnutt, having died in 1887. At his spacious Park Lane house he used to entertain lavishly ; and when he was not entertaining his own friends the house seemed always to be lent for meetings to further one or other good and charitable cause. His own hospitable designs were admirably aided and abetted by Lady Brassey, who was the very model of all that a London hostess should be. His voyages and his Australian Governorship had brought him acquaintances from every Colony of the Empire, and they always found a warm welcome when they came to the Motherland and sought out Lord Brassey. It was not in Great Britain alone that his loss was lamented, but in all the Colonies to which the *Sunbeam* had ever sailed ; and I can think of none which she did not at one time or other visit.

CHAPTER XV

WHEN we were small boys at school we used to hear of teams of the best rifle shots in England, Scotland, and Ireland going off to Wimbledon to shoot for some mysterious thing called the " Elcho Shield." As soon as we grew to be bigger boys and arrived at the age when young human beings begin to ask themselves something about the meaning of some of the words that they have been using in a parrot-like way for a long while past, we were informed that this Shield was the gift of a certain Lord Elcho, who was "keen on volunteering," as we said, and had given the Shield as a challenge trophy to be held by the country whose team should make the highest score in a special competition during the great annual week of rifle shooting on Wimbledon Common. He gave it as an incentive to make the soldiers and volunteers practise and improve their rifle shooting. Wimbledon in those days, it must be understood, was what Bisley is to-day : the place where the great rifle-shooting competitions of the year were held. Queen's Prize-men made their names there. Later, as Wimbledon became more built over and more walked over, and as rifles attained longer ranges, life and property were deemed to be rendered insecure by the great shooting week on the Common. Its venue was changed to the wilds of Bisley.

The great man of these Wimbledon shooting gatherings, no doubt, was the then Lord Elcho. We have rather forgotten him by that name now, by reason of all the years during which he was so striking a figure under the name of Lord Wemyss. He succeeded to the title in 1883. Besides, there was another very well-known bearer of the Elcho title, he, namely, who is the present Lord Wemyss and was then Hugo Charteris, and, in the early Eighties, at Oxford.

Lord Elcho—I speak of the Elcho of the Shield— held very high official rank in those gatherings, for he was Honorary Colonel of the London Scottish. This London Scottish Corps had their depôt, or headquarters or whatever it should be called, in a lowly, corrugated-iron building that was scarcely consistent with their honourable dignity. But no doubt it served their ends. And, these volunteers being Scottish, and seeing the noble expanse of Wimbledon Common spread out before them, it was but right and patriotic that they should think the opportunity for the playing of their national game too good to be lost. Therefore they laid them out a golf course on the Common, and instituted the London Scottish Golf Club, composed, I think, at first of members of the volunteer corps solely, but afterwards widely expanded. When rifle-shooting Wimbledon went to Bisley, the golf club and not the corps became the chief tenants of what then began to be called the Club-house. Lord Elcho, as keen a golfer as he was a rifle shot, was as leading a figure in the golf club as he had been in the volunteer corps.

He had led that corps because he was its honorary colonel ; but he had also led it because he was Lord Elcho—that is to say, a personality. He always had that great quality, personality, even as a young man, and as the aged Lord Wemyss he acquired it in ever growing measure. He had a remarkable figure, tall, upright, broad-shouldered, always spare

LORD WEMYSS.

and lean, and of fine slender bones, but large of frame.
His features were yet more notable—Sargent's picture
should have made them known to everybody. There
was a hawk-like character and keenness about them,
and right into the second decade of the twentieth
century he wore those long whiskers—Dundrearys—
which were the fashion of the Sixties. As some one
said of another well-known but much younger man,
also the subject of a very fine painting by Sargent,
Lord Ribblesdale, he looked like a portrait of one of
his ancestors—and a splendid portrait at that.

My uncle, Colonel Hutchinson, who, though not a
Scot himself, had married a Scottish wife, had been
for a time adjutant of the Fife Militia, and in that
capacity had learnt golf at St. Andrew's, took me
down to Wimbledon as a boy to play golf, and there
we met Lord Elcho and I had the honour of playing
with him. I speak of myself now as a boy at that
time : I think I had just gone to Oxford, so probably
I should not have spoken of myself as a boy then.
Naturally Lord Elcho did not remember me, though,
no less naturally, I remembered him, for when I
met him again, long afterwards—he had then become
Lord Wemyss ; and I, though a mere Englishman,
had in the interval impertinently perpetrated some
didactic writing about the national game of Scotland—
he said, " You're not that infernal fellow, are you,
who writes telling people they ought to take the turf
with their iron clubs in the approach strokes ? "
I was " that infernal fellow," and had humbly to
confess it, whereon I received the most awful castigation from his tongue. Lord Wemyss, to speak of him
now by the title under which he was by this time best
known to all except the small volunteer circle, could
not bear to see turf excised in the playing of the
approach strokes. His own golf dated back to the
days when men approached with wooden " baffy "

spoons, and he both maintained that old tradition faithfully in his own practice, and also commended it, with a fine natural force and flow of words, to all and sundry. He even went so far as to devise a wooden approaching club with a specially rounded sole, in order that the turf should be spared by it.

So naturally he castigated me, and thoroughly enjoyed the castigation, when he caught me and had me thus self-confessed of preaching the doctrine which he particularly abominated. I maintained to him, with such small and shamefaced eloquence as I had at command, that the ball could be controlled in its flight, and in its behaviour on alighting, with a jerk stroke in which the turf was excised as it could not possibly be controlled with any stroke which followed through. I might talk—or, to say truth, I was not allowed to do much of the talking—but of course made no impression whatever on Lord Wemyss' conviction, except to deepen the already formed impression that I was an " infernal fellow." I did not mind the castigation in the least. I do not think that anybody ever really minded what Lord Wemyss said to them, because of that great personality he had about him. It was a personality as charming as it was forcible, indeed more so. It was grace rather than strength, both physically and intellectually, of which he gave you the idea. Certainly he did not measure his words. One of the great arguments which we, the great majority that approach with iron clubs and cut out junks of turf in the process, used as against Lord Wemyss' wooden club proposition, was that junks thus solidly excised could be as solidly replaced, the roots of the short-rooted grasses not ruined by the excision, so that when the piece was restored, like a bit out of a Chinese puzzle, all grew together again and the turf was not " one penny the worse." With the wooden club, on the contrary, if the stroke was played in a " sclaffy " fashion and the turf were taken at all, the consequence was a bludgeoning into little atoms of the portion of soil thus stricken, with fatal destruction of all grass roots affected by the concussion. So the controversialists furiously raged together, with equal heat on the one as on the other side of the argument, and some wicked rhymester actually had the audacity to make Lord Wemyss the subject of an irreverent nonsense rhyme, as follows :—

> There was an old Scotsman called Wemyss,
> Whose language was all *in extremis*.
> He approached with the baffy,
> But when he hit ' sclaffy,'
> The turf went in small smithereemys.

To " sclaff," it may be explained, means, in golfing jargon, hitting slightly beneath the ball so as to take the turf at the same time.

Lord Wemyss never, so far as I know, expressed any resentment of this gibbeting. Indeed, his own position was not such as to give him ground to insist on the most extreme points of courtesy in debate, for he set no narrow bounds to his own liberty of attack. But Lord Wemyss could say things in the heat of argument without giving serious offence which would have been deadly wounding in another man's mouth. A certain licence always seemed to be conceded to him. When he passed, by succession, into the House of Lords, he was a frequent speaker. Anything that touched the interests or dignity of his beloved volunteers was as a gage of battle thrown down to him, and he eagerly took it up. Now and again their dignity was rather apt to be assailed. The portly citizen decking himself out in uniform, with rifle on shoulder, was a subject that lent itself to humorous illustration. Our great comic journal *Punch* has had an almost unblemished political record, apart from party questions, in regard to which no man or publication can appear without blemish from both points of view. It has almost without exception been on the side of right, and has chastised with the pen and pencil of ridicule only such things as are evil. But in this particular case of the volunteer movement even Mr. Punch's warmest friends will not deny that he made one of his very rare mistakes. He held up the unfortunate volunteer as an object of chronic derision. Perhaps the keenest arrows of ridicule had already been discharged by the Eighties, and the points of some of those yet to be fired were a little blunt from previous use, but still an easy laugh could be raised by a cheap jibe at the volunteer, and the poor fellow had suffered so many pricks that his skin was likely to be in a state of abnormal sensitiveness. Be that how it may, Lord Wemyss was always ready to rise in his place among the Lords to speak for him—with eloquence, with humour, often with extravagance.

It was not only the volunteer movement, by any means, on which Lord Wemyss was ever ready to address the House in this, his eager characteristic manner. Any army regulation which affected it even remotely interested him. He was always in favour of enforcing that Militia Ballot, which had been instituted as far back as 1757, and was really a form of compulsory service rather similar to the French conscription, though far less drastic. He was clear-sighted enough to perceive the danger lurking behind that insidious alliteration " peaceful picketing," when the legislation connected with the Trades Unions came on the *tapis*, and fought it, though vainly, with all his force. His natural sympathies were with his own class, yet this sympathy did not preclude a large and kindly view, and in the measures passed and projected for regulating the

relations between master and servant he was earnest
and eloquent in favour of giving to the employed
equal liberty of contract making and of contract
breaking with the employer.   And here his eloquence
was not spent in vain.   As a Scot, and a large land-
owner in the Lothians and in Perthshire, the battle
became a personal one for him whenever the debatable
ground was on the north side of the Tweed.   And
further, in addition to these topics of his constant
and, as it were, natural interest he would often surprise
the august assemblage of the Peers by rising to speak
on subjects wherewith he seemed to have no association whatever.   Thus he constantly astonished that
House of Peers, which breathes an atmosphere too
high and rarefied for many such emotions.   He
surprised the House by taking part at all in many of
the debates, and surprised yet more by the part he
took.   For Lord Wemyss could usually be relied upon
to say the fresh and the unexpected, and to avoid the
obvious and the hackneyed.   I have been told that
there was always a little thrill of expectancy in the
House when he rose.   But by far the most astonishing
thing of all was the very advanced age to which he
retained this evergreen freshness and originality of
outlook.   " My young friend, Lord Wemyss," as
Lord Rosebery spoke of him at a time when he must
have been just knocking at the doors of ninety, even
if he had not already been admitted through it to the
honours of a nonagenarian.   It was a humorous
stroke which had every justification.   His mind
seemed to be as quickly responsive to a new impression
at ninety and past as it could have been at nineteen.
So the House was delighted when the very striking
and handsome figure of Lord Wemyss rose to its feet
and he began to hurl, it might be, extravagant maledictions, broadcast.   Nobody, that is to say nobody
with an ounce of sense in his head, ever minded Lord

Wemyss' maledictions. There was nothing that was
not excused him ; for no matter what extravagances,
nay even impertinences and almost insolences, he
might utter, it was never possible to forget or doubt
that he was a great gentleman the while. He could
say things without lowering himself from that altitude which another might not. In every generation,
as it seems, there are one or two to whom this kind
of licence is given. Lord Wemyss enjoyed his large
share of it in his.

But, of course, a free-lance who wages war in this
gueiilla fashion does not write his name so large in the
annals of Parliamentary fame as the leader of a
campaign which sets out to attain some big particular
objective. So far as I am aware, Lord Wemyss'
name was never particularly associated with any
great legislative measure, although he was for very
many years in one or other House of Parliament. At
the beginning of the Eighties he was member for
Haddingtonshire, but, three years later, passed, by
his father's death and his own succession to the
Earldom, to the Lords. He took with him from the
Lower House a fame already established as a graceful
debater, deft in quick riposte, keen in attack. He
had long experience, for he entered the House of
Commons at the age of twenty-three, almost directly
after leaving Oxford. Within less than ten years he
was a Lord of the Treasury. Earnest politicians had
high hopes that he would follow the staid paths
leading to more important offices of State, and no
doubt it was well within his power, had he so chosen,
to attain them. But he chose otherwise. Perhaps he
was of nature too impatient either to bear the trammels
of office or to endure, long or often, the toil needful
to win it. Speaking came easily and was no effort
to him, but all the dull business of preparation and of
" cramming " would have been very uncongenial.

Wisely perhaps, therefore, he took a line of his own in which such spade work was not required. His great natural gifts could not have been developed in the slow processes of sap and siege. His way and his bent was, rather, to jump in, after the battle had been solemnly set in array by others, to engage, to deal a few masterful, brilliant strokes, and so out again ! And neither side, perhaps, could be very confident, when he entered into the fray, whether they or their foe was to be object of his attack. It is a mode of warfare which has its merits : it had the merit, for one thing, of lightening and brightening debate ; but it also had the quite obvious defects of its qualities. And then it is always to be remembered that Lord Wemyss had the perilous gift of humour, a possession blessed indeed, both for self and company, in all the common circumstances of life, but of very dubious value for the carrying through of any big piece of legislative business. Just in what measure humour may handicap a man for the purposes, if he wishes to take them gravely, of Parliamentary life it would not be easy to say, but beyond question the handicap is heavy. It is a melancholy but indisputable fact that wherever any measure has to be carried by the consent and with the aid of a large body of men, it is by a majority of dull men, men who have no appreciation at all of humour, that it has to be put through. It is not really enough to say that such men have no appreciation of humour : their attitude towards it, if they perceive or suspect its presence at all, is more than negative ; they have a positive distrust of it ; often they suspect and resent it, when no humorous intention is in the speaker's mind : they do not know when he is speaking seriously ; they even doubt whether such a person is capable of a serious view at all. Having convicted him once of levity, they can scarcely credit him with being grave ; and at the back of their minds, perhaps only subconsciously present, lurks ever the awful apprehension that their own selves and their own opinions may be the covert objects of the humorist's attack. The only professed and accredited humorist that either House of Parliament ever seems to have consented to take at all seriously in the Eighties was Sir Wilfrid Lawson, but he was a teetotaller. I have always thought that this was the saving clause in his case, by virtue of which the dull majority was able to be convinced that he was in earnest. Moreover, the great object for which he was for ever fighting was temperance and teetotalism, and even to the dullest this presented itself as an object the most serious and even tragic that could possibly be imagined, for they were not by any means a water-drinking majority themselves.

The mantle of humorist which Lord Wemyss wore so gracefully in the Lords descended upon the shoulders of his eldest surviving son, then Lord Elcho, in the Commons. For several years in succession, one of the annual events in the Commons was Lord Elcho's speech in favour of the suspension of the sitting of the House on Derby Day, in order that members might attend the classic race. He generally took the line of arguing that their constituencies would think far better of their representatives if they saw them enjoying themselves like reasonable beings at Epsom than if they read of them mewed up in the House passing measures of a very dubious utility. He always twisted the stock arguments about with a whimsical ingenuity which won ready and spontaneous applause, even though it may not largely have affected votes, an object to which, be it said, the speaker was entirely indifferent. And then—I forget the year, but it was not very long after the introduction of the Irish Home Rule Bill by Mr. Gladstone which divided the Liberal

Party so that a section faithfully followed their venerable leader in his Home Rule proposals, while others, under the title of Unionists, bifurcated off, seceded, and left him—I was staying at Mells with Mr. and Mrs. (now Sir John and Lady) Horner, and Asquith came down on the day after the usual motion for the adjournment of the House for the Derby Day. They were stirring political times, all kinds of agitation were in the air, but he would tell us little or nothing about Parliamentary alarums and excursions, so full was he of Elcho's speech on the Derby Day motion.

There had been something almost like a " scene " in the House. I am not quite certain of the procedure which led to the situation. The situation is what matters however. The procedure is a detail, but I believe it to have been thus : that when the moment came for seconding the proposition that the House should sit, instead of adjourning, on the day of the great race, Lord Elcho rose from his seat so quickly that he could not fail to be first in catching the Speaker's eye. He suffered grave rebuke from the Chair, being reminded that he was out of order, that it was not the moment for the opposer, but for the seconder of the proposal to say his say. I believe that to have been the way in which the situation arose. In any case, Lord Elcho, unperturbed by the rebuke, kept his feet and succeeded in putting in a few words which quite changed the aspect of his act. He rose, he said, not as an advocate for the adjournment of the House over the Derby Day, but as urgently opposing it on the highest grounds of moral principle. The House was first petrified with astonishment, then delighted by the *tour de force*. Yet again had Lord Elcho achieved the unexpected, on a theme which seemed worn tolerably bare with time and repetition. " Why not ? " was the question that he asked in very well-affected surprise at the consternation into which he had thrown his audience. Why should he not alter his view towards this proposition ? he asked. It was true that hitherto he had favoured the postponement of business to pleasure, of legislation to racing for the one day in the year. With age he had come to take a different, a riper view. " Honourable members opposite," he said, fixing with his eye the very recently converted group of Gladstonian Home Rulers, and selecting, as we were told, Sir George Trevelyan for his special optical attention—" honourable members opposite have had the courage, I might almost say the audacity of their changed opinions. Why should I not change mine ? "

It was a very deft stroke. Of course Lord Elcho, in the Commons, never got over the effect of that speech. It was thoroughly appreciated, but it was impossible that it could be either forgotten or forgiven. Whenever he rose to his feet again—and I do not think that he rose often—a beatific smile must of necessity go round the House : his Derby Day face-about must be remembered ; he might talk of what he would—even, like Sir Wilfrid Lawson, of tee-totalism, although I do not know that he ever was at all tempted to stray into that particular by-path— still the House would persist in keeping that smile upon its face until he resumed his seat. Even if he did not actually induce the smile to stretch itself to a grin, they were always apprehensive that he would be on the point of so widening it, always fearful that they might miss the point, and be convicted as dullards for so missing it ; in a word, they incorrigibly insisted in regarding him as an incorrigible humorist, incapable of a serious view—which he was not. He did some very good work later, on the London County Council, and much later again, after his father's death, made a very good speech in the Lords on the truly awful muddle created by the joint efforts of the Home and the Indian Governments in the first part of the Mesopotamia campaign in the Great War. But no man, since the patriarchs, has ever lived long enough to succeed in quite living down such a reputation as Lord Elcho acquired by his Derby Day speeches.

In the case of Lord Wemyss, the father, it is not so possible to turn up Hansard and put your finger on the page and the paragraph, and say it was here, and here, and thus, and thus, that the character of a wit and a popular entertainer of the House, whether in the Upper or the Lower Chamber, was won. With him it was rather the cumulative effect of multitudinous small witticisms and whimsicalities ; but the result worked out much the same in the end. Surely Lord Wemyss must have greatly enjoyed the knowledge that the audience which he was about to address always settled itself down in the comfortable conviction that some minutes of good entertainment were before it, but " you cannot have it both ways," as the colloquial phrase goes : people will not laugh with you and take you seriously at one and the same time. There have been witty and humorous men in Parliament, who have made a success there ; witness Lord Rosebery himself. It is sure that no one can read him and still doubt that he is gifted with these qualities, and yet less can one doubt them who has heard him as an after-dinner speaker. But he kept his humour very much below the surface of his speeches in Parliament and in his utterances on political subjects even without the walls of Westminster. Now and again he might indulge himself in letting a glint strike out, as in the above " my young friend, Lord Wemyss," or when he remarked, discussing certain unfavourable comments made about dukes by Mr.

Lloyd George at Limehouse, that though he, Lord Rosebery, naturally knew little of dukes, from what little he had seen of them he judged them to be a poor but honest kind of people. Now and then he might let his natural bright light shine forth in this way, and very pleasant it was when it appeared, but as a general rule he kept it well hidden under a good thick bushel of opaque gravity ; and perhaps it is only on the condition of this voluntary eclipse that a humorous man can hope to be taken seriously in any assemblage of men who are taking themselves, and the purpose for which they are gathered together, at all seriously. It is a sacrifice which neither the Lord Wemyss nor the Lord Elcho of the Eighties was prepared to make, and both paid, with perfect cheerfulness and content, the penalty.

I should imagine that Lord Wemyss—I write now of the father, the great volunteer—found life by far too variously interesting to settle down to make anything like a serious business of politics. He worked for the volunteer movement, because his heart was in that and because it made an appeal to his imagination ; he gave to the House of Lords the decently sedulous attention which became his position ; he had on his hands all the business which large ownership of land involves. He had extensive possessions in East Lothian, where he built himself the very fine modern house of Gosford, looking northward over the Firth of Forth ; and he had a property, besides, in Gloucestershire, with the delightful old house of Stanway, where Lord Elcho lived for many years. This latter is close to that village of Broadway, which is perhaps the most famous of all " professional beauty " villages in the country. Then he loved society, and to entertain hospitably at Gosford ; he loved art, and amused himself collecting *objets*; he was a sportsman ; he shot and he played golf ; he travelled ;

he loved music ; there was scarcely a human interest
to be named which did not make its appeal to him.
Really he enjoyed too many sides of life to be able to
set his face very steadfastly towards any one point of
the compass. Possibly he might have accomplished
more, had he been able, or had he cared, to face more
steadfastly in any single direction, but in that event
he would almost certainly have enjoyed less. And,
when all is said, he did a great work : its extent has
scarcely been appreciated. What he effected on
behalf of the military volunteers may fairly be set
alongside of the work that Sir T. Brassey (afterwards
Earl Brassey) was doing at nearly the same time for
the naval volunteers, to supplement the strength of
the naval reserve. It is not perhaps to be claimed
for him that the land volunteers were in the same
measure the creation of one man's idea and energy
as the naval volunteer force was Sir T. Brassey's
creation. Lord Wemyss did not count for so much
in the strengthening and support of the former as
Lord Brassey in the very making of the latter. He
did not count for so much, but he did count for much ;
and it is a record with which any man might pass to
his rest content, even if he had no other deed well
done to his credit.

It is my immediate business to deal with Lord
Wemyss as a figure, and a very striking one, in a
portrait gallery nominally devoted to a certain decade,
the Eighties, but as a matter of fact his activities
came near to spanning a full century ; he might appear
in the gallery of many decades. He was born in 1818,
and in due course went to school at the Edinburgh
Academy. In those days it was not much the way
of Scotsmen to send their sons to English schools.
Nevertheless he went on to Eton and thence to Christ
Church. In 1843 he married a daughter of Lord
Lichfield's. He was in Parliament, as member of

the Lower House, from 1841 to 1883, at first for East Gloucestershire and from 1847 onwards for Haddingtonshire. For three years, in the Fifties, he was a Lord of the Treasury. The first Lady Wemyss died in 1896, and four years later he married Miss Grace Blackburn, a daughter of Major Blackburn and niece of Lord Blackburn. He died in 1914, being thus short of the century by only four years. The Eighties saw him therefore at the height of his mental power and activity, though in point of fact scarcely any diminution of his intellectual faculties could be noticed till very near the end. In the country he adhered to a style of dress not so much to be called youthful as personal. It was rather peculiar to himself. A characteristic of it were very full and wide knickerbockers, and he claimed to have been the inventor of these garments without which we can hardly imagine ourselves going stalking, shooting, fishing, golfing, or pursuing any of the ordinary vocations of a British country gentleman on foot. I do not know what some of the old " knickerbockers " of the United States would say to this pretension, but probably it is at least to be conceded to Lord Wemyss that by example and precept he brought these raiments, so very convenient for field sport, into vogue. We look at our ancestors by Raeburn or Scott or what painter you will and we see them going a-fishing in long pantaloons so close fitting to the leg that the first wonder is how ever the wearer got into them, and the second wonder how ever, once in, he is to get out. Similarly we see them portrayed as going a-shooting in trousers drawn trimly down by the buttoned strap passing beneath the instep of the shoe. Either, we may think, they did not go a-shooting or a-fishing in wet weather or on any holding and damp soil, or else their lower limbs must soon have been in a very damp and dirty and insanitary condition. On top they were not crowned in a manner much more convenient, with the eternal top-hat from which they appear never to have parted. That top storey of the edifice Lord Wemyss seems to have left to die its own very natural death in field and moorland, but we certainly owe him much if it is due to his initiative that we trudge the plough land and the heather in knickerbockers and shooting boots rather than in pantaloons and pumps.

CHAPTER XVI

"THE idle singer of an empty day." Thus, if you will have a look at the beginning of the *Earthly Paradise*, you will see William Morris describing himself. And he is so convinced of the aptness of the description that he repeats it five several times. The Eighties was a period of stress and zeal in politics, science, and art generally, but if you wished to point to one among all the prominent men of the time as foremost in zeal and stressful energy I do not know whom else you would indicate than William Morris. I once remarked to one of his few intimate friends that I wished I had the privilege of knowing him better—of knowing him well. "Knowing him well!" he repeated after me, "you might as well speak of knowing the North Wind."

It was a very good metaphor for him. He went past you like the wind, boisterous, bothering about you not at all, intent on arriving at his own goal, pushing anybody out of the way to get there. Not that he was an unkindly man at all—far the contrary. Not that he was egoist at all—his sympathy for the working folk and his socialistic campaign are evidence to acquit him. Only he was so entirely concentrated in attention to the purpose which he was aiming at the moment to achieve, that he was indifferent to all else, would push all else aside, and was indifferent to anything in the nature of his own personal comfort more than all.

(*By G. F. Watts, R.A.*)

WILLIAM MORRIS.

Thus ne was like the wind, blowing every obstacle
out of his way, going " where it listeth " ; and also
he was very much of the North. Distinctly it was a
North Wind. He came upon you with all the tonic
and bracing of the gale from that pole—no soft and
soothing zephyr, with a breath of the lotus flower on
it, but with a keen and biting tang, as if flowing from
the snowy peaks overlooking Scandinavian fiords and
picking up a taste of the briny foam in its passage
across the sea. So he went by you, like a cold gust
of air, and on to one or other of his multifarious arts
and crafts—intensely pre-occupied worker, in many
arts, of a day crowded to the very limit of all its
moments. Many men have miscalled themselves
before : none have ever more widely missed the
mark than Morris in this description of himself above.
Of course we do not take him to have meant it very
seriously. It is a nice, sing-song phrase ; it suggests,
poetically, the idea of some troubadour—though the
Provençals had not yet come on the stage at the date
of this " empty day " that he speaks of—beguiling
the leisure hours with songs of Atalanta and the rest
of the delectable people of that paradise. He never
was at all meticulous about his phrase. So long as
he could induce it to express his meaning, which was
seldom a very subtle thought, and so long as it was
Saxon rather than Latin phrase, he was content with
it. It was not in his way, nor in his nature, to go at it
again and again with polishing file, to make it brief
or pointed. In so far as that he was " an idle singer,"
and in so far he sang as if the day was " empty " of
all else than his singing, as if he had " all the time
there was " in which to sing his song out—that is
the reason why, no matter how deep our admiration
of Morris's verse, we shall not find many passages in
it apt for quotation. He needed large room for his
singing, and he took it. He did not pack his thought

up tight in those neat little parcels which other poets
arrange for us to take away and unpack again, and
set them between quotation marks, to the greater
glory and good advertisement of their makers.

With all my profound admiration of Morris and my
love of his verse, I am not at all disposed to claim for
him a place among the greatest poets. He was very
melodious, but his melodies were not so full and noble,
nor anything like so varied, as those of Swinburne,
who was in some sort his disciple, or of Tennyson. He
was nothing like the equal in mastery of phrase and
technique of either ; or if he had, in fact, somewhere at
command such mastery, he did not produce it for our
edification. Moreover, his rigid faithfulness to the
Saxon words, though it gave his verse a force, yet bereft
it of a greater flexibility and variety which it might
have shown if he had not been so strictly one-tongued.

The best of it all, if I may speak of my own judgment, is *Sigurd the Volsung*. It must have been a
year or two before 1880 that this was published,
for I had the good luck of reading its proof sheets
before publication. That luck came my way because
I was a friend of Cormell Price, the " Crom " of the
Pre-Raphaelite brotherhood. Morris sent the proofs
to " Crom," and " Crom " let me read them, saying
at the time that this would be, in posterity's judgment,
the second epic in the language to *Paradise Lost*.
So it may. I suppose that posterity has not yet given
its final verdict on Morris as a poet. But he always
seems to me to be greater and to be more at his ease
when dealing with Scandinavian story than with any
other.

The world of readers of English may be divided into
two parts : those who love the Sagas and see ultimate
and most entrancing reality in all their myths,
and those to whom the Sagas seem dull, wearisome,
and unmeaning, untrue tales. I have to confess myself

wholly on the former side. And just as men deem
of the Sagas, so they will deem of Morris, for his
soul was steeped in the Saga literature and feeling,
and his spiritual home was there, in the great wastes
and mountains of Iceland and Norway, the bitter
cold foam and breeze of the northern sea. He wrote
beautifully of classic story in his *Earthly Paradise*,
and I love his Odyssey and his Æneids. Perhaps the
best of all that he did in treatment of Grecian legend
was that which, if I remember right, came out just
before *Sigurd*; that is, *The Life and Death of Jason*.
But I am sure that he was happier when the Norse-
men's tales were his theme. He had the very spirit
of them, as it seemed. He had been to Iceland in
1871, and again two years later : he had visited the
Thingvalla and stood where the dooms were pro-
nounced. He never forgot the experience. Norway
I do not think that he ever visited ; but, after all,
it is the island that was the source of the best of the
Sagas and that is still steeped deep in their traditions.
Its position, its mountain ranges, with plains between
strewn with huge lava blocks, its narrow fiords with
the emerald green strips of pasture beside them, all
go to make it the abiding home of Scandinavian
romance, and to guard it from too swift intrusion of
the modern spirit. When I saw it in 1912, it is true
that the telephone wires, reaching over the lava-
strewn wastes to the scattered farms, gave a strange
air of modernity and scientific apparatus invading the
primitive wilderness, but the very sharpness of the
contrast somewhat served to throw into high relief
the grimness of the waste. Anyhow, there were no
telephones when Morris went there in the Seventies.

At that time he was just touching forty years of
age, but still he was not past the age of impressions
and enthusiasms. It may be said that he never did
pass it. And the importance of an impression
12

received by Morris consisted in the first and most vital
place in this, that he was wonderfully capable, by
reason of his talent, his impetuosity, and all the
attributes bound up in his very remarkable personality,
of passing that impression on in first instance to the
small coterie of which he was not only a member,
but the very centre of its inspiration, and thence,
by their mediumship or more directly by his writing
or other art, distributing it as a national (and even
wider than national, a more or less universal) possession.   I claim for him no less than this.   I claim that,
although a minority enjoy his writings and still live
between his wall-papers, and though many hear his
name with reverence and honour, and more or less
know what he accomplished, yet that only a very few,
if any, quite realise in what measure, how widely, and
how deeply the influence of Morris is still about our
path, about our bed and board, and is over all
our ways.   If you look here, there, and everywhere
you will hardly rest your eye on an object created
since the day of Morris, which is at all worth resting
it upon, that does not owe something, and very often
the most important thing about it, to his genius.
I say this, with full realisation that it is saying a
great deal.   I do not believe that it is saying at all
too much.   The papers on our walls, the carpets
beneath our feet, the curtains which drape our
windows, the chintzes upon our chairs and sofas, the
forms of our furniture, our chairs, our tables, our beds,
our table-glass—all owe their debt, usually a large
debt, and the larger the more beautiful they are, to
Morris.   Every colour scheme by which we are
surrounded in nine houses out of ten is his, realising
in more or less imperfection his idea of the House
Beautiful.   It almost goes without saying that few
pictures painted since the Pre-Raphaelites formed their
brotherhood would have been just what they are had

William Morris never lived and painted and been the fervid inspirer and goader on of other painters. He was a driving force as well as infectious exemplar of energy to all whom his gusty north-windy temperament breathed upon. Swinburne I have claimed as in some sort his disciple in another branch of the arts, though far excelling the master in the art which they had in common ; and from Swinburne we may derive much of Kipling, and from these two, therefore ultimately from Morris, how many legions of pious devotees ? Kipling very likely owed to him quite directly, for Kipling, as a boy, was much in touch with all the set that he would meet at his uncle Burne-Jones's house, though perhaps it was not there that he picked the gems which he wove into Barrack Room Ballads and the like firstfruits of his wonderful head. There was one Muse that, so far as I know, did not attend Morris's christening and shower her gifts upon him : this was the Muse of music. He loved it, I believe, but did not set his hand to it. All the rest of the sisterhood were at the ceremony and in their most freely giving mood. I am sure, had he been so drawn, he would have set his hand to some musical instrument or composition, for the one thing that he never could abide was to be a spectator, to look on and see " the other fellow " work. He must put his own hand to it.

The modern taste seems to have gone a little past the Morris wall-papers now ; we are apt to find their spaces too crowded ; we ask a little more rest for the eye. But, apart from the this or that of form and colour that Morris has given for our eyes to dwell on round about us, it is a bigger gift than this, a gift not of details, but of a general point of view, that he has been so forcible in bestowing on us : that is, the appreciation that there actually is a beauty which can make a difference to our lives in forms and hues. It is an appreciation which we know quite well to have been hid from the eyes of very many of our forefathers, and it is our great debt to Morris that he has been so largely the means of freeing our own eyes from the like scales. The early Victorians had something of the sour look of the Puritans towards any work of art. The forms and hues among which they lived bear abundant witness to that unhappy attitude of mind. Even Morris himself had to encounter and overcome some opposition on the part of his family when he announced his intention to follow art, at first in the noble form of architecture, instead of the Church, as his profession. His early inclination, however, towards the religious life had its manifest influence on him throughout. His interest in church architecture, church brasses, church music, church rites, and painted windows was formed in his early years and never left him. All pageantry appealed to him. We are told that as a small boy one of his prized possessions was a child's suit of armour, and, donning this, he used to go riding on his pony, a knight errant in little.

So his mind received its bent, and all through his very varied work in life, all through the devious ways along which it led him, we see at least this unity binding the many aims together in the one personality— a deep love of the mediaeval. He looks to reform the world by leading it back to mediaeval beauty. Really this is the keynote. He himself strikes it keen and clear for us in the Prologue of *The Wanderers* :

> Forget six counties overhung with smoke,
> Forget the snorting steam and piston stroke,
> Forget the spreading of the hideous town ;
> Think rather of the packhorse on the down,
> And dream of London, small and white and clean,
> The clear Thames bordered by its gardens green ;
> Think, that below bridge the green lapping waves
> Smite some few keels that bear Levantine staves,
> Cut from the yew-wood on the burnt-up hill,
> And pointed jars that Greek hands toiled to fill,

And treasured scanty spice from some far sea,
Florence gold cloth, and Ypres napery,
And cloth of Bruges, and hogsheads of Guienne ;
While nigh the thronged wharf Geoffrey Chaucer's pen
Moves over bills of lading—mid such times
Shall dwell the hollow puppets of my rhymes.

Those are just the times and just the scenes in
which he did love to let the puppets of his thoughts
dwell. He was a mediaeval, and of all the mediaeval
scenery in which his mind moved it was most at home
in that of the Northern fells and fiords. He had no
Scandinavian blood in his veins, as I believe, but he
had his Celtic inheritance, from the Welsh. His
forebears had styled themselves Ap-Morris. Save
for such artistic stirrings as such blood must, as it
seems, bring, he does not appear to have had any
large artistic heritage, unless it were in music, which,
curiously, made less vivid appeal to him than other
arts and crafts. Personally he had a good deal of
the look of a Scandinavian, almost of a Viking, with
that towzled head of hair which got him the name of
" Topsy " as early as Oxford days, and his big frame
and quite uncommon strength of muscle. He had a
passionate temper, too, which was rather primitive,
and with his strength he must have been a terrible
fellow to offend. And in equal measure, by compen-
sation, he had the joyous love of life.

I have written of him as engrossed in his projects
so as to have little thought to spare for the personal
concerns of other people, or even for his own ; but
it would give a wrong idea if that were to convey
that he had not warm affections. In his own family
he was very loving as well as very much beloved,
and no one can well say that he had no capacity of
warm friendship who is aware that when he and
Burne-Jones were not living under one roof in London,
and yet were within reach of each other, they never
failed to breakfast together on Sunday mornings, and

to spend all the forenoon in talking—*de omnibus rebus et quibusdam aliis.* He was a man of few friends, but to those few he was very dear and they were very dear to him.   His letters to Cormell Price show a great affection.   In fine, the few friends he had counted for a great deal more with him than do the many friends of a more friendly man.   Outside the circle he had many acquaintances perhaps, many people who knew and recognised him, but very few whom he knew or recognised as he went through the streets in a terrific hurry, with his eyes, under the shadowing brim of his squash hat, bent inward, on his thoughts. Yet if any detail of architectural or other beauty caught that eye, that detail was impressed very deep. He did not lose it again.

But he would hardly ever be seen in those parts of the town frequented by the people who called them-selves " the world."   He seems to have carefully coasted round them, as a kind of dangerous centre, to be avoided.   Thus he was brought up, in boyhood at Epping, or close by.   Then, with Burne-Jones and some others of the brotherhood, he was in Red Lion Square, W.C., and Queen Square.   Again we catch sight of him out in the Holland Park direction, and in Bayswater. Again in Hammersmith, es-tablishing his printing shops, and at Merton Abbey. Thus he carefully skirted round the danger zone where men wore that ridiculous head-piece the high hat, and that no less absurd toga the frock coat.

It is worth while looking for a moment at the programme that he put out of the work to be done at Merton, in order to see how various it was.   Or, at least, I will say that it is worth my while to cite it, in order to endorse my claim of a few pages back about the almost universal extent of Morris's effect on the houses in which we live to-day :

(1) Painted glass windows ; (2) Arras tapestry

woven with high-warp loom; (3) Carpets; (4) Embroidery; (5) Tiles; (6) Furniture; (7) General house decorations; (8) Printed cotton goods; (9) Paper hangings; (10) Figured woven stuffs; (11) Furniture velvets and cloths; (12) Upholstery.

He never embarked on any of these ventures for money's sake, for his father had been a rich man and he had enough. Yet he wished to make them an economical success as an object-lesson. His great idea for the regeneration, both of crafts and of craftsmen, out of the ugly monotony to which mechanism and the conditions of modern industry had reduced both the one and the other, was that the workman, for a fair wage, should do a fair day's work at labour which should interest him. It is a lovely idea. Like almost all of Morris's ideas it was mediaeval. It was an idea entirely unsuited for to-day's conditions. It was all very well when industry was called on to support relatively few workers, when the population of the world was scanty. It is an idea which may perfectly well be realised again if the world consents to cut down its human population to something like its figure when the mediaeval conditions prevailed, and when the workman was an artist and worked on the product of his hands for the love of its beauty and the zeal of creating. That is a very far more pleasant way of life for the worker. But at present there is no sign that the world proposes to seek its salvation on such lines : the lines on which it is working are still to increase and yet further to increase populations ; and it seems that such multitudes can be fed only on the condition that work shall be done in circumstances which make life doubtfully worth the living. That, at least, is the view that Morris took of it. And the circumstances are certainly no more pleasant for the worker, in the way of making his work more interesting to him, than they

were in the Eighties, though he has the very considerable advantage of a larger wage and more
leisure.

I have to confess—I feel the confession to be almost
impious—very little affection either for Morris's type
of socialism or for the products of his Kelmscott
Printing Press as practical things.   I have the greatest
admiration for them in the abstract.   *The Dream of
John Ball*, and so on, are beautiful, as dreams.   They
were beautiful realities in the Middle Ages perhaps ;
but to-day they " won't work."   His theories are
laughable, considered as solutions of to-day's problems.
Similarly the Kelmscott Press productions are things
of perfect beauty : they entrance us to look at as we
turn their pages, while they lie in their majesty on a
table.   But when we try to deal with them as a
book—that is to say, as a vehicle to our eyes of the
printed thought of the author—they are frankly a
failure.   They are immense : two hands for a reading
desk are required to bring them within reading range
of our eyes ; they are as ill adapted to our modern
use as his socialism.   I hate writing thus, because of
the almost hero-worship that I feel for Morris ; but
it is no use trying to draw a portrait of a man and
instead of his own snub nose giving him some one else's
Roman, because it looks more handsome.

It was in the Eighties that he was most actively
engaged in his socialistic campaign.   It need not be
said that the idea which inspired him was noble : he
had a warm and a generous sympathy with all whom
he saw to be squeezed nigh to death in the great
modern industrial machine.   In very many of his
writings we may hear the note of the relief of suffering
ringing like a trumpet call to action, and this inspiration of the knight errant he brought into his projected schemes of industrial reform.   That they
progressed no farther than the project stage was not

the fault of any lack of enthusiasm. The fault was in the schemes themselves, that they were not fitted to their times.

When the theme was not socialism, which we may rejoice that it seldom was, his prose was no less poetical than his verse. It was fully as inspired by fancy and by the spirit of romance. I have said that he was no subtle poet. There is no weaving and inter-weaving of thought with a complexity in which the pattern is very difficult to follow, as in Browning. There is a big simplicity about it, and it is almost always narrative, never introspective. It is all simple to read, in spite of the air of mannerism which is given by his love of the Saxon and sometimes archaic word. For " hanap " *e.g.*, which means a cup, usually of wood, many a reader will want a dictionary.

When he ground stories out from the stocked mill of his own head he generally wrote them in the prose form. He went into verse more when he was translat-ing or transcribing. Greatly as I admire his verse, and his *Sigurd* particularly, I love his prose romances more—*The Well at the World's End, The Roots of the Mountains, The Wood beyond the World*, and so on. What a *flair* he had for a title that takes you at once into a realm of romance and invites you to go with him through it ! He sets you wondering, from the start. He came into his literary heritage very early. Almost the best are the *Early Prose Romances, The Hollow Land*, and the rest of them. And although I have written that he was not a very quotable poet, still it must be allowed that he interjected into the prose of these early stories some verses which haunt the memory, very persistently calling to be recited, and which were in fact constantly in recitation on the lips of his friends of that time. They were pub-lished in the *Oxford and Cambridge Magazine.*

Take this for example :—

> Christ keep the Hollow Land
>   Through the sweet Springtide ;
> When the apple-blossoms bless
>   The lowly bent hillside.
>
> Christ keep the Hollow Land
>   All the Summertide ;
> Still we cannot understand
>   Where the waters glide.
>
> Only dimly seeing them
>   Coldly slipping through ;
> Many green-lipped cavern mouths,
>   Where the hills are blue.

For sheer beauty and hinting of a picture to haunt the mental eye these lines are not easily to be beaten. And again, there are those others from the same tale. One is heard singing :

> Queen Mary's crown was gold,
>   King Joseph's crown was red ;
> But Jesus' crown was diamond,
>   And lit up all the bed
>   *Mariæ Virginis.*
>
> Ships sail through the heaven
>   With red banners dress'd,
> Carrying the planets seven
>   To see the white breast
>   *Mariæ Virginis.*

Even if literature's debt to Morris was no more than what is due for his translation, with Magnusson collaborating, or by his own hand as he grew to know the Icelandic better, of the great Sagas, it would be large. His *Grettir the Strong* keeps wonderfully what we must believe to be the spirit of the original.

His English was so individual and so little borrowed that it is hard to liken it to any other writer's. In form of sentence it suggests Carlyle now and then ; which we may perhaps take to be because both followed the Teutonic, so much more than the Latin, of the diverse elements of our speech ; but the writer of whom he reminds most, though here again the reminiscence is only occasional, is Cobbett, of the *Rural Rides*. Here again the reason, doubtless, is that Cobbett loved the pure Saxon and always used it of preference when it would serve him for what he had to say.

Of the men prominent in the Eighties Morris is certainly one of the most remarkable, on whichever of the many sides that he presents we may consider him ; and certainly it is he above them all that has made most difference in the surroundings of our daily life. Others, especially Darwin, who died very early in the period, have modified our mental outlook far more deeply ; but, little as we may be aware of it, the influence of Morris is scarcely ever absent from us in our homes.

CHAPTER XVII

SWINBURNE AND MEREDITH

WHEN Mr. Theodore Watts-Dunton took Swinburne to lead the sheltered and suburban life he no doubt deserved well of the world and of the poet himself, but it was a fearful and a wonderful thing to do. The very name of the house, " The Pines, Putney Hill," was pathetic as the home of a flaming genius whose proper address would be " The Rigi, Switzerland." It was like taking an eaglet from the eyrie and putting it in a hen-coop.

Not that this particular eaglet seemed to mind. He appeared to domesticate himself, very readily, to the surroundings of Putney Heath, and tripped about them with his peculiar short-stepping gait quite happily. Did his verse lose fire by it ? One can hardly say. Even at its least fiery it had inspiration, and to spare. Watts-Dunton's devotion, at all events, was very touching. It was as whole-hearted as it was rare, and we cannot suppose that at all times the poet was quite easy to live with. People with the " temperament " seldom are.

There is no doubt, moreover, that this eaglet was quite unable to fly, or even to walk, alone. He needed a guiding, sustaining hand, and he would not allow his own family to extend that hand to him. It is not very evident that they would have done so if he would. His Bohemian ways were not at all those of the patrician nest in which he was reared.

Beyond question, Watts-Dunton saved him from himself, and from the irregularities into which he had fallen. It was just the kind of steadying influence that he needed. Almost physically and literally he needed a hand. He never did so much walk as trip on his peculiarly small feet, and they always seemed not quite adequate to his support. His head was quite splendid, with its apparent size increased by the redundant way in which it pleased him to wear his hair. His body looked too small for the fine head, and the feet too small, again, for the body. It was as if Nature had started off with the head-piece and had spent so much care on its modelling that she grew increasingly tired of the job as she worked downward, and so finished him off with a pair of child's feet that she found lying about. He looked always ready to tumble, and the first time that I met him he actually did tumble, and hurt himself severely, down the stairs from the billiard-room at the hotel at Westward Ho !

That must have been rather before the Eighties, and before the Consulship of Watts-Dunton. It was during the Eighties that he went to live at " The Pines," and from there he published much during the decade—*Mary Stuart, Tristram of Lyonesse, Century of Rondels, Midsummer Holiday, Marino Faliero, Miscellanies, Locrine,* among the poems; and I think it was then that he was engaged in that painstaking analysis of Shakespeare's methods, which produced his *Study of Shakespeare* and *Age of Shakespeare.* Perhaps it was not such flaming stuff as some of the *Poems* and *Ballads* ; but for most men it would serve, and surely it was good singing for Putney Hill. Of course Watts-Dunton himself was a poet, although he was not a Swinburne, and his prose, in the instance of *Aylwin* at all events, was quite as poetical as his verse. There must have been much give and take between the two friends, however we may think that Swinburne was the greater giver. That is spoken, of course, of the intellectual exchange. In material and moral ways it was otherwise, perhaps.

Swinburne, as we all know, began with the Pre-Raphaelites. He was the singer then of protest against all that was conventional, all that was tyrannical; against kings, priests, and lawgivers in every garb. It was a spirit of terrific iconoclasm, strangely incarnated in the small but great-headed, tripping figure. He was a perpetual delight to friends of his own way of thinking—that is to say, of the iconoclasts—a perpetual terror as to what he might do or say next to those not of that way, and especially to those who cherished and respected the idols. These last were heartily relieved when he passed under the brooding wing and was taken to the domestication of Putney.

Beaudelaire and his like, I suppose, were Swinburne's earliest influences. Then came the distinct Victor Hugo phase—the worship of the heroic, the compassion for the toiler, the identification of heroism with toil. Something of all this is expressed in *Songs before Sunrise*. But it is curious : the small personality and the burning passion of it all seem not to be of a piece. Of course that appearance only arises from our almost consciously imperfect way of viewing such relations. In truth, however, genius, especially the poetic genius, is the very quality which defeats and upsets, by reason of its originality, all our formed concepts of relations. We may almost say that it is just this upsetting which makes it genius.

Swinburne caught something of the mantle of these earlier singers—a fringe from the robe of Rossetti, and also of Morris, were about him too—but he was not therefore to be called a borrower. He took their forms ; he was always experimenting, and nearly always successfully, with strange techniques in verse,

even with that *terza-rima* of which the Ettrick
Shepherd observed with point that it was " an infernal
measure"; but he expressed his own thought and
white-hot emotion. Of course he borrowed the old
stories in his narratives and dramas, as *Tristram*
and *Mary Stuart*; but every one is a borrower in
that sense. All the stories have been told a thousand
times : only now and then some inspired teller, like a
Kipling, comes along and tells them in a new manner.
Swinburne, at worst, might take to himself that
moderate encomium bestowed on a very different
poet : *Nihil tetigit quod non ornavit*. And he *ornavit*
in very truth. It is a marvellous cascade and wealth
of words that he pours out in melodies most entrancing. We actually hear the waves of his dear ocean—
" Mother and lover of men the sea "—with her pearly
surface, her opalescent depths, her eternal mystery,
and her moaning as with eternal sorrow. He takes
us to some island of the Lotus-eaters, where " it is
always afternoon." He laps us in slumber ; he fires
us with passionate emotion. He shows us " the
light that never was on land or sea." And then it
occurs to us to ask : What does it all lead to ? What
does it all mean ? What is its message ?

We find ourselves strangely at a loss for an answer.
His message seems to be just as empty of any affirma-
tive sense as that of Bolshevism. He is ready to
crack all crowns, to knock down all conventions, but
we never win from him any definite idea of how he
would propose to rule the world when this is done.
He gives us splendid visions, glorious music ; and
that seems to be about the end of it. Still it is very
much, and if we thus criticise in the name of truth,
we need not lose our sense of gratitude in the criticism.

He was critic himself too, and assuredly he did not
err in criticism on the side of forgetting gratitude—
that is, be it said, when his criticism was approving.

Indeed he was so enthusiastic in approval and in gratitude that the balance needed for sane criticism was sometimes lost.   Nor was it otherwise when the criticism was disapproving. Disapproval left no room at all for gratitude then : indeed he could not see that any claims on gratitude remained.   As critic, therefore, although he is so appreciative, or trenchant, as the case may be, and gifted with an insight born of sympathetic imagination and of trained experience far beyond most, he still stands liable to be corrected in his verdicts by more prosaic persons, to whom these scintillations of genius do not come with their bedazzlement. We may learn from his criticism in a thankful spirit, and yet may venture to give it only a qualified endorsement.

The language of his prose is only less splendid than his poetry.   There have been very few such wielders of the English word, in either mode. He lived and wrote long beyond the decade with which I am trying to deal.   His death came in 1909, watched over by his ever faithful friend, who survived him.   He was an old man, past the age that the Psalmist has allotted as our mortal span ; and it is most unlikely that he would have reached it had it not been for the touching care and devotion of that friend.   It is due to the same cause, no doubt, that he was able to leave us so large a legacy of song.   No man of letters has ever been more fortunate in this respect than Swinburne ; none has ever had the material worries of life so cleared from his path nor has been able to give himself up with more complete detachment to his calling. We have to remember that not only was the bulk of Swinburne's poetry very large, but that his verse was often cast in forms which required very attentive workmanship. It has the air of running easily off the pen, but we know that this is but an instance of the perfection of art concealing the effort of art.   The metres were often difficult and elaborate and not to be framed by even the most practised and inspired hand without much labour and polish.

As I read over the foregoing lines, I have a guilty feeling that I have been unjust to Putney Hill. The name has a suburban sound, but in the Eighties, at all events, Wimbledon Common, at the eastern edge of which is Putney Hill, was a place of unbelievable beauty and wildness to be so near Charing Cross. In some of its birch-crested, heather- and gorse-clad ravines you might believe yourself in Scotland. If only you could forget, and imagine—and a lesser poet than Swinburne might do this—it was not so unromantic a setting after all.

MEREDITH

How it may be with others I cannot say, but for my own part I find that when I come back to a novel by George Meredith, not having read one of his for some while, I always find after I have finished a page or two that I am asking myself how it is possible that I have ever wasted my time reading any other novels when I do not know by heart all those of this amazing man. That is a mood which endures during half, or it may be three quarters of the book, and then I find that I begin to slacken a little, not in my wonder and admiration of his sheer cleverness, but in zest of interest about the characters. I grow critical, which I never was at first—criticism being swallowed up in admiration—and ask myself whether the characters are real, whether they and the situations in which they move are possible. That is not the kind of question about which it concerns us to seek an answer in many novels ; but George Meredith is such a realist that he demands that everything in his stories shall be real. The romantic haze is not their atmosphere. He wants all clear-cut.

13

I know I am uttering heresies in the view of the pure Meredithian. For one thing, the pious devotee of those works would never be in my position : would never let the fire of his cult die so low that he would come to any novel of the master as to a new thing. But, also, the word realist applied to that master would not be allowed. The disciple would claim him as the prince of idealists. But I mean realist as a term of pure praise. I mean by it that Meredith strives and toils and polishes, with chisel and file, to make all most actual ; he elaborates phrase upon phrase in the endeavour to make clear to us the definition and the interfusion of " the fine shades " of those ladies who so intolerably patronise Emilia in England ; he idealises, and then he works and works to make that most idealised motive or sentiment as real as, say, the posed figure of Roy Richmond for the statue of the German prince. That is what I mean by his realism, and it need not conflict with the purest conception of his idealism. It is indeed but the finish of it—the last word.

Refining thus, however, he does grow, if not obscure, at least difficult. We begin to wonder, too, whether this extreme clairvoyance into emotion and sentiment is the real thing. Even if that wonder is subconscious, still it is there, subconsciously suggesting scepticism whether the atmosphere is quite real, whether it is not a little too translucent for life. We live our common life in rather a haze ; Meredith would take all that sometimes kindly fog out of it and bring outlines clear and distances close as we only see them on a day when the glass is very low and the air is made lucid by a great mixture of water vapour. As we read we almost begin to wish for some of the Scottish mists of Sir Walter, or even some murk of the " London peculiar " as served out by Dickens or Thackeray.

Coming to details, and to plain speaking, though

GEORGE MEREDITH.

plain speaking is not quite the Meredithian way, did any people ever live as some of his people are related to live ?   For example, in *Harry Richmond* we have the question arising whether it be possible to get rid of the Countess, from a house in which she is a guest, within a month.   And she had already been there for a good long visit !   Did people in those days —and they were not days of so very long past—stay so interminably ?   Then is the Countess possible ? Are any of those three sisters possible ?   Or again, are they possible in their reincarnation in the three sisters in *Sandra Belloni* ?   Of course they are the same three, equally as of course Roy Richmond is another incarnation of " the Great Mel."   Meredith was economical.   He would invent his characters once, and then he would make them serve twice, or even more often.   Possibly there is some autobiography about the three sisters and the magnificent parent.   I do not know, but it has been so hinted. A good deal about Meredith's early life has not been told us.   Why should it be, if he had any reticence about it ; as it is exceedingly natural that there should be reticence.   We marvel at reticence about any one's private affairs to-day, and are apt to suspect all kinds of mystery behind it in these times when no affairs are private, and all the secret details of domestic life are set out in public print.   It was not so in Meredith's early years.   He was born in 1828, and lived until 1909. Thus he enjoyed his full span. We do know this, of his boyhood, that he went to school in Germany : and that is of interest, for it lets us into the secret of his knowledge of the little German Court in which Ottilia was bred, to be the worry of Harry Richmond's soul.   It also gives us a hint of the origin of some of the occasional obscurity of his style.   It is cast in Teutonic forms, now and then.   By reason of his obscurity, he has been likened to Browning ; but the resemblance is perhaps too obvious to be profound. Browning's thought comes crowding on thought in such hurry that the last seems to impede the articulate utterance of the one foregoing.   And sometimes he is obscure because he tries to pack his thought into such few words that it really has not room to show itself.   Also it is thought of a very deep nature, often of the nature of divinity.   Meredith is concerned with the nature of humanity purely, which is a difficult matter enough, but not quite so high nor so deep.   It is true that the divine in man is his quest, but he does not travel quite so far into the ultimate mysteries as Browning.   Neither does he pack his thought so tightly.   Really it is his poetry which is obscure rather than his prose, although the man who claims full understanding of all the first chapter in the *Egoist* is bold.   There is no obscurity about some of the later published verse, such as that volume in which *Love in the Valley* is probably the best known piece.   And well does it deserve to be known —a beautiful lilting metre, and delightful thought ! But certainly some of the *Poems*, published in 1851, are difficult.   Probably it would come as a surprise to most readers to find how large was George Meredith's production of verse.   That is because he was, and is, so far better known, as he deserves, in the rôle of novelist.   His first published essay in pure literature was, I think, in verse, namely a poem called " Chillian Wallah," which came out in *Chambers's Journal* in 1849.   In all justice to both " obscurantists," it is only just to say that they could be lucid enough when they so chose.   There is no mystery about the way in which they " brought the good news from Ghent to Aix," for example, any more than in *Love in the Valley*.

Just as we trace the source of some of *Harry Richmond* to Meredith's school days in Germany, so

we may find some hints as to his Emilia in Italy in
the fact that he served as correspondent to the
Morning Post in the Austro-Italian war. Some
of these letters might be well worth republishing, if
only for the sake of the Meredithian phrase and point
of view, and they would be of particular interest at
this moment when Italy has won her own back again
from the " White-Coats."

It is rather difficult to say whether it would be
proper to speak of Meredith as a popular writer, even
now. He has earned an appreciation which is very
much better than mere popularity : that goes without
saying ; but his books are scarcely to be counted in
the ranks of the " best-sellers." He was winning
his slow way to the recognition of his genius all
through the Seventies, but the novel which is certainly
one of his greatest, *Richard Feverel*, was published
as far back as 1859. In the early Seventies *Beauchamp's Career*, which is said to be that work of his
hands which he, personally, rated highest, was coming
out serially in the *Cornhill Magazine*. The most
Meredithian of them all, as it has been called, *The
Egoist*, appeared in 1879. This is regarded by those
of the true faith as the touchstone, the test piece : if
you can conscientiously write yourself an admirer
and appreciator of *The Egoist*, you are ready for
admission at least into the Outer Court of the Temple.
If you fail to answer to that test, you are lost to hope.
And surely it must be a very dull person who cannot
admire " with much amazement " the relentless skill
with which the author of this wonderful book has
stripped the skin of self-satisfaction from what little
of soul there is in his Sir Willoughby Patterne, and
left it so bare for his dissection. The crowning
triumph and testimony to his unrivalled science as
an operator in this kind is that the small soul of the
man who supposed himself so great is found, thus laid

naked, to be not altogether an unlovely thing. It
has its pathos : it is a thing that moves our pity
rather than our scorn. It would have been an easy
task in comparison, as we may suppose, to show it
altogether ugly and base. But he has not made it
so ; and that is how it is that it is such a very human
soul, after all. It is a holding of the mirror up to
nature withal ; for he must be either a very perfect
or a very blind man who cannot see in that soul, thus
exhibited, qualities which he may now, for the first
time, detect, with shame, in his own. If there be a
moral purpose in Meredith's writing, it is surely this—
to lay pretension bare, to expose it for what it is and
make us see it as a loathly thing which we have to
slough off from us, like an out-grown snake's skin ;
and in none other of his books does he accomplish
this end quite so perfectly as in this amazing
Egoist.

I have spoken of *The Ordeal of Richard Feverel*
as one of his greatest novels. To the person whom
I have called the true Meredithian I believe that *The
Egoist* must seem greatest of all. Meredith himself,
as we have seen, gave first place to *Beauchamp's
Career*. But in the opinion of such general public as
he commands I suppose that the novel which he
published in the middle of the Eighties, *Diana of the
Crossways*, is that which will be ranked together with
The Ordeal as showing his genius at its very highest.
He is a very earnest and interested student of women ;
that is seen in every one of his books without exception ;
and the best, the most true, the most lovable perhaps,
in spite of her one desperate and yet truly feminine
act of treachery, in the revelation of the State Secret
to the great editor, is Diana. Diana is avowedly
the presentment, in fiction, of the famous Mrs.
Norton. I suppose that it is impossible to affirm
how exact the portrait is : probably Meredith himself

would not claim precision in the outlines and the shades. The most that he would ask us to admit is perhaps that he has given us a character which expresses the fascinations and the weakness of its original. Whether it is exact in material detail I presume it is hardly worth inquiring. It was not his purpose to make a contribution to history. In the main his purpose was, as I take it, to show a woman of a character which would explain to us Mrs. Norton, as he imagined her to be, and in the scenes wherein he gave her a rôle. We cannot, at the very least, deny that he has given us the picture of a real, vivid, and a delightful woman ; and with gratitude we may leave it so.

The popular estimate, ranking together *Richard Feverel* and *Diana*, no matter what the relative place of the two in comparison with *The Egoist, Beauchamp's Career,* and any of the others, strikes me as a very correct one ; and it is curious enough that it should be so, seeing that they were written—or at any rate were given out to the world—at dates so far apart. The one was published in 1859 ; the other in 1885. I may be very wrong, but they appear to me to show a very similar maturity of genius. Had I been asked, knowing nothing of the dates, I should have said, in my ignorance, that they were the products of very much the same period of the author's life. Is it possible that after many years, and many books given to us in the interval, his mind reverted to a mood of twenty-six years earlier ? It is possible. Perhaps what is far more probable is that my estimate of the two, and of the similarity between them, is far astray from the truth.

As this *Diana* was one of the greatest of Mr. Meredith's novels, so it was, I think, the last of the super-excellent ones. In 1891 came *One of our Conquerors,* and after that several more, but none, as most of us would judge, to be placed quite on a level with those already named.

By friends who used to visit George Meredith towards the end of his life, at his home near Dorking, I was told that he grew more and more aloof from the occurrences in the world, and increasingly absorbed in his own creations. His mind restored them again and again, speculating as to whether they would or would not, being such as he had made them, act just as they did in his writings, in the successive scenes in which they took their part. Thus he mentally revised again and again, and it would be of the keenest interest if we might know the outcome of those revisions. But that knowledge he has borne with him to the grave, together with the gratitude of a growing company of readers to whom he has given great entertainment and, it is to be presumed, some clearer insight into the hazy workings of their own souls.

CHAPTER XVIII

SPENCER WALPOLE AND ANDREW LANG

THE fortune of men is very different, and very carelessly adjusted to their true merit, in respect to that degree of fame which each is permitted to enjoy during his lifetime. To some it is given to reap this particular kind of reward for their achievement as soon as their fame-worthy deed is performed. From others the meed of recognition is withheld till they have passed to another life, in which we do not know how high its value may appear to them. It is, perhaps, more than probable that the eminence of one who was—what shall we say?—here, a Prime Minister, will then seem somewhat equal to the glory which we, who are adults, now deem to have been the due meed of the captain of our private school eleven. No Prime Minister, by the way, in the estimate of his Cabinet and his country, was ever a man of such importance as that small emperor in the eyes of his subjects and contemporaries.

This brief preamble is suggested by the thought of the name of Sir Spencer Walpole, for it is a name which will not mean very much to many who read it. There is no Civil Servant of his time, it is true, who can think of it without the idea arising in his mind of a most charming and kindly personality, an able official in various capacities, and so forth. But to the general reading public his is a name but little known. Yet, as an historian, I do not hesitate to claim for him that he is in the first rank. How many have read his history or consider him as a great man ? There are certain " household words " which fit them out with all that they deem it necessary to be acquainted with in the way of writers of history—Macaulay, Froude, Lecky, Stubbs, and so on. But who is Walpole ? they may ask.

Of course no historian asks the question. No moderately well-informed man, perhaps, asks it. But I am writing of the many, who are neither historians nor moderately-informed. And I maintain that they have hardly, if at all, heard of Spencer Walpole. So saying, I appear to have imposed on myself the burden of telling them why it is that they should have heard of him. I have already said that he was a great historian. In a little more detail what he has done to achieve that greatness, is mainly this : he wrote the *History of England* from the year of Waterloo to 1858 ; and supplemented this some eight years later by his *History of Twenty-Five Years ;* these twenty-five being the years that followed the last date dealt with in the former publication. Thus he gave the history of sixty-eight years in all. They are the years in which the events occurred that are the most immediately important in making our country what we find it to-day. Further, he wrote several studies in biography, such as the *Life of Spencer Perceval*—who was, if I mistake not, an ancestor in some sort, collateral or otherwise, of Lord John Russell—and others, as well as many articles on political and historical subjects.

That is what he did, but what makes the doing important is the way in which it was done. Historians know. They give every credit to the solidity of the work ; to the width of grasp and the understanding of the relative proportions of the great questions discussed and involved ; to the impartial

SIR SPENCER WALPOLE.

and judicious opinions, always stated with a moderation and a modesty which are no more than the
natural expression of the writer's own nature; to the
accuracy of the finance; and, above all, to the very
scrupulous care with which every fact and figure and
detail have been verified and confirmed. This,
mainly, is what makes the history so valuable, that
its every sentence, its every date and figure, may be
taken in the absolute trust that they are exact. The
labour which he lavished on it all, in order to achieve
this triumphant result of precision, was immense.
I used to see him mainly when it was the *Twenty-
Five Years* on which he was engaged. I used to ask
him what he had been doing. The answer was always
the same for I should be afraid to say how long :
" Oh, proof-correcting, proof-correcting." Three
several times, as he told me, he went over every fact
and figure that he had quoted, tracing each back to
its farthest discoverable source ; and this, although he
was the last man in the world to need to go again over
ground that he had already traversed, because his
memory was so remarkable that I cannot imagine
him failing to observe any discrepancy between
two readings. It happened to me once to be looking
up in *Bradshaw*, while in his house, a certain obscure
station. I mentioned it to him. " Oh," he said,
" you will find it on page so and so ! " " How in the
world do you know that ? " I asked. " Oh," he replied, " I looked it up for myself only a fortnight ago."
A fortnight ago ! And he had remembered the
number of the page ever since, though he had no
motive whatever for making a mental note of it, and of
course had, in fact, made no such special note. What
struck me as so extraordinary was his surprise at
finding that I deemed it at all surprising in him to
remember it. He seemed to think it a matter of
course that any man, having looked up a station a

fortnight ago, would still remember the number of the page on which it was to be found. To me, who retained a figure of this little importance within my sieve-like brain for a maximum of, say, five minutes, the fortnight's retention which he seemed to regard as almost inevitable appeared almost supernatural. And I still think that it was a testimony, in itself trivial enough, to a memory of quite uncommon quality.

Only second, as an element in the value of his history, to this extraordinary exactness and truth, is the fortunate balance of his judgment and opinions. Of moderate views, inclining to the liberal and to the democratic, is the verdict which would be, and which actually was, passed on his standpoint towards events. That means a very sane point of view, and a point of which the sanity becomes increasingly conspicuous as the opinion of readers veers in the democratic and liberal direction. And no one, whether they like the admission or not, is able to question that general opinion has moved in that line since the Eighties and the days of Spencer Walpole's writing.

He was actually engaged in the compilation of the first and main part of the history from 1878 to 1886. It was in the last of these years that the last volume of that history was published, and it was in 1904 that he gave us the *History of Twenty-Five Years*.

It is rather amazing, considering the amount of work which he got through as a Civil Servant, that he should have found the time for so much production of a literary kind, and particularly as it was a kind which demanded so much original research in the first place and so much attention to detail and correction in the second. He went as Governor to the Isle of Man in 1882, and later, when there arose need to find a place for Sir West Ridgeway, he was brought

back to be Secretary to the Post Office. I believe
that he found time for a good deal of writing while
in the Isle of Man. He was far away, indeed, from
his original sources, but he made a good deal of use
of the London Library, of which he was a pillar of
support from the earliest days of its most valuable
institution. He always said that the committee
had treated him very well (he was a leading member
of it himself) in letting him have more books and
keeping them longer than he was strictly entitled to
do. It is merely a wise and justifiable stretching
of that usually inelastic substance, red tape, in favour
of a man thus engaged on literary work of real
importance.

What vexed Spencer Walpole most was the
question of his style. I write of him without the
" Sir," which came to him later in the form of a
" K.C.B.," almost forced upon him in 1893. He had
not been dubbed knight during the Eighties. I write
" forced upon him," because that word really represents
the fact. He hated the dubbing. He would not
accept a " C.B.," which was pressed on him earlier,
but consented reluctantly to the " K.C.B." because it
was pointed out that the King could not well make his
subordinates " C.B.," however they had merited it,
while leaving him, their superior, letterless.

He disliked the dubbing simply and solely, I believe,
from modesty. He was, I have always thought, the
most modest man—truly modest, really humble,
with regard to his own powers or performance—that
I ever met. Affected modesty and humility is as
common as blackberries, and the tribe of Uriah
Heep increases merrily, but the real humility is a very
rare fruit, and I never saw it in such perfection as in
Spencer Walpole. And it was by reason of this
humility that his style was a question of so much
vexation to him. He used to complain bitterly

almost tearfully. " It is so heavy, so dull!" he used
to say. I do not find it so. I have no personal
acquaintance whatever with the Muse of History,
but, as I conceive of her, she is a dignified lady,
not to be wooed in any light flirtatious manner, but
with weighty, well-considered words.

It was thus that Spencer Walpole wrote. His
style is dignified, worthy of its theme. It has not
the lightness and the sparkle, it is true, which is
imparted by epigram, but does not that sparkle often
give a rather dazzling look to what is not very deep
or sound below ? The dazzle and the epigram are
all very well for a work which we mean to glance at
and to lay aside after some hours or so of entertainment. If we want a history to read, to put up on the
shelf, and then to take down again and again—not
merely, however, a " book of reference," as it is called,
but a solidly and well-written and well-considered
story of events and reflection on their causes—we
have it, as it seems to me, in these books of his, and
have it as it would not have been, had he succeeded
in lightsome sparkling.

People, in the wide sense of the reading public,
do not know him to-day ; but people, in that wide
sense, will know. His day will come for popularity,
as it has already arrived at a really better than merely
popular appreciation.

He did, no doubt, achieve much popularity, and
some official dignity, during his life, but the popularity
was personal, and the dignities were conferred for
official work done unsparingly and with ability.
After his retirement from the Post Office he found
himself with larger leisure, and went on the Boards of
several Companies, where his good judgment and his
capacity for figures were very useful. His personal
popularity was great. He was a very sociable man,
with something of that interest in his fellow men and

love of gossip of his relative, Horace Walpole. But he would have been kindlier, even if not quite so witty in comment, than that immortal diarist and letter writer. Nor do I think that he would have perpetrated the Gothic of Strawberry Hill. There was no trouble that he would not take to serve a friend, and I believe that he would have done as much for an enemy. The only difficulty in the latter case being that he would probably have been quite at a loss where to find one. A more unselfish man could not be.

Early in his career he had been associated as one of the Fishery Commissioners with Frank Buckland, and used to tell wonderful stories about the queer aquatic things that would tumble out of Frank Buckland's coat pockets when they went to stay as fellow guests at a house where a friend of one or the other was entertaining them in the course of their peregrinations inspecting rivers and fisheries. The flavour of Frank Buckland's coat in consequence came to be such that his association with things fishy could be perceived at a considerable distance. In spite of this association, Spencer Walpole was not keenly interested in any branch of natural history. If a mind could be said to have but a small range which took in the whole of English history, and all foreign history that had any connection with it, as its province, it would be then true to say of him that his intellect worked within a limited circle, for nothing outside this tolerably large circumference made any strong appeal to him. Probably it was, in part, on account of that limit that it was such a thoroughly effective mind within its range.

His death came with alarming suddenness in 1907, when he was still engrossed in his literary work and his Company directing, and when he still appeared to have vigour beyond his age and to spare for many years to come. He had the strong, stout figure, with moderate height and broad chest development, which usually promises a long life. To the last he kept the ruddy colour of a young man and a look of youth in his singularly blue and kindly eyes. The greyish hair and beard were the only signs of age.

ANDREW LANG

I hardly know why I thus couple up Andrew Lang with Spencer Walpole, unless it be that both were historians—of a sort. But it was of a widely different sort, and they would not have jogged in double harness together. Walpole's rank and mode as an historian I have just discussed. Andrew Lang was historian by accident rather—the accident that some of the people who caught his quick fancy and incited him to write about them were engaged in great historical drama—Mary Queen of Scots most notably, also *Pickle the Spy*, and others. Andrew Lang was a number of things intellectually, for the versality and range of his mind were extraordinary, but of all things that which he was not was an historian at all of the type of Spencer Walpole. He did not care a bit about the measures or the political games in which the people that interested him were taking in hand, or cared only in so far as they were the setting, the scenery, for his actors. It was the actors themselves and their doings that appealed to him. And yet here again we have to make a qualification : he was interested in the activities of these persons, in the scrapes into which they fell and in the puzzles, as in a detective story, which they presented; but he was not really very interested in their characters and their motives. As he himself confessed to me once, " I can do nothing with human nature." He meant, as a writer of the novel. He was quite right in his estimate of himself.

ANDREW LANG.

Few people probably are aware that he ever tried his
hand at a novel ; but he did, and very bad it was.
I think it was called *The Brand of Cain*, or something
of that kind, and I well remember his amazement
to discover that I had read it. It was not altogether
gratified amazement either. He was actually sorry
that any one for whose opinion he cared even the least
bit should have read it, so convinced was he of its
badness. Of course it was only because it had his
name to it that it ever got itself published.

To be sure, he wrote *The Disentanglers*, an ingenious
idea, ingeniously worked ; but it is hardly to be called a
novel, or a study in humanity. He collaborated with
Rider Haggard, too, in *The World's Desire*, but his
personal share is not obvious ; and, after all, its theme
is a type only, and perhaps not a very probable type.
And all this disability to " make anything " of human
nature arose, in all likelihood, from the fact that
motives and character did not present problems of
real interest to him. He did not go probing down
deeply into the springs of conduct ; he found much
more excitement in the material and the obvious.
It is singular that it should be so, with his very acute
intellect, but so it was.

It appears to me that I am, so far, saying everything
that is negative about Lang, recording everything that
he was not. It is a way, like another, of sketching a
portrait, to begin with determining the lines to be left
out, and having thus begun, I may continue. He
was, then, as unlike as possible to Spencer Walpole,
because he had not the real historian's bent of mind,
he had not the weighing, judicial sense. With all
my deep admiration for Andrew Lang—and let me
say at once that I did admire and love him greatly—
he was the last man to whom I would go for a judicious
opinion on men, women, or affairs. He lived in a
curious detachment, although he touched at so many

14

points the various interests of very different men. His was, in truth, one of the most remarkable personalities and intellects that we shall find in all this portrait gallery. He touched at so many points, and yet he drove in deeply at none of them ; he was really aloof all the while ; and he made this merely surface contact in spite of possessing an intellect most penetrating and incisive. So, in his historical studies, if we call them so, though we should be more right in saying " studies of historical persons," he picked the actors up, let his graceful fancy, his fine intellect, and his delightful style play about with them for a time, and then dropped them back again into the welter of history for the true historian to deal with them. I have heard the term " scrappy " applied to his methods, and it was not misapplied. He himself confessed to habits of carelessness and inaccuracy in detail. I think that he exaggerated this inaccuracy : he was really far more conscientious as a writer than he gave himself the credit of being ; but it is certainly impossible to think of Andrew Lang going over his proofs three times, and verifying and re-verifying his figures and citations, as Spencer Walpole did. He wrote as easily as Walpole wrote laboriously. He was indeed the quickest writer that I have ever known. I have heard him say : " Is it humanly speaking possible to write an article before dinner ? " —taking out his watch—" Twenty minutes before we need go and dress ! Yes, I think it just is." And off he would go—I think it was for the *Daily News* that he was writing at this time occasional articles about all things in general, and a few more—and scribble down the article, and as a rule these lightning articles of his were the best : these forked-lightning articles, perhaps we should say, for all his writing had the speed of merely common electricity. The reading of them did not go quite so fast. For days I have

kept a letter of Andrew Lang's by me, wondering at
its meaning, making intelligent guesses from time to
time, and usually, at each new look, discovering the
significance of some new hieroglyphic, until all was
unravelled. But it was a very tangled skein, and my
pity for his compositors was sore.

In its own way, Andrew Lang's intellect was the
most brilliant and the most delightful that I have had
the luck to encounter. I say that deliberately and
with no hesitation. His fancy was so graceful, his
taste so perfect. The world in which his spirit really
lived was a kind of fairy-land. He came down to
this terrestrial business only now and then, always
with a spectator's interest in it rather than an actor's.
There was a pathetic side to this. He had a great
leaning to the athletic and to the primitive ; the
life of the savage and of the gipsy appealed to him.
I am not sure but that he had some strain of gipsy
blood in him. His singularly handsome dark face and
large dreaming eyes gave suggestion of it, and gipsies,
even of royal race, moved a good deal among the
Border Scottish families to which the Langs were
akin. He was thus drawn by his disposition ; and
yet his health was always delicate, so that the life
even of the ordinary athletic man of civilisation was
forbidden him. He had to be very careful in his diet ;
he could not travel very long distances in a day, I
think because the rattle and jolt of a long train
journey were too much for his head. It was all a very
delicately balanced organisation, of the very finest
constituents. I believe he had once been a fair
bowler, with a slingy, fast action : never more than
moderately good, I imagine, and less effective than
his brother T. W., who was in the Oxford Eleven as
a medium-paced bowler. But with this exception
I can think of no form of athletics in which he took
part.

And yet there was no form that did not interest him. He wrote delightfully of golf, of cricket, of fishing—he was something of a trout-fisher, by the way, though very rarely catching a trout—especially he wrote well of golf, so far as a man can write well of a game which he cannot play at all. Even a stroke a hole handicap would have complimented him too highly. But it was always the writing of an artist, though his art was not golf, but literature. He loved Sagas, and all deeds of derring-do. He loved the classics, such as Homer, because they tell stories of heroes, and he loved them even better than the Sagas, because they are heroic stories told with art, while the Sagas are absolutely artless. He would have been perfectly at home had he lived in ancient Greece, or in the Iceland of the Vikings, or in the Provence of the Troubadours—only, he would not have lived, for the climatic and sanitary conditions would have been his immediate death. But in any one of these environments he would have been more at home than in modern England, and especially in modern London. "Why people live in London," he wrote to me once, "I wonder; and my wonder ever grows." Yet he lived there, and in Marloes Road, Kensington— not one of the most romantic streets. "Where is Marloes Road?" I heard some one ask him, who wished to call on him. "You go along the Cromwell Road till you drop," said Andrew Lang. "It's there!"

So there he lived and wrote and dreamed; and it was in his dreams—by which I mean waking dreams, of course—that he was happy. He lived in Kensington, and I think that if one had asked him what life he would like best to have lived or be living—he might have said that he wished to be going with Herodotus, the old father of history, on that pilgrimage to Egypt, about which he tells us in his fourth book :

> He left the land of youth, he left the young,
>   The smiling Gods of Greece ; he passed the isle
> Where Jason loitered and where Sappho sung ;
>   He sought the secret-founted wave of Nile,
>   Of that old world, half dead a weary while ;
> Heard the Priests murmur in their mystic tongue,
>   And through the fanes went voyaging, among
> Dark tribes that worshipped Cat and Crocodile.
>
> He learned the tales of death Divine and birth,
> Strange loves of hawk and serpent, Sky and Earth,
>   The marriage and the slaying of the Sun ;
> The shrines of ghosts and beasts he wandered through,
> And mocked not of their godhead, for he knew
>   Behind all creeds the Spirit that is One.

That is how Lang himself writes of this bewitching adventure in the sonnet which he prefaces to a reprint of an old translation of that fourth book. The sonnet gives us a good deal of the real Lang and of his psychical cravings. He would go with the traveller for the very adventure's sake, for the brine and the tossing of the sea, for the peril by water and by land. And he would go to satisfy his yearning intellect with knowledge. He would hear stories. He would learn folk-lore, and that was of deep interest to him. Finally he would be living in a fairy-land, as remote from Marloes Road as may be.

He made up, in a measure, for Marloes Road, by going to St. Andrews in the winter—in the winter of all seasons for the East Neuk of Fife. Yet it had its delights, I know, because he used to let me come and stay with him there. The house that he took stood right on the cliff, with the splendid old ruin of the Castle on its eastern side, and northward the Firth of Tay, and Forfarshire opposite. That was a fitter habitation for a man who was dreaming of going a-Viking. He went from London, but he never went for a holiday. A holiday would be impossible for a man whose imagination worked so perpetually,

and whose artistic impulse drove him to constant
expression in words. He must write, and he did write,
whether at St. Andrews or elsewhere. He also had
the air of abundant leisure ; he was always ready to
talk and to idle : he took his work and his art with so
little apparent seriousness that he actually never had
a study, apart, to write in, either in London or anywhere else. He always seemed to regard himself
rather in the light of an amateur, whose production
was worth very little, so that it did not matter a jot
to the world whether it was produced or not. He
said to me once : " People ask me why I do not write
some big book. Why should I write a big book ?
I have no particular message for the world."

Perhaps he had not, unless it be the common
message of all artists, to make the world realise the
beauty of the world as it never would do without the
artist and his revelations. And yet it always made
me angry to hear people talking of Andrew Lang as if
he were a literary trifler, a minor poet, a writer of
Ballads in Blue China, and no more. He was all this,
but he was a great deal more besides. People who
judged him thus had forgotten, or did not know, those
serious books of his on ancient religious ceremony and
so on : *Custom and Myth*, and *Myth, Ritual, and Religion*. They did not know, or did not think of, his
share with Butcher and Leaf and Myers in the transla-
tions of the *Odyssey* and the *Iliad*. They did not
remember his brilliant record at Oxford, nor recognise
the range of his learning, stored and kept brightly
ready for use by a very retentive memory. He knew
old French literature, both prose and verse, better
than any other man I ever met, though of course he
made no speciality of it, nor of any other one subject
of study. The truth is that he was so very quick
of apprehension that he could grasp a subject with
about half the attention that a common mind had

to apply to achieve anything like the same mastery. But he worked far harder than people thought, and was far more conscientious than they supposed. For instance, I happen to know that he toiled for weeks and months over a projected history of the Jewish tribes. He did not like the point of view of Renan in his *Histoire des Peuples d'Israël*, although he had an unbounded admiration for it as a work of art and storehouse of knowledge. I had left him keenly engaged in this. A short while after I met him again and asked : " Well, how are the children of Israel ? Are they out of the desert yet ? " He had been humorously bemoaning the apparently quite unnecessary length of their sojourn in those inhospitable arenas. " Oh," he said lightly, " I have given it up, given up all idea of it ; I have torn up what I had written. I have come to the conclusion that no man ought to write about it who does not know Hebrew."

He spoke thus lightly, but it was no light sacrifice that he had made. He had sacrificed months of toil, and destroyed MS. that any publisher would certainly have given good money for, even in its fragmentary style. But money, and what most men regard as the good things of this life, interested him hardly at all. Folk-lore, crystal gazing, psychical research, and old story of all kinds were the things of the spirit which really seemed to him to matter. A certain material comfort he was obliged to have, if he was to live, by reason of his delicacy of constitution, and the devoted love of Mrs. Lang assured him these, without any personal attention of his own. She shared, too, in all his literary interests, and published several books, of which *Dissolving Views* probably won most fame.

I do not suppose that it is possible for any one to have the least knowledge of Lang and of his work without realising the brilliance of his intellect. What

I do not think has been nearly enough recognised is the warmth and kindliness of his heart. It is to be admitted of him that he was at times impatient and even petulant. Much of this, doubtless, may be put down to the score of his always rather indifferent health. It is true, however, that he habitually suffered fools badly, very badly ; and also that fools were apt to suffer badly from the caustic wit which ran so readily from his pen. But there are scores of writers alive and at work to-day who would bear witness to the help which his kindly encouragement gave them at a time when their inexperience was in much need of such aid ; and he was as liberal of his money as of his counsel. The contributors to his *Red, Blue,* and all sorts of coloured *Fairy Books* were rewarded with a generosity which left very little balance for the editor, and the assistants of his musings under " The Sign of the Ship " in *Longman's Magazine* often ate up all the guineas that the publishers gave him for this monthly " feature."

His interests ranged widely, but two of the sides of life which are the main concern of very many men, politics and finance, appealed to him not at all, and when either of these came on the *tapis* he made not the slightest effort, not even so much as mere courtesy might demand, to conceal his boredom. In some ways he was more like a supernaturally brilliant child than a grown man—possibly a slightly spoilt child. It was a child's world in which his spirit moved, and moved with a whimsical fancy quite delightful.

Some of his *obiter dicta* are worth quoting : " This book is good, though powerful," was the opening sentence of one of his reviews of a novel in the *Saturday.* Of another he wrote : " A touch of the supernatural is added by the hero finding the book he wants in the London Library." This was in the early days of that admirable and now very well-equipped institution ; and we may well believe that Lang, in his quest for old and little-known books on old French literature and the like, may have been a sore thorn in the side of the librarian and his ever attentive staff. He was appointed Gibbon Lecturer in Natural Theology at St. Andrews. "What line did he take?" I asked Rider Haggard, who had been at the opening lecture. "He commenced," Haggard answered, "with ' Once it began to thunder ; and men began to wonder.'" It was a characteristic start for Andrew Lang to make, and perhaps the large and vague topic could not be broached much more auspiciously.

I had heard nothing of his last illness until its fatal end, and the news was very grievous. It seemed as if an element of lightness went with him from the world. But he had little reserve of strength to fight any serious attack, and, for all his gaiety and wit, he was by nature disposed to melancholy. I should imagine that his vitality was always rather below the normal. Many others have made a larger figure in the world, but there have been few in our generation of such an interesting and attractive personality.

CHAPTER XIX

WATTS, MILLAIS, AND BURNE-JONES

MR. WATTS was the oldest of the three great painters, Watts, Millais, and Burne-Jones, who were producing glorious works for our delight in the Eighties. I am not forgetting that this period saw the rising genius of Mr. Sargent. His picture, of or about this time, which I seem to remember best is Mrs. (now Lady) Agnew—a beautiful portrait of a beautiful woman. But Sargent happily is painting still, and should have many years of work before him. The other three are gone.

Watts's production may be split up not so much into periods as into phases. He had the phase in which he did symbolism; another phase in which portraiture attracted him, yet another in which his zeal was all for the presentment of virile force. Perhaps we might better call them moods, than phases. But they cannot strictly be called periods, because there was no regular succession about them. The one mood or the other might possess him for a while, and then all his production would be of works that were the expression of that mood. And then another mood would come and another kind of production, and the former, now laid aside, would be returned to later.

In the Eighties, when I used to see him, he was greatly occupied with the physical force idea. Thus he was working—when indeed, for months and years,

. WATTS IN HIS STUDIO.

was he not now and again so working ?—at that great
equestrian figure of which we see the replica in
Kensington Gardens. He called it " Physical
Energy," and the expression of energy is abundant
both in horse and man. I like to think that the original is far away on the Matoppo Hills, watching the
grave of Cecil Rhodes, the Empire-maker. Then he
had also in his studio at the time the big canvas of
the two huge dray-horses and the only little less huge
drayman, looking like an advertisement to the blood-
making qualities of beer. There is no keen energy
manifest in either horse or man here : it is rather the
massiveness of force in repose that they exhibit.
They are moving nothing, not even themselves, for
the moment, but you are obliged to feel that battering
rams could hardly move them. It was perhaps a
curious form for Watts's genius to take, because there
was none of this great robustness about him, personally. One could suppose it much more naturally
the expression of Millais' nature, who, however,
never did anything of exactly this kind, so far as I
know. Of course this picture and this statue in
which physical force were so typified were symbolical,
but in rather a different way from those frankly
romantic and allegorical figures, the " Love and Life,"
the " Love and Death," " The Minotaur," and so on.
It is especially this class of picture with which the
name of Mr. Watts is associated in the minds of
most people. He had faith that they carried a moral
message with them. If we think of each, we can see
easily what the message is that he means it to carry,
but it is doubtful whether nine out of ten of those
who look at them ever think of it. I have a suspicion
that although he flattered himself with the opinion
that he was painting them primarily for the sake of
the message, it was really the joy of colour and form
that inspired him. He was an immense admirer of

the Venetians, and it is their rich colours that he aims at. He was very strong and correct in his suggestion of the form beneath the skin. His knowledge of anatomy was perfect ; and you can always " feel," so to say, where the bone lies and where the chief muscle is attached under his flesh surfaces ; but his real joy was in the colour. He could take delight in it as expressed by other modern artists, as well as by himself, for he was unstintedly generous in his praise, even extravagant maybe.

" Have you seen the exhibition of Lady Waterford's pictures ? " he asked me one day. It was shortly after the death, if I remember right, of that gifted lady.

I said " No," and further confessed, to my shame, that I knew nothing of her. " But you must," he said. " It is imperative. You must not miss it. It is at Lord Brownlow's house in Carlton House Terrace. She is the greatest colorist we have had since the days of the great Italians. I have seen nothing like it. They say that she cannot draw. I don't care for that. She draws quite well enough."

Of course I went, and of course I fervently admired. Equally, of course, it is not for me to state my private judgment beside that of Mr. Watts. That Lady Waterford was a very great colorist, no one will doubt. That she drew " quite well enough " is open to rather more question. But I quote the opinion of Watts by way of example of the warmth of appreciation which would carry him now and then to an extreme that some will perhaps call not quite balanced. In any case, this contented criticism of Lady Waterford's drawing is rather striking, and very typical, from one whose own drawing was so very perfect and whose conscience, in connection with his drawing, was never at ease unless that perfection was reached.

And then there was his phase, or mood, of portraiture. If we were able to collect and range to-

gether a gallery of his men's heads, that in itself
would show a noble achievement for any painter.
An excellent example is the head of Lord Lawrence
in the National Gallery. With women he was not
quite successful ; but then, what painter is ! One of
his best was of Mrs. Coltman Rogers, whose beautiful
and refined face greatly attracted him. The shoulders
wear a cloak of a blue that makes a wonderful
harmony with the corn-hued hair. But this is a
story of a day later than the Eighties.

Mr. Watts had a very delightful gentleness, courtesy,
and dignity of manner. It was the manner of a man
who lived entirely out of the world, engrossed in his
art. He was offered a baronetcy, but declined it ;
and one cannot conceive a motive for him to accept.
He had no children, and could not care for it personally, since it certainly could not give him added
honour.

There were a few ladies by whom he was devoutly
worshipped. They called him " The Signor," or
" The Master." It is a situation which very few
men are able to support without appearing slightly
ridiculous ; but Mr. Watts accepted it without loss
of dignity. I think that he found it agreeable,
though he did not value it at all above its worth.
Still he appeared to accept it seriously : possibly he
had not a very keen sense of humour. The wor-
shipping ladies were a little ridiculous at times,
inevitably ; but I do not think that Mr. Watts ever
was.

" Posterity is a funny fellow," as some one has
sapiently said. One never knows just what its
verdict is going to be. But the production by which
posterity is likely to judge Watts, and by which it
will surely rank him with the immortals, is his portraits, that gallery of men's heads. There were those,
and good judges of art, too, among them, who could

not tolerate his allegories, which made him popular.
I suppose it must have been a little later than the
Eighties, probably in the following decade, that
I was going through the Tate Gallery with Sir John
Day, the judge. Sir John was a great judge, not only
of law but also of art, and a considerable buyer of
pictures. He had, especially, a very fine collection
of the Barbizon School, which he had made long before
there was any vogue for that style. Mr. Obach,
from whom the greater part of the collection had been
bought, told me some twenty years ago that Sir
John's collection must even then be worth quite
double what he had given for it. Sir John, however,
took no financial interest in his acquisition. He was
a lover of beauty for its own sake, and had either
published, or had printed and privately circulated,
a small book named *The Idea of Beauty*. Thus he had
every right to speak with some authority on a matter
of art, especially the painter's art. And when we
came on these grand allegories of Watts, with their
Venetian richness of colours, what he did was to lift
up his hands with an expression of comic horror on
his always most humorous face, and exclaim, " Well,
well ! Well, well ! If that's what painting's meant
for ! " He became almost inarticulate in his dismay
at the splendid canvases.

To me, at that time in rather a fervent state of
Watts-worship, the comment from a man whose
opinion in art I was obliged to reverence piously, was
rather shocking. I tried to say a word or two of
protest, and in defence of these glowing splendours.
He would listen to none of it. He would not take a
second look at the pictures. He hurried past them, as
though the sight of them pained his eyes, as indeed it
did. Mr. Watts, however, can afford to be judged by
other work than this, and his fame is secure. A few
curious by-products of his art are to be found in the

cricket pavilion at Lord's. They are curious, because, so far as I know, he never cared greatly for cricket. But he did greatly care, as we have seen, for virile energy, and thus it interested him to draw sketches of the cricketer in the poses of the different strokes with the bat. There is much vigour of action about them, and every one is a perfect representation of the portrayed stroke as it should be played.

Mr. Watts worked much alone. He was not of a school, unless his continuance of the Venetian colour tradition assigns him to that noble heritage, nor was he at all obviously the founder of a school. There was no eminent originality in his methods. But in all his phases he was, beyond all question, a very noble painter, to be ranked among our greatest.

MILLAIS

Was there ever a man who looked less like an artist than Sir John Millais ? I cannot think it. Had one met him in the street, not knowing him, and been told to guess at his profession, one would have said, " Country gentleman ; fox-hunter ; good man of business in county affairs."

That was his look—big, bluff, very intelligent, and most remarkably handsome. It was impossible to pass him without a second glance. His manner was to match with his look, genial and hearty ; again the manner of a good-hearted English squire. But artist—no ; anything but !

I am not sure but what his most intimate disposition accorded with his look and manner rather than with his profession as artist. He loved the country, and he loved sport—the sport of fishing best of all. At one time he rented Murthly from Mr. Walter Fotheringham. It was there that he painted his "Murthly Moss," and one or two other very beautiful pictures. But he

took it for the sport rather than for the picturesque.
It is on the Tay, and good salmon fishing goes with it.
I fished with some of his gillies later, and they used
to tell me wonderful stories of Sir John's keenness,
perhaps to stimulate my own. It did not need much
stimulus, when a possible salmon was in question,
but I cannot claim that it was equal to Sir John
Millais'. I would fish when there was the barest
conceivable chance of a salmon ; but he would fish
when there was absolutely none at all. When the
water was perfectly gin-clear, they told me, he would
come down, day after day, under a burning sun, and
flog it steadily down with his fly just as eagerly as if
a fish might be expected to rush at it on every cast.
Of course it is not given to one man to know the
intimate heart of another : it may be that he thus
flogged and flogged to get rid of superfluous energy,
or it may be that his work, his painting, had such firm
hold on his thoughts that he resorted to this means
of shaking it off a little and getting quit of it for a
while. But I do not think so. I do not think that
he was a painter, an artist, a poet, of such a nature
and conviction that his art would fasten on him with
this strange grip. In one sense that was the pity of
it, perhaps—that his art was not all in all, and his
whole life and all that mattered in it, to him as it was
to his great contemporaries Watts and Burne-Jones.
He was a stronger man, physically, than either of
these ; more virile of aspect ; looking as if he had more
blood in his veins. Thus he was perhaps able to throw
off a load of work and of thought better than they.
He would not need the relaxation for the same reason
that they might need it, though I do not know that
either of them was a fisherman or lover of sport in
any form. I believe that he fished for the pure love
of fishing, and cast when there was not the faintest
chance, humanly speaking, of a salmon, in the dim

(By Charles R. Leslie, R.A.)

SIR JOHN EVERETT MILLAIS, R.A.

hope that the supernatural might happen, that a miracle might be vouchsafed, and that ⟨salmon⟩ salmon, contrary to all the laws of nature and o⟨...⟩s kind, might even in these impossible circumstances attach itself to the far end of his line.

It is hard to tell, as I say, what the temperamental gifts of Millais were for the art of which he was so great a master, but that is the only question about his gift which can be in any conceivable doubt. In all other ways, at all events, he was opulently gifted— gifted, as I am disposed to think, beyond either of the others I have named with him. His colour was so fine and so true, he could carry it so far at both ends of the scale ; his drawing was so good and facile, his range was so wide. He could do portrait or landscape or what you will. Anything that man has done with brush and colour seemed as if it came perfectly easily to his hand. He deals with it all like one to whom it was no effort. That is the impression that it gives, and it is an impression that all evidence points to as correct.

Behind it all there is still the hint of pity, still the feeling that with such transcendent gifts of hand and eye and mind he might have done more, very much though he did.

It does not do to be ungrateful. He has given us glorious pictures. Just because of his landscapes and his " subject " pictures, or drama-pictures, or what- ever they should be called, such as his " Huguenots " or " The Black Brunswicker," people are rather apt to forget how much he did in portrait. He painted Mr. Gladstone three several times, once right in the middle of the Eighties, in 1885, and once just before that period, in 1879 ; and again just after it, in 1890. And he did portraits of Lord Salisbury and Lord Beacons- field about the same time. For his " subject " pictures he often took one or other of his own

15

daughters, especially Miss Effie Millais, afterwards Mrs. James, a very beautiful woman, for his models. The effective portraiture of women's faces did not seem to present the difficulty to him that it did to many artists who have been well able to cope with the more rugged and marked male face. He dealt with all ages and both sexes with equal apparent ease and success. Those little boys blowing " Bubbles," and extensively used by Messrs. Pears to advertise their soap, were his grandsons, and the sons of that Mrs. James who was born Miss Effie Millais. He was a charming painter of children. I tried once to get him to paint a little girl friend of mine, now the wife of a general, with boys at Eton, telling him that she was the most lovely child that had ever been seen. " My dear fellow," he said, " I am pestered morning, noon, and night by people coming and telling me that they have found the most beautiful child that ever was seen, and asking me to paint her."

So he would not ; but he was wrong, for I am still sure that she was the most beautiful child that ever was—in spite of all those others. I quite admit the probability that each of the parents of those others thinks quite the same in regard to theirs. But this was no relative of mine ; I had at least that advantage for impartial judgment.

If Millais himself had little look of an artist, his studio in Kensington Palace Gardens had even less likeness to the typical *atelier*. He built the house himself. It was very commodious and comfortable, and, I suppose, of the style that the house-agent would describe as " sumptuous." The studio was like a very nice large room in a very nice large house, with nothing very suggestive of art about it, except the big easel and the chair on rails so that he could run it back easily away from the canvas when he wanted to have a real look at it, and forward again to bring him within brush-range. The house was finished, and he went into occupation of it, in 1879, so he was there all through the Eighties. And all the Eighties through he also had Murthly. It is in Perthshire, and Lady Millais was a Miss Gray of Perth, living in a house on the north side of the river with a beautiful and very peaceful garden, which is the original scene of one of his best-known pictures, "The Vale of Rest." He was made Sir John, and a baronet, in 1885.

We are rather apt to forget, under the impression of his later work, that he not only started as a Pre-Raphaelite, but that he even started Pre-Raphaelitism itself. It is, of course, a little difficult to say with precision who were the real immediate parents of a movement of this kind, or the exact moment at which it had its first being. It does not spring on the world at any single instant fully grown and armed like the unfortunate goddess who never had a childhood but jumped straight out of Jove's head. Generally, however, the initiative of the brotherhood is ascribed to Millais, Holman Hunt, and Rossetti. Millais' talent developed very early, and, born in 1829, he was already originating, with those others, these new ideals in art in 1846. Some of his pictures of that period are vivid beyond belief, until looking at them compels belief. His "Autumn Leaves" is a gorgeous riot of colour. Personally I care far less for his "Ophelia," though probably I am quite wrong, because so many good judges admire it immensely. But I cannot believe that Hamlet would have thought it did Ophelia any kind of justice, or that the story would have been as it is if Ophelia had been as Millais shows her. The statement of the Pre-Raphaelite aim, to which he, in common with Hunt and Rossetti, committed himself, runs thus, and simple enough : " To present on canvas what they saw in Nature."

Well, yes—and Millais, looking at "Autumn Leaves,"

painted each leaf just as he saw it, and splendid the result is, but it is not the result that a man's eye receives from looking at a heap of autumn leaves, of which his painting purports to be a picture. It is the sum of the result which the eye receives from looking at each leaf severally—and that is quite a different result.

This, however, is not the place, nor has the writer the least ability, to discuss the fundamentals of Pre-Raphaelitism, which in effect amounts to the discussion of the principles of the whole art of the painter.

Millais himself did not long remain faithful to the principles which he had thus stated, nor to the fellowship which he had helped to found. After 1860 he was no longer to be numbered among the brotherhood. He died while he was still of an age to give us many more pictures, in the fullness of his power.

BURNE-JONES

We might suppose it impossible to conceive a man more whole-souled and single in his devotion to art and to the cult of beauty than Watts, and yet I believe that the Eighties had such a man to show us in Burne-Jones. Seldom as the former permitted himself a side-glance down the ways that are frequented by ordinary men, the latter probably allowed himself that distraction even less often. Then, too, we see phases, or moods, in Mr. Watts' work : the moods of allegory, of portraiture, and of the admiration of the glory of great strength. Burne-Jones, save for a few pencil drawings of faces that interested him, had no mood other than that which inspired his presentment of beautiful form and line and colour, and beautiful story. Further, he never was afflicted, so far as I am aware, in any one of his sets of paintings

with the burden of a definite moral purpose ; which
Watts had to carry at times, not to the furtherance,
as some thought, of his best effort in art.   Much
incidental morality he gave us, no doubt, but it was
by the way ; it was not part of the essential aim.

On a day to be numbered with the highest note of
red, among days of good fortune and happy coincidence, there came up to Exeter College, Oxford,
two Freshmen, of whom one was named William
Morris and the other Edward Burne-Jones.   I do
not think that either had any previous knowledge of
the other ; but it seems that they were not long in
finding each other out and in discovering that there
was in each of them a spirit disposed to the worship
and pursuit of beauty, as it is not likely that they
would find it in any other undergraduate.   It is a
great bit of luck that there should have been this
coincidence to draw them together.   It is hardly to
be supposed that Morris, such a man as he was, would
have been any other, or much other, than the Morris
as we know him, even had Burne-Jones not happened ;
but it is equally difficult to think that Burne-Jones
would have been just what he was, or would have
given us that series of romantic pictures, to be a joy
for ever, had Morris not happened—and happened
just when he did, so that their common " freshness "
brought them into close intimacy in the strange
Philistine company.   The binding of the bonds of
the friendship thus commenced has been told to
perfection by Mr. Mackail and others, and is a story
long precedent to the Eighties.   The name of Burne-
Jones was already known, already " made," as we
say, by this decade ; but it could not fairly be said
to be " made " until some very few years before.
There were all the trials and the struggles of these
lean yet delightful (as they surely must have been)
years, under the masterful ægis of "Red Lion Mary,"

the "cook-general," as I suppose she should be called, of that house in the Square of the Red Lion, which some of the brotherhood of the Pre-Raphaelites shared.

We must call Burne-Jones Pre-Raphaelite—I suppose he would so have called himself—for he was brought up with them; they were his friends; but do we see very much of the special influence of that school in his work ? I, at least, cannot. And it is curious that, if he professed himself of a brotherhood whose aim in art was defined as being " to present on canvas what they saw in Nature," he should have given us a full gallery of beautiful things that most certainly he never did see in Nature. Almost of open avowal, he gave us " the light that never was on land or sea " ; went in quest of it, and determined that it was the ultimate principle of art to find it and present it, in order to gladden and lift the hearts of those who had not the genius to seek and find it for themselves. I do not know how he would have defined his art : I suspect that he had a wholesome hatred of definitions. His wish, I believe, would have been to live emotionally rather than intellectually. I remember, on one of the few occasions that I had the privilege to meet him, mentioning an article that I had lately been reading in *Mind*. Upon which he asked, with a most wearied and pathetic emphasis on the title, " Is there a paper called *Mind* ? " As much as to say, what a fearful thing that a whole journal should be so given over to the things of the intellect as even to dub itself with such a name !

Nevertheless, Burne-Jones was the possessor of a delightfully humorous and fanciful mind of his own. He was the best of company, in that particular and whimsical way. He was not the company for all men, for he had very few dealings with the Philistines, and no sympathy at all with them. For the most part he was happier in the society of women than of men. But the men whom he did like were real friends, and most of all that friend whom he made on his first day of going to Exeter, at Oxford, Morris. I believe that Morris came every Sunday to Burne-Jones or he to Morris when both were in London, all through their lives, and they would talk art all the morning through. It does not seem as if either went much to church, except to paint a window. Yet both, I imagine, were religious men.

I think it was in 1877 that the Grosvenor Gallery was opened, and from that opening we may date the popular recognition of Burne-Jones as a painter of individual genius and a depictor of scenes and figures of uncommon beauty. In the first year of the Eighties he was exhibiting the " Briar Rose " series and the " Perseus." He was born in 1837, so he was not young when the full measure of success came to him ; that is to say, not young as measured by the age at which many artists have commanded fame.

It is hardly necessary to name any others of his works, for he was not a painter of many modes, and these are typical of that mode in which he worked so perfectly. But he had many applications of this mode, sometimes under the direct influence of Morris, as in the window work and in his illustrations for the *Chaucer* and other classics that Morris printed at the Kelmscott Press. There is a lovely piano, which he painted for Mrs. (now Lady) Horner. That was exhibited, so the world has seen it, and fortunately it escaped being devoured by the fire which disastrously burnt down Sir John Horner's beautiful house—Mells, where the piano used to be.

There is no painter more easy to appraise. I do not mean to say that it is easy to assign him his precise rank in the immortal hierarchy of great painters. Far be such presumption from me ! But it is not so difficult as with many others to see where his greatness lies, and where his weakness. Both the many qualities and the one defect are alike obvious. I do not speak of the technique, as of his use of water-colour, very dry, for the sake of the texture, used in conjunction with oil-colour—to the despair of some of the cleaners of his canvases, who have dealt with them as if they were wholly done in oil-colour. That cleansing has been to the undoing of the picture, too. All this is a mystery into which I am not suffi-ciently initiated to pass judgment on it, further than to say that as there are

> A hundred thousand ways of making tribal lays,
> And every single one of them is right

—I quote from an execrable memory—so it does not seem to matter, granted you achieve your effect, what your technique, what your mode of laying on the colour, and what the medium for its mixture. And Burne-Jones' technique achieved its end to a marvel. So we need say no more about it.

And that end which it achieved was this : he presented us with a very large series of large canvases telling us tales from the classic epics, from mediaeval legend, or from Scandinavian Saga. Whenever or wherever a beautiful story had been told Burne-Jones would illustrate it beautifully. He would illustrate it with the finest possible delicacy of line and richness of colour and grace of form. His fancy decked it with lovely trappings and set it in the fairest scenery. His figures carried suggestions of marvellous purity and refinement.

All this is on the side of the qualities. One might write of them at much length, but it would be little more than an expansion of this brief precis. And with the last of them we begin to touch on the defect—on the one weakness in so great strength. Surely,

in his devotion to refinement, he has refined too far !
In the intent of showing us the virginal he has given
us the leanness of middle-aged maidenhood. These
are heavy-eyed, heavy-lidden maidens, moreover, as
though they had shed tears for sin of which we feel
convinced that they are not guilty ; they express a
humility or a bashfulness, by an inability to hold
their heads straight upon their shoulders ; it is as
though their necks were without bone and sinew.
His men, his very Vikings and heroes of classic story,
have the like negative characteristics. He has put
away from them all fleshiness to such extent that they
appear as anchorites clad in the garb of fighters,
figures in armour with a covering of skin over the
bones, but no flesh between. If these indeed be
warriors, it is as most unhappy warriors that we have
to rate them ; we can scarcely regard them as victors
in the fight ; certainly not as delighting in any joy in
victory. They are fine-drawn to the point of
emaciation ; they would all be the better for what
is vulgarly called " a full meal." We have to recognise that it is done in noble aspiration to show us all
that is highest and most spiritual in humanity.
It is a lofty aim that he has placed before him. His
error surely has been in going too far in the one
direction in seeking it. By this ultra-purity which he
has endeavoured to make his beautifully executed
figures express to us, he has really abstracted all that
gives purity a living value. These men and maidens
of Burne-Jones are not only without sin : they give
us the idea that they are without the wish to sin,
and that is a condition which makes sinlessness of
little worth. We can take little interest in Sir
Galahad if we suppose in him none of the temperament and none of the temptation of Sir Lancelot
Moreover, we are quite unable to believe that these
Burne-Jones maidens will be mothers of fair women

and strong men. They have a delicacy which suggests phthisis and anæmia rather than the healthy coursing of red blood. When their banns are published, we have a feeling that a tribunal of Eugenists would be quite justified in forbidding them, on sight.

I know that this is presumptuous criticism, that it will sound sheer blasphemy in the ears of the devout worshipper of the beauty which Burne-Jones has revealed to us. I contest neither the beauty nor the revelation : I am a deeply grateful admirer of both ; but that his types of men and women are such as we can accept as representing humanity's best—that is a claim with which I cannot, in all conscience, agree.

Singularly contrasted, in their outward aspect, were those three great artists whom I have brought together in this chapter. There was Sir John Millais, frankly and obviously a man of the world, Mr. Watts, with a style of dress rather individual to himself and somewhat reminiscent of those old Italian pictures which he loved. He sometimes wore a long robe rather like a priest's cassock. I do not know whether it was this that suggested the name of " Signor " by which those adoring ladies called him. He had an Italian look, undoubtedly. Then there was Sir Edward Burne-Jones—both he and Mr. Watts wore beards—the only really at all Bohemian figure of the three. He was careless in dress, as neither of the others was. Both those others, each in his own way, were singularly handsome, which " B. J." (as his friends loved to call him) was not. There was, however, a curious charm about his thin face, and a great gentleness that was very attractive. Despite that gentleness, there was more real humour in Burne-Jones, and humour with a piquant sauce to it, moreover, than in either of the other two painters. His letters were delightful ; always whimsical and never ordinary ; sometimes illustrated with pictures drawn as a child would draw, and incredibly badly for one whose serious drawing was so very earnest and so very beautiful.

Some have tried to see a parallel, in comparing these artists with each other, between their personal physical traits and the types that they adopted in their pictures, finding the Millais type the most vigorous and full-blooded, next that of Watts, and finally that of Burne-Jones, the painter of the ascetic type and himself with the lean look of an ascetic. It is all rather fanciful perhaps. At all events, ascetic though he may have been in appearance, I do not think that we have to charge Burne-Jones with any sins of extreme asceticism in practice. He appeared to have an enjoyment of life which the unhappy warriors and drooping maidens of his paintings might envy him. But he was always a delicate man. I think it was at The Grange, Fulham, where he had lived nearly all through the Eighties, that he died—at sixty-five years—an early age for a painter, for painters are a long-lived race. Still, Millais' life was but a year longer. Watts alone of the three completed more than the full term, dying within three years of ninety.

CHAPTER XX

NELLIE FARREN AND SOME OTHER PLAYERS

[" Edmund Gurney said one evening, and Butler said he believed he meant it seriously, and saw no fun in it, that the world had produced four great un-self-conscious artists, viz., Homer, Raphael, Wordsworth, and Nellie Farren."

SAMUEL BUTLER, *A Memoir*, vol. i. p. 232.]

IN the early Eighties I was undergoing the process called " eating dinners for the Bar " at the Inner Temple. To say that the dinners were " plain " is to pay them an almost extravagant compliment. Messes of four at a table were arranged in the fine old hall, and a single bottle of anæmic claret was set at each table to be the bountiful liquid complement of this number of very plain dinners. Usually two or three friends would mess together at a table, and for the fourth place there was great competition to secure one of the Indian students, from an idea, which we often found grievously mistaken, that the religious convictions of these Orientals forbade any looking upon the wine when it was red—in which case the munificent single bottle might less inadequately serve to make glad the hearts of three white men. The dinners were eaten at the mediaeval hour of six, and if you were late the meal did not count in the keeping of your term. I dare say all these anachronisms have been corrected now, even to the plainness of the dinners and the one bottle of acrid claret among four, but I do not know. The law moves slowly.

There was, however, amidst all these trials, one compensating merit about the mediaeval hour for dining, that the meal was concluded in perfect time to

allow a consolatory smoke before turning in at the
Gaiety Theatre nearly opposite. We were even
young and trustful enough in those days to have faith in
the qualities of the coffee of the Gaiety bar as an anti-
toxic to the Temple dinners. So we smoked and sipped
our coffee, and at eight o'clock went into the theatre.

The Gaiety Theatre means to us comparatively little
in these days, so that the reader may well wonder
why I make all this preface and palaver to it ; but
in those days the Gaiety Theatre meant wonders. It
meant Nellie Farren, Fred Leslie, Kate Vaughan.
They were a great trio, but far and away the greatest
was the first. I often ask myself—and, comparing
notes with my contemporaries, I find that all of us
have done the same, and always with the same result
—whether it was all an affair of the glamour of first
youth : whether the reason why Nellie Farren appeared to every one of us, without exception, as the
most marvellous woman, in her line, that ever came
upon the stage, was that we had seen so few others ;
that our enthusiasm was in reality the child, merely,
of our inexperience. We have asked ourselves the
question as dispassionately as we may—I quite admit
that such dispassion is difficult—but the answer
which every one of us, still without exception, is
obliged to find is that there really was some quality
or qualities in this wonderful little lady which no
other has had in degree at all like hers. I believe
the answer to be correct because, after all, we did see
others, we had our opportunities of comparison.
Moreover it was not only we, young students of the
Temple and scarcely out of Oxford, who judged thus
of her in our inexperience. Our youthful verdict
was endorsed by the middle-aged and by the elderly
who had seen all sorts of stars rise and fall—Vestris,
Taglioni, or whom shall we name ?

It is not quite possible to name another ; a true

comparison with artists gone before is scarcely to be drawn, because none of the earlier ones had just the same opportunities. The kind of musical comedy which we saw and heard at the Gaiety was rather a new thing in those days. Really it was the precursor of the Gilbert and Sullivan series which was very soon to follow. I would not so much as say that *Aladdin*, *The Forty Thieves*, *Ruy Blas*, and so on, as presented at the Gaiety, were the inspiration of all those other comic operas. No one can rob their joint authors of their right to fame as creators of an original thing. But I do think that the Gaiety series educated and prepared the public for a proper appreciation of the comic operas when Gilbert and Sullivan did form their ever-blessed combination. In that sense the one may be looked on as the parent of the other.

But whatever degree of kinship those plays at the Gaiety might claim with what came after, nothing exactly like them had gone before ; so that Nellie Farren, with her supporters, appeared as a new gem in a new setting, and the effect was heart-searching. Naturally it is an effect which you cannot hope to recreate by any description ; it had to be seen to be realised. It is easy to say that she was a fine comedy actress : it almost goes without saying, for she could have had none such success as she achieved had she not been to that point accomplished. But it is after saying that obvious thing that the difficulties begin. What else was there " to her " ; for evidently there must have been much ?

Even when all that is said, we can still say something else not wholly to her advantage : she had no voice worth talking about, and certainly none to be enthusiastic about. And yet she sang her songs, such songs as she had to sing in those comedies—or burlesques, or extravagancies, or whatever name is right for such nondescript productions—to perfection,

to fascination, even to tears. There was a " tang "
in her tones, which I think came quite naturally, of
purest and most delicious Cockney. People took
up her songs, they would sing the chorus with her,
they would not be denied sharing in the positive
delight with which she appeared to give them out.
They were Cockney songs, for the most part, and the
voice was a Cockney voice, but behind the Cockney
" tang " and the Cockney humour there was ever
present the pathos which is always there in the life
of the poor of London. That is where she touched us
—with her pathos. Actually in the very " tang " of the
Cockney itself the pathetic note would wail out—in-
describable in the method of its production and impression, but most unmistakably and impressively there.

> Let me hold yer nag, Sir ?
> Tike yer little bag, Sir ?
> Won't yer sky a copper ?
> Thank ye, Sir.

They are not notable words, hardly on the level
of high poetry, but as Nellie Farren gave them to you
—probably as a verse appropriate to some incident of
the Arabian Nights Entertainments, for the sacred
unities of time and place were not very faithfully
observed in the Gaiety Nights Entertainments—as
she gave them they went straight to the heart.
She would have you laughing happily the one moment
and the next very near tears. That trick of touching
the emotion, however it was done, no doubt was the
trick that made her what she was, and what no one
else in her own line ever was. Calvé or Destin are the
artists, if it is possible to compare great opera with
little, with whom one might class her.

And she never was in the least degree vulgar. It
was an age of almost grosser vulgarity in the music-
hall stage than this. It was an age of dancing on
the stage in tights, an age of less feminine nudity,

both on the stage and off, than this ; but most of
what there was of the dress was worn, by the stage
dancer, skin tight. So, of course, Mrs. Grundy was
shocked. After all, is not that what an institution
such as the Gaiety stage and such an institution as
Mrs. Grundy exist for—to shock and to be shocked ?
Nellie Farren appeared to have among her gifts that
of eternal youth. She kept the stage for very many
years, and for some reason Mrs. Grundy seemed to
think it more heinous for a middle-aged than for a
youthful lady to exhibit the admirable contours of
her leg and form. But I think that really a shrewd
old Scottish woman, an aunt by marriage of my own,
put that matter in what we have to regard as its
right light. Another old lady, of her own age but
with very much less than her own large views and
incisive insight into the core of a subject, was visiting
her, and the talk turned on the stage of the day.
" Dreadful ! Shocking ! " said the visiting old lady,
at a certain juncture in the conversation. " There's
Nellie Farren—dances in tights on the Gaiety stage,
and she, a grandmother ! "
" Oh, well, my dear," replied my aunt, " if you
mayn't dance in tights when you're a grandmother
I'm sure I don't know when you may."
It was good argument, as well as good repartee, I
venture to think. Whether Nellie Farren really had
grandchildren I do not know. What a grandmother
she would have been, by the by ; what fun to be her
grandchild ! She married. Her name in private life
was Mrs. Soutar. But I do not know whether she
had any family. I think not.
The charm of her voice, then, so far as one can put
it into words, was this keen, nasal Londoner's " tang,"
with a note of the pathos and the hardness of street
life just audibly ringing, here and there, through it.
Some part of her fascination rested on that. And

then there was her tremendous energy, vitality, " go " !   It was " go " that was dreadfully infectious : it was bound to make you want to " go " too ; you could hardly sit still in your stall, so delightfully catching was it.   It made you feel as if life was indeed worth living and that you must set to work, or to play, at once, and begin to live it for all it was worth. I remember one night being at the Gaiety with a friend, and Nellie Farren on the stage in some act in which part of her business was to bang a tambourine —and she did bang it.   She was a little creature, but the energy that she put into her fist work on that parchment was wonderful to see, and it must have been a wonderfully tough piece of ancient sheep-skin to stand it without breaking.   The next day, in the afternoon, I met my friend with whom I had been at the Gaiety.   " Whom do you think I saw to-day ? " he   asked   me.   " Whom ? "   " Nellie   Farren ! " " No ! where ? "   " She was in a phaeton, rather a high phaeton," he told me, " and she was driving a pair of horses down Bond Street.   She was driving them just exactly as she banged that tambourine last night, exactly as if she and her phaeton were the only things that there were in Bond Street.   Why she didn't kill herself and a dozen other people and run into a dozen other carriages I'm sure I don't know. But I suppose the Lord looks after her."

Happily some kind providence did ; happily Nellie Farren, whether grandmother or not at the date when my aunt's silly old visitor came and gossiped about her, lived on to a ripe old age, although illness prevented her from acting for very many years. Towards the end, long after she had retired from the stage, some of the profession had the good thought of getting up a " star " benefit performance for her. It was a touching affair.   There always was, as I have tried to hint, a pathos attaching to Nellie Farren,

16

though she was nominally a burlesque musical artist, and the pathos was very much in the air that night of her benefit. Her fellow players did themselves much honour in honouring her as they did.

She was not, according to any classical canon, beautiful, but she had far more than her fair share of that natural charm which is more than a mere matter of facial lines and is so much more fascinating than any beauty of feature. Off the stage and on, she had this goodly heritage. Her slight, energetic, boyish figure was perfectly adapted for her favourite parts, and she moved with a virile grace. But she, of course, was not the attraction of the theatre as a dancer. The dancing of that day was quite different in style from that which we have seen more lately at the feet of Maud Allen or of the ladies of the Russian Ballet ; but no dancing has shown us more grace than Kate Vaughan's. Neither she nor Fred Leslie could ever have brought people to the Gaiety as Nellie Farren compelled them, and Nellie Farren might have compelled the appreciation and attendance of her public even without their help ; but none the less were they admirable aids and complements to her mastery.

Fred Leslie, besides an excellent burlesque actor, was an accomplished man in many lines, a good sketcher, and very agreeable companion. Essential vulgarity was just as far from him and his art as from Nellie Farren's own. I lost sight of him quite early, and fear that he died very prematurely and without real fulfilment of his high promise.

It was the day, too, of another Ellen—for the Nellie of Miss Farren's first name really was derived from the dignified Ellen—Ellen Terry, fascinating us all in more serious drama. She happily is with us still, and occasionally on the boards even now, in parts, such as the nurse in *Romeo and Juliet*, befitting her years. Her voice also was, and is, part of her charm. It has

ELLEN TERRY 243

none of that *gamin* note which the Nellie of the
burlesque made so effective—no Cockney, natural or
acquired—but a most moving and deep tone that we
seldom hear from a woman's lips. It was no stage
trick, for it was equally audible and compelling in her
every-day talk in ordinary life. It is not my business,
however, to attempt an appreciation of this most
gifted lady who so enchanted us in the Eighties, for
the happy reason that we may still see her at times.
It is not the features of the living that I am trying to
sketch. It was obviously impossible, however, to
speak of the stage of the Eighties without the introduction of Ellen Terry, and it is yet more impossible
to speak of that stage without mention of Henry
Irving. And Henry Irving, though he would always
have been original and great, never would have been
all that he was, never so complete, without Miss
Terry. No actress of her day could have taken her
place in the parts which she played as complement to
Irving. Of all the rest, perhaps, her own sister Marion
might have been her best understudy ; but we can
hardly think of her as Ellen's equal, though she acted
finely. She had not all the fine subtlety nor the distinction of her sister.

These were just the qualities that Irving needed in
the lady that was to lead to him, for whatever else
we may say of his acting, fine subtlety and distinction
were there, not to be questioned. What was questioned, even furiously debated to the severing of
family ties and the dissolving of friendships, was
whether Irving could act at all. With his strange
figure, his voice of the occasionally affected *basso
profundo*, the singular drag that he affected, both in
his stage walk and in his stage speech, all these were
mannerisms of which some men said that they were
intolerable, that he was a mass of tricks, that they
never would go and see him again.

Now in all the former part of that statement these critics were in some measure correct—he had tricks and mannerisms that were most tiresome—but in the last part of this statement these same persons were strikingly incorrect, for, in spite of all they said, they always did go and see him again and again and again. Whatever else he might be, Irving was always compelling and attracting. You might feel a repulsion, you might say you did not care to look at him, but look at him you would, none the less, all the while that he was on the stage, partly by reason of these very mannerisms. For you never quite knew what he might do next, and did not wish to miss the new trick or action or piece of business when it came. I have always thought that there was a good deal of likeness between Disraeli and Irving : both deliberately developed the mannerisms which came natural and easy to them into a pose calculated to attract attention, the difference being that while Irving was a professional actor and on the stage, Disraeli was an amateur and off it. But Disraeli would have been great in some of Irving's best parts, had he gone on the boards of the Lyceum instead of the floor of Westminster. Irving, just before the Eighties, had taken the management of the Lyceum Theatre, and forthwith he began to set us a new idea of acting, a new idea of some of Shakespeare's characters, and a new standard of stage decoration and the setting of the various acts. Perhaps he overdid the pomp and elaboration of the setting—that at least is my own opinion ; perhaps Shakespeare plays better in that simplest possible scenery for which he wrote. At all events Irving, as an actor and manager, completely realised Aristotle's idea of the " magnificent man." Whatever he conceived was on the magnificent scale : there was nothing ever small about it, just as there was never any of the obvious in his way of presenting the characters. Incidentally there was this further point that he had in common with Disraeli, both were singularly apt, agreeable, and witty speakers after dinner or on any like occasion. So far as I am aware Irving wisely left politics quite untouched. An actor cannot afford to make friends with the one side at the cost of having the other pass by the doors of his theatre as though the plague were raging within.

Irving's face was such a very striking one that it is difficult to imagine him playing any rôle just as another man would play it, or not looking singular and original even in the most natural action. The extraordinary length of the face, from the arching eyebrows to the end of the chin, was the departure from the normal which made it so interesting. The forehead was low and wide, appearing lower than it really was because of the hair worn rather long and heavy and brought rather far down. The nose was long and straight. The chin very long, and the line from the nose right down the chin remarkably straight also. So, too, the line from the forehead down the nose. Seen full-face, the contour was an elongated oval, the chin going away rather narrow. The head gave the appearance of no great brain capacity ; but I think that there was some capacious room at the back, though the way in which he wore his hair did not give a good chance for phrenological study.

Irving, I imagine, must have deemed the Lyceum a lucky house for him. It is quite certain that he was a lucky man for the Lyceum. Back in the Seventies, when Bateman was the manager, its prospects were not too cheerful. Then came Irving, in *The Bells* ; and at once people flocked to see him. Matthias, in that play, was one of his best parts throughout his career. It was hardly the first part in which he had a great success, for he had already made a hit as Digby Grand in *The Two Roses*. But it made the success of the Lyceum. Then began those friendship-severing discussions as to his merit as an actor. People might say what they liked of him, but they must go and see him. The fortunes, both of Irving and of the house, were made.

It was just prior to the Eighties that he took over the management from Bateman, and at once he began the sumptuous staging of plays for which that theatre quickly became known to fame.

The plays with which he " took the town," to use a pleasant phrase in vogue long before the Eighties, were *Hamlet* and *The Merchant of Venice*. These two, no matter what Macbeths and Iagos he might play later, were enough to establish him. Never had Hamlet been seen played in that manner before. His spare figure did not much realise the Queen-mother's description of her son as " fat and scant of breath," but that is thrown out as a very curious *obiter dictum*. The over-thoughtful character of Hamlet is of the kind that we associate far more easily with the lean and sallow man, as Irving was, than with the stout, so much so that I have always thought that Shakespeare must have had some acquaintance of his own in mind, when he thus sketched Hamlet with this obese physical aspect. And I think that Shakespeare's fat friend must have had " a liver," which led him into those too anxious introspections. So, perhaps, even to this minute detail, the super-student of human nature was exact. Nevertheless a fat man supports his dignity on the stage with far more difficulty than a slender, and we may recall that in all the interest and curiosity that attached to Sarah Bernhardt's manifestation of Hamlet, the fact that made it occasionally hard to accord sympathetic attention, and that invited the smile which is so fatal in a tragedy-audience, was that she had tried to conform herself to something like the contour of

figure which the mother's words suggested. Irving
made no such mistake as this. We may remember
that although his chief rôle was in tragedy, he was
splendid in comedy also ; and a man with the sense
of humour which is thus implied would hardly peril
the sublimity of his Hamlet by stuffing cushions
round his middle.

So Irving gave us the new Hamlet, to gaze on, to
wonder at, to admire, or otherwise, according to taste
—at all events to talk over, again and again. And
Miss Terry was his Ophelia. But then, if it was not
enough to invent a new Hamlet, forthwith he gave
us a Shylock who was yet again a novelty. What
will not this man reveal to us, of the unexpected, in
Shakespeare, we began to ask ? And was it revelation
in the sense of unfolding Shakespeare's conception,
or was it a creation of his own that he was giving us,
not in Shakespeare's intention at all ? We asked
that question also ; and most of us answered the last
clause affirmatively : this was a Shylock according to
Henry Irving rather than a Shylock according to
William Shakespeare. Already we had seen the
dramatist's Jew alternatively presented. The old
idea had been of the crawling, cringing creature,
ready for any man's tongue to abuse or toe to kick.
Then we had a new revelation, with a cruel, hard,
remorseless, bloody-minded Jew, scarcely human,
and only to be admitted as a fellow creature because
his own inhumanity was somewhat condoned by the
inhumanities Christianity practised on him and his.
We had seen these two ; and then Irving came on the
stage, presenting us with a dignified, patrician old
Jewish gentleman—cruel, to be sure, but with a cold
and polished cruelty perhaps quite as deadly but
certainly not nearly so brutal as the former. I do not
say that this was the Shylock of Shakespeare. I do
not think that he was. Nor, of course, was it a

rendering likely to give all satisfaction to those whose idea of the Jew of Venice—as Shakespeare meant him—was already fixed. But at least he gave them cause to think. Again he roused friendship-severing debate. Again he posed a problem.

Unquestionably he was a genius, no matter what definition we adopt of that elusive quality. He had the originality of genius, its high ideals, and its infinite capacity for taking pains ; for there was no pains that he would not take to get the setting of his scenes, the robes, and so on, just right, even as he would spare himself no personal pains in polishing his performance to the last point. No actor ever paid the public greater respect. There was no detail in which he neglected them or treated them lightly, saying, " This is good enough for them." It was not good enough for him, unless it were the best that he knew, and he would give them no less.

Irving's Shylock was a creation of genius, and it was supported most fascinatingly by the Portia of Ellen Terry. That great and charming actress never had a part more adapted to display her delicacy and her dignity. She really was the very incarnation of the youthful " Daniel come to judgment " with her deep grave voice, her slender young grace, and her consummate art. Those tones, now witching, now damning, as she modulated them to the occasions of the baffled murderous Jew, seemed almost to hint at a prevision on Shakespeare's part that some such creature as this would some day step to the boards for the portrayal of one of the most finely conceived and finely executed persons of his stage.

So Irving went on, generally with Miss Terry beside him, acting and entertaining and interesting us all through the Eighties, and the Nineties also, although interrupted for a long while towards the end of the century by illness. With Miss Terry he went to

America more than once, and played to full houses
and appreciative audiences there as here. He was
in harness—actually on tour—when he died at
Bradford in 1905, a man of whom even those who
disliked his acting would admit, perforce, that he did
more for the stage of England than any other single
man, the playwrights apart, has ever done.

There was one side of Henry Irving, the kindly side,
which the public did not know. Neither did I know
it. But I do know from what many have told me
how grateful they have had occasion to be for kind
and helpful words from the great actor when they were
making their first little essays in the art of which he
was master. What is better known is his generosity
in giving to charitable objects and in aiding struggling
players. Friends of his early days in Bristol have
told me that the good which he did without his name
appearing as a donor was far greater than any one
knew, or than more than a very few suspected. That
highest honour which our nation pays its great dead, of
burial in Westminster Abbey, was surely well deserved
by Henry Irving. Other men, in other walks of life,
in the Eighties, may have made a larger and deeper
impression on the history of the time : assuredly no
more striking or interesting figure appeared upon
its stage.

Irving dominated the theatrical stage of this
decade, just as certainly and completely as Mr.
Gladstone dominated what we call the political stage ;
but it was a period of production and performance
of a very high level of merit at other theatres besides
the Lyceum. There was Charles Wyndham at the
Criterion ; Hare and the Kendals at the St. James's ;
Beerbohm Tree, towards the latter end of the
Eighties, at the Haymarket, and so on. Tree carried
on the splendour and elaboration of scenery and setting which Irving had introduced. His best parts

were those in which a strong melodramatic interest blended. He had not quite the subtlety nor the simplicity required for the playing of modern domestic life. He was always a theatrical actor. His Gringoire was perhaps the best thing that he did. Later, his Svengali in Du Maurier's *Trilby* was a great piece of acting and haunted one for days. It made a very satisfactory kind of nightmare for Frank Lockwood, the Q.C., as he has recorded in one of his humorous sketches. But the parts which we used to go to see him play in the Eighties were such as he took in *Jim the Penman* and *A Man's Shadow*. These were melodramas that gave him just the opportunity of which he was able to take the best advantage. However, it is but fair to his memory, after thus criticising his acting of parts which were not relieved by strong " character " touches, to say that it was in the presentation of a figure which had little of these aids for the " character " actor to lay hold of that he made his first hit, namely in *The Private Secretary*. That was his first real success. But no other actor that I can remember so effectively realised the Fat Boy's ambition of making your flesh creep. He was aided in this by a figure as unlike that of the original fat boy as possible, who really must have lived under a rather cruel handicap against the achievement of his aims. Tree was tall and dignified. His Svengali really was terrific. One wept for Trilby. He was a kindly and beloved man in his private life and welcome for a curious, absent-minded, whimsical humour. Beerbohm was the family name, the Tree merely taken on for the stage, and his brother (or is it only half-brother ?) Max Beerbohm made it a very well-known name later, by his caricatures and by his witty essays on men and things.

A delightful face, with an ironic blend of humour and cynicism, was Charles Wyndham's. It grew

to wear a look of great pain and stress towards the end,
and it is to be feared that he had to suffer much
physical pain. These lines were not writ upon it, or
only lightly and incipiently, in the Eighties. But
even then it had its very expressive and keenly
intelligent aspect. And surely if trouble were to
write them—trouble of a domestic character, trouble
of his own seeking and well-deserving—then surely
they had every reason to be graved on Wyndham's
countenance, for his life on the stage seemed to be
spent in perpetual hot water. He was always
delightful in the midst of his worst villainies : always
it was he, who was singularly ill-deserving of it, that
had all our sympathy—never his victims, who merited
everybody's pity. Through it all, he was always a
gentleman. He failed to disguise that distinction
even in that most painful scene in *David Garrick*,
where a high sense of chivalry demands that the
hero shall show himself to deadly disadvantage before
the face of his beloved : even there it was no worse
than a drunk gentleman, never a drunk cad, that he
could force himself to appear. It was in that rôle
that he touched the highest level of his art. His
innate and expressed refinement only added to the
pain of all who had to witness this really heart-
rending performance, admirably, almost too admirably, as it was given. Another classical part in which
he was quite first-rate was that of Charles Surface.
He produced at the Criterion most of Henry Arthur
Jones's plays, such as *The Liars*, and *Rebellious Susan*.
Sometime in the Eighties he engaged as his leading
lady Miss Mary Moore, as her stage name was, and
this was as happy a combination as that of Miss Terry
and Henry Irving at the Lyceum. Miss Moore was
then, I think, the wife of James Albery, the playwright.
Had Wyndham only been given better health he
might have gone on delighting us many years after

he virtually quitted the stage. It was not given to him, as to Irving, to work up to the end. But in the Eighties he was at his most effective and most delightful best.

If one had taken a referendum of all the actors of that day, I believe that the man whom they would have voted top of their profession, as the supreme artist and craftsman of them all, was none of those that I have named, neither Irving, nor Wyndham, nor Tree, nor any other than John Hare. He was a favourite with the public, a popular actor enough, and in private life a very well liked man, but it was among the actors, among those who were professionally trained to appreciate the points of fine acting, that Hare was so appreciated. He was great in those parts which did not seem constructed to give opportunities for an actor to show greatness. He could make a character live when it had no particular saliencies of disposition, no peculiarities, no oddities, no attributes excessively emphasised or thrown into high relief. He could act the ordinary, every-day life, and yet make it seem like life and not the mere strut and squeak and gesticulation of a puppet. Therein lay his strength. It was the kind of performance that would not take the eye of the ignorant and the uncritical, but it won enthusiastic appreciation from those who had the training or the insight needed for the recognition of its merit. Hare was with the Kendals at the St. James's all through the Eighties ; but I must confess that it was a little later, in the Nineties, that I have my most vivid recollection of him. He had then migrated to the Garrick, where he was manager, and brought out several of Pinero's great plays. But the play in which I remember him best was *The Pair of Spectacles*. It was perfect art. Just as the play itself was Grundy's finest production, so it brought out the best that Hare ever touched.

And it seems difficult to imagine how that best could be improved on.

Among the several theatres that came into being at just about this fortunate period of the drama's history in England was Toole's. Toole was a delightful man, cheery and humorous, off the stage as on. We did not see a great deal of him in London, for though he started the theatre there which he called by his own name, he spent most of his time on tour, with one or other of his companies, in the provinces. He really seems to belong, chronologically as regards the stage, to an earlier date than this, because he was in some sort a survival of an older and almost extinct school of comic actors. He was quite a " type," but typical rather of the earlier past than of the Eighties, although he well outlived that decade. You might almost think him one of Dickens's characters stepping out of the novels on to the stage. But though his art was not " up-to-date "—to use that ugly useful piece of slang which America has given us —it was art which achieved its end, of drawing audiences and keeping them excellently amused. Toole's name was never mentioned without sending a happy smile round the faces of a company, and he was loved for his kindly nature as much as he was appreciated as an entertainer.

And then there was another theatre which appeared as the setting for some very bright particular stars in the Eighties : this was the Savoy. But the story of the Savoyards is one that must have a chapter of its own.

CHAPTER XXI

W. S. GILBERT AND THE SAVOYARDS

A LREADY, when we were undergraduates at the beginning of the Eighties, and before we had even started to eat those mediaeval dinners for the Bar which were so convenient for a look in at the Gaiety Theatre afterwards, we had begun to sing, not too melodiously, at our " Wines," by way of a change from more time-honoured ditties :

My name is John Wellington Wells,
I'm a dealer in magic and spells ;
    In ready-filled purses,
    And blessings and curses,
In prophesies, witches, and knells.

So if any one anything lacks,
He'll find it all ready in stacks,
    If he'll only look in
    On the resident Djinn,
Number 70 St. Mary Axe.

Thus, or somewhat thus, it went, from that delectable opera *The Sorcerer*, which was one of the earliest that W. S. Gilbert produced in his most fortunate collaboration with Arthur Sullivan. But many years before, almost in our nurseries, and certainly in our schooldays, we had been reciting :

Amongst them was a Bishop who
Had lately been appointed to
The balmy isle of Rum-ti-foo,
And Peter was his name.

(*From a photograph by Messrs; Russell & Sons.*)

SIR W. S. GILBERT.

This Gilbert was born actually as long ago as 1836. One could not well believe it in the Eighties. It was then that I had the fun of meeting him first, and I hardly regarded him as at all older than myself. No doubt this was partly because the man was at heart so young and gay—not only then, but a great deal later, even to the last. Who might not keep young if his mind was for ever turning and twisting itself about in such whimsical and metrical caprices as he used to give us ? Surely the reader does not need to be told that that second quotation, about the dignitary of the Church, is taken from the immortal *Bab Ballads* ! The name exactly fits the spirit of the poems, but it was not coined for the book. " Bab " was the pen-name which Gilbert took when he wrote in *Fun*, that extinct and not always funny journal which, with *Judy*, was at one time rival of the great *Punch* who, unlike the poor hero of the puppet show whose name he bears, seems to live even more vigorously and gloriously on the dead and buried bodies of his foes. Gilbert's father had been a man of letters and had written a novel or two, which no one now remembers. But this gives us an idea that W. S.'s talent, though, truth to say, not lacking in originality, was in some small measure an inheritance. For what career the son was intended I find it rather hard to guess, for at one time, if I mistake not, he was in the Forfar and Kincardine Militia (and why in a Scottish corps when, so far as I am aware, he had no Scottish connection—who can say ?) ; and then again he was at the Bar, one of the relatively briefless. I think that he had a turn in some Government office, too. So his experience was varied.

Providence perhaps was working for him in its mysterious ways all the while, though at the moment he probably did not see its guiding hand very clearly or very gratefully ; but may we not perceive how each

and all of these professions and these professors
became grist to that slow-grinding mill of ironies
which was subconsciously on the twirl all the while
in Gilbert's brain ? The men of the sword, the men
of the gown, the men of the office stool, all come in
for his satire and for our entertainment, in their turn.
" They'll none of them be spared," to parody his own
words.

I have said that *Fun* was not always funny—had
it been it would be living *Fun* to-day—but Gilbert,
with the signature of" Bab," never failed to be funny.
Over that signature the ballads came out which were
published later in the book. And he could draw, too :
his gift for comic strokes was only second to his
gift for comic words. He had even begun with the
strokes before the words, for I think that he had
comically illustrated some of his father's books before
he " commenced author " with his own pen.

I have said that he looked far younger, in the
Eighties, than he was, and have said, too, that no man
could well feel other than young when he had such
humorous conceits ever dancing in his brain ; but I
do not know that he invariably made every one about
him feel young and gay. I understand that in the
common composition of ink there is a modicum of
acid, but it seemed as if that modicum had been
increased to a maximum in the composition in which
Gilbert steeped his pen. It was his pen-work that
went out to the public, by which they judged and
extolled him, but his tongue, in conversation, was quite
as aspish as his pen. The man John Toole, the outlines of whose portrait I just suggested at the end of
the last chapter, was one of those of whom it might
be said that he went through life without making an
enemy. That is by no means to be said of Gilbert.
Life, just at first, does not seem to have used him very
kindly. He was disappointed in an ambition to

enter the regular army and to become a gunner, in
the Royal Artillery ; as barrister he had to go through
all the embittering processes of hopes deferred ; I
believe that he found the career which a Government
office promised dull to the point of suicide. And in
each of these attempts at making good he had found
men, whom he must have known to have brains of
not half the agility or subtlety of his, making better
than he, for one reason or other, was able to. It
is not the kind of youthful experience which sets
a man at peace with his world. Gilbert was certainly
never wholly at peace with it even after he had made
very good, and a great deal better than any of those
who had outstripped him at the start found any
possibility, in their talents, of making. The youthful
impressions go deep and they do not easily get worked
out. So we may imagine him, I think, in those days
of his disillusionment turning what appeared to be
the ill-favours of Fortune over and over in his mind,
finding them very bitter, and at the same time coining,
in an extraordinarily ingenious and prolific mint,
biting criticism of those who seemed to be leaving him
behind. That they did not in the long run defeat
him, that he came at length to a goal of fame which
they could not even hope to see afar off, did not
make any difference. The natural milk of his
human kindness had gone just a little acid. He was
never quite able to correct it. With that ironic wit
of his, the temptation to the biting word must have
been very hard to resist. As a matter of fact I do
not know that he ever made any very determined
effort to resist it. A man generally enjoys the use of a
tool or weapon with which he is conscious that he is
adept. Gilbert had all this consciousness of mordant
wit, and appeared to have full enjoyment of it. One
might quote endless instances. Many have been
quoted already. Of a famous actor, essaying the

17

rôle of Hamlet, while a company of people were condemning and ridiculing the personation, Gilbert, with the air of one trying to introduce a little more Christian charity into the criticism, remarked : " Oh, I don't think ——'s Hamlet is so bad." Then added : " It's funny, without being vulgar." That, with the semblance of a kindly comment, has a barb of wit which makes the malicious arrow stick, while all blunt damnation of the poor actor's well-meant work would be long forgotten. I am afraid this is too well known for the reader to have the least difficulty in filling in the name for which I have set a blank. That is the worst of quotation of Gilbert's gibes. Unless one has his own callousness to the pain that he gave, one must leave out the names, and with that omission some of the point goes, too. How excellent, but how acid, was that reply to one who asked him " Which do you think the best of R. L. Stevenson's books ? " " Oh, Travels with —— " (naming an enthusiastic appraiser of R. L. S.'s writings) " in the Cevennes." The companion whom that agreeable book of travel has made immortal had, it may be remembered, long ears and four legs.

In company with an American friend, to whom he was showing the sights of London, he was being taken over Westminster Hall by a member of the House of Commons, who drew attention to the fine roof. " Of what wood ? " the visitor from the States asked. " Oak, I think," said their guide. " Some say it is English chestnut, but I don't believe myself that at the time when this was built there were enough old chestnuts in England to provide the material." " Probably not," put in Gilbert, " ——'s Memoirs had not been published then."

These and the like little comments are very apparent examples of the " gentle art of making enemies," as Whistler called it, at just about the same time.

Gilbert probably did not mind. He had much enjoyment out of life, but universal popularity was not an element in it.

As a rule, when the Creator puts out a piece of human workmanship of an uncommon quality He sets His hall-mark upon it. The exceptional man does not usually look just like the rest of the crowd. But I do not think this final pains had been taken in the issuing of Gilbert. There is no doubt whatever that he was a man of quite uncommon gifts, of wit and irony, but I never could see that his lines and features gave token of any remarkable capacity. It may have been my own dullness in deciphering them, and perhaps keener eyes saw more. To me he had the aspect of a sensible, solid country gentleman—one who might be good at Quarter Sessions. As a matter of fact Gilbert, from all I have heard, was this : he was a magistrate, and did his work well in the county; but he was also a good deal more than this. We may imagine his fellows on the Bench standing, or sitting, in considerable awe of him. He was not a man with whom one differed very readily, nor without fear of some sharp punishment. I do not know what his family motto was, but I do know very well what motto I should have handed out to him personally, if he had applied to me for one as a member of the Herald's College : *Nemo me impune lacessit.* That would have fitted him admirably, and at the same time, if he would have worn it legibly on his shield, might have served as a salutary warning to others. As it was, his rather harmless and by no means formidable aspect was such as to dispose unwary strangers to quite an opposite opinion of him, and tempted them to indiscretions, that cost them dearly, which they would not have ventured if he had only looked a little more dangerous. The wolf is especially to be feared when he wears the fleece.

I believe Gilbert to have been essentially, and at heart, an exceedingly kind man. He would do any friend, and very likely a foe too, if he did not happen to have a quarrel with him at the moment, a kindness ; but it seemed to be very hard for him to say a kindness. And it never seemed at all difficult for him to say an unkindness, if only he might point it with a glint of wit. A kind man in deed, not a kind man in word, is a summing up that we might make of him, and at least that is better than its opposite.

But if this seems only a grudging estimate, we may give him thanks with no grudging, no reserve at all, for all that he did for us in the way of our delight and our entertainment. A dull man, or a man of no more than ordinary powers, might work his life long in acts of kindness, yet never do one tithe of what Gilbert did towards making the world more joyful and more happy. It is rather pathetic that it should be so, but it is all part of the pathos of life's handicap which we can never throw off us. This *Sorcerer*, which I have mentioned, was not the first of Gilbert's production in partnership with Sullivan, but it was among the first. The actual first was *Thespis*, as early as 1871, of which I have no personal recollection at all; and it was followed in 1875 by *Trial by Jury*. Then, in 1877, came *The Sorcerer*. It was a distinct advance on the *Trial by Jury*, and, as I believe, on *Thespis* also, in its aim and its scope. It had a plot, and it was a connected piece of several acts. It was a play.

The Savoy Theatre as yet had no existence. *The Sorcerer* was given at the Opera Comique—I think under D'Oyly Carte's management. So, too, were the next three—the three P's : *Pinafore, The Pirates of Penzance*, and *Patience*. The success of each exceeded that of the one before. Then, in 1881, D'Oyly Carte opened the Savoy, which had been expressly designed for the operas of Gilbert and Sullivan—a glowing testimony to the favour which they had already attained and the permanent hold of that favour which this very clever and experienced theatre manager deemed that they, or their successors, would maintain. Certainly he was not deceived. *Patience*, in high tide of booking, was transferred to the new Savoy : the Gilbert and Sullivan opera had come to its own home, and had " come to stay." I do not think that the next two, however, *Iolanthe* and *Princess Ida*, were quite up to the same level. They never hit the public taste quite as hard. But *The Mikado* which followed them has been perhaps the most popular of the series. Then came *Ruddigore*, followed by *The Yeomen of the Guard* ; and lastly, so far as the Eighties went, *The Gondoliers*.

The conspirators who had done so excellently well for our entertainment and, incidentally, for their own pockets, began to fall out among themselves about this time over the distribution of the spoils. I believe Gilbert's only ground of complaint with Sullivan was that Sullivan did not sufficiently join in the complaint that he, Gilbert, made against Carte. At all events, as between the author and the musical composer, the rifted lute was soon set to rights again and gave us more music in the Nineties—*Utopia Limited* and *The Grand Duke*. It is a wonderful record.

I am very sorry that I never knew Sullivan at that time—only later, when he was in no good health. Indeed I believe that his health was never robust all through life, which makes the merit, as well as the amount, of his compositions the more remarkable. I know nothing at all of music, but have heard many musicians regret that he did not devote himself to great opera, so gifted was he. Perhaps they were right, but I can feel no share of their regret. For a great opera or two we might have lost all those lesser works that I have just put on the list. Gilbertian opera without its Sullivan would be rather like *Hamlet* without the Prince of Denmark. I do not mean by that that Gilbert did not write some very pleasant dramatic pieces in collaboration with other composers : I know that he did : also that he was himself personally responsible for a few of the songs and melodies, and not the least alluring of them, in some of the operas in which Sullivan was working with him. For instance, it was he, entirely, as I believe, that created that haunting melody of the " I have a song to sing, oh ! " But still, none but a composer of very special gifts, and probably none who had not given himself professionally to the composer's art, could possibly hope to maintain that wonderfully high level of freshness, grace, harmony, and brightness which Sullivan carried through all his collaborations with Gilbert.

Also, on the other side of the count, we have to appreciate all that he actually did in more serious musical modes. We cannot deny him, for instance, the glory of *The Golden Legend* ; when a whole congregation joins in unison to sing, " Onward, Christian Soldiers," they are Sullivan's notes that they are bringing out with all their chest powers. *Oh Mistress Mine* is a song which of itself would keep his memory green ; *Orpheus with his Lute* is another of the same series of five songs from Shakespeare ; the sacred cantata *The Martyr of Antioch* is his ; the oratorio *The Light of the World,* and very many pieces of less or more importance. These instances are enough to show how astray from the facts is the popular verdict which has judged him as if he were the co-worker with Gilbert and very little else. He actually accomplished enough to make a very high reputation with the whole Gilbertian series left out of the count altogether. Sullivan, in short, would have been as great a man as he is (some would say that he would have been far greater) without his Gilbert : we can hardly imagine Gilbert as great as he is without his Sullivan. Undoubtedly Sullivan was far more popular socially and had more devoted friends than Gilbert. He was quite unusually well beloved, and by the consensus of all whom I ever heard speak of him he was a man of extraordinarily lovable nature. He had none of the caustic wit of Gilbert, and probably he would not have been loved so widely and so well had that perilous gift come his way, but he had a bright spirit which made his company welcome wherever he went. One of his claims on the gratitude of all true lovers of music I had almost forgotten : he discovered, or helped to discover, some lost musical scores, in manuscript, by Schubert. Perhaps the peculiar claim of his own work on the gratitude of music lovers in a wider circle is that he revealed the possibility of writing music which should be " popular " and yet be good. As a rule, which had few exceptions up to his time, the music which had found favour with the people, if not bad, had been distinctly cheap and second-rate. He proved that it was not necessary that it should be so in order to hit their taste.

I suppose that any attempt to range the Gilbert and Sullivan operas in an order of comparative merit would be quite futile, even if one had the musical ability to estimate them correctly on that side. *Iolanthe*, I believe, was considered by some of the musical critics the finest, but it was by no means the most popular. *The Mikado*, with its bright dresses and dances, its extravagant burlesque of the popular idea of things Japanese, its thousand and one whimsicalities, was the most appreciated by the people. My own humble taste inclined to the three P's,

Patience, *The Pirates*, and *Pinafore*, in the order named. In *H.M.S. Pinafore*, the first of them to be produced, we have distinct echoes from the " Bab Ballads," and especially from that " good Captain Reece, Commander of the *Mantelpiece*." In *The Pirates* there is less of the Ballads, and by the time we come to *Patience* the writer seems to have shaken himself quite free of their lingering influence.

None of them is altogether without some mild, and never obtrusive, moral purpose. Gilbert had a very shrewd eye for all that savoured of humbug, and always had the wit at command to show it up to ridicule. I do not know that he cared so much for the moralities, if only he could make his point, and especially if he could make fun of high office. " Stick fast to your desk and never go to sea : and you all may be the rulers of the Queen's Navy," was a gibe at W. H. Smith as First Lord of the Admiralty. But it is not to be supposed that Gilbert deemed W. H. Smith to be other than a very good First Lord. That statesman did indeed admirably realise the successive rises in station by which Gilbert led his office-boy to his elevation, for he did his successive jobs, one and all, excellently well, and culminated as one of the most successful and well-liked leaders of the House of Commons ever known. But Gilbert perceived that a laugh was to be got out of this lands-man and man of the City made nominal commander of the High Sea Fleet, and wrote his libretto accordingly. That was enough for him, and enough, too, for his audience. Now and then the humbug that he castigated was a pernicious piece of humbug, and then the castigation was an agent for good. So he achieved, here and there, a moral end ; but laughter and entertainment, far before morality, were the aim of all he wrote.

In *Patience* he had as attractive a target for a

sardonic humour to shoot at as the heart of wit could desire in those singular people of the Eighties, who were called, and who even called themselves, the "Æsthetes." They were the subject of Du Maurier's endless ridicule in *Punch*, but no one ever made them appear so supremely absurd as Gilbert, with his " greenery, yellowy, Grosvenor Gallery, *je ne sais quoi* young man," his " out-of-the-way young man," and so on. Perhaps it was no very high end of morality that he achieved in knocking all the stuffing —if ever they had any—out of those poor posturing figures—after all, do we not owe some gratitude for our merriment to those at whom we laugh ?—but he was out to attack affectation and pretence wherever he found it, and he found it very ready to his hand in the households of the Postlethwaites.

I often used to wonder whether it ever happened to Gilbert to be worsted in an encounter of wit, whether verbal or in letters. I never heard of an instance, and should be rather grateful, even after this lapse of years, if I could—just for novelty's sake. All the stories went the other way, telling of Gilbert's scores over opponents. There is one which, so far as I know, has not found its way into print about a certain Bishop who wrote expostulating with him, soon after the production of *Ruddigore*, for the choice of such an unsavoury title. Gilbert wrote back a long and, in form, exceedingly courteous answer, explaining to the Bishop that all depended on the sense in which the title was understood—that any possible offence, in fact, existed in the mind of the reader and not of the writer. The case was purely one of *honi soit qui mal y pense*. " So much," wrote Gilbert, " I would remind your lordship, must always depend on the sense in which words are understood. I will, if you will allow me, give you an instance in point." Before going farther I must ask the reader to pardon me if the telling of the story involves the mention of the favourite adjective of the British Army. That is Gilbert's fault, or the Bishop's—I am not sure which—and Gilbert's own argument to the Bishop which I am about to quote may be cited in its excuse. " If I were to say to your lordship," he wrote, " who has done me the honour to address me about the title of my play, that I admired (which I do not) your blooming complexion, your lordship might be graciously pleased to accept it as a high compliment ; but if I were to say precisely the same thing to your lordship, in a slightly different form of words, and were to affirm that I wondered at (which I certainly do) your lordship's bloody cheek, your lordship might not be at all disposed to accept the sentiment with equal gratitude. So much depends on the sense which the mind of the recipient conveys into the words." I do not remember hearing what, if any, was the Bishop's reply. Possibly it took the form of excommunication, but in that case I do not think that Gilbert suffered greatly from its effects. But in truth I never did hear of one who had " the last word " in any such encounter with him. A most dangerous man to meddle with ; a man whose edged wit the prudent would ever prefer to leave safe-sheathed rather than do anything to invite its keenness on themselves ; but a man to whom millions have cause for profound gratitude, for his contributions to the gaiety of the world, contributions which are even yet not exhausted, for it is quite lately, as I write, that some of the operas have been revived and we find that time has not withered their infinite variety. They have killed the æsthetes, and many another mode of affectation, stone-dead, but the witty word that killed them and the bright music to which the word is set are still vital, and are enjoyed by a generation that never knew the " æsthetes."

We may speculate what, if anything, Gilbert would have been without his Sullivan, and what Sullivan without his Gilbert. Yet a third problem for our speculation immediately presents itself : What would either, or both, have been without their Grossmith ? I believe it is Disraeli who is credited with saying that there is no such thing as " a necessary man." If he did say so, and claimed any credit for it, he took credit for stolen goods—French goods. Be that how it may, it is scarcely to be believed but that George Grossmith was a necessary man to those Gilbert and Sullivan operas. It is impossible to picture them without him ; or, at least, if we are able to draw such a picture, it is a picture different from any of those at which we laughed so heartily with him in its very fore-front. There is no argument to the contrary in the fact that in the later revivals, which I wrote of just above, of these operas they were without Grossmith. He, poor fellow, died at no considerable age, with many good years left in which he might have played for our entertainment. But though he was not bodily on the stage when those operas were given again lately, his spirit was there. He had created the parts, and his tradition was handed down and in some degree brought to life again. He was the hero of the various pieces, even from that very first of the important ones, such as *The Sorcerer*, right on to the end of the Eighties, when he left the Savoy and went into the entertainment business on his own account, rather on the lines of Corney Grain. Apart from the ladies, who were really subsidiary, though charming, the other stalwart support of the operas was Rutland Barrington. His cheery presence and stout figure is with us still, and in all bodily substance came on the boards when some of these operas were recently played again.

Never was there a happier contrast than these two,

Grossmith and Barrington, presented. Each was just made to be the other's foil. Corney Grain, poor fellow, a very Yorick of good company, comes into one's head very readily on mention of Grossmith by reason of a very excellent and very well-known caricature of the two together early in the Eighties, done by Leslie Ward, the " Spy " of *Vanity Fair*. There is Corney Grain, colossal in size, smiling down indulgently on a tiny George Grossmith, whose insect-like tenuity of limb and waist and feature is exaggerated by the art of the caricaturist, and who is looking up at the smiling giant with a chiding fore-finger raised in protest at some enormity committed by the enormous man. It is very pleasant fooling. And very much like this contrast, which " Spy " has turned to such good account, between the two enter-tainers, was the contrast between the figures of Grossmith and of Barrington on the stage. Barring-ton was not quite so tall as Grain, but he was tall enough, and just as bulky. Anything more waspish than the thinness and fragility of Grossmith it is impossible to conceive. Perhaps it should be gnat-ish, rather than waspish. He did not suggest a creature with any envenomed sting, but rather a restless, buzzing thing, ever about your head, ever ready to give you pin-pricks. He would dart and dance around the stolid bulk of Barrington in all directions, bewilderingly agile ; Barrington standing unmoved and unruffled the while. It was like the encounter of Dignity and Impudence. In one of his acts, I think in *The Mikado*, he had developed the faculty of sitting down into the cross-legged tailor's attitude with a suddenness that was scarcely human, and scarcely like a living thing at all : more like the action reversed of a Jack-in-the-box, jumping down into his box instead of up and out of it. And he used at times to play this trick while in perfectly serious conversation with a friend, or even with a stranger, who would, of course, be terribly disconcerted. At one moment you found yourself looking at George Grossmith's face, more or less on a level with your own ; the next moment it had vanished, and, going in search for it, you found it away down looking up at you from a figure in straddle-legged contortion at your feet. It was the act of an elf, and Grossmith really was most delightfully elvish in all his ways.

A very great feature of these operas, as goes almost without the saying, was the songs. Everybody with any ear at all caught their rippling melodies and whistled or sang them. And it is a curious thing that though they made of these songs such delightful and infectious things, still Grossmith and Barrington did not seem to have enough lungs to make one able-bodied man's voice between them. Yet Rutland Barrington, at all events, had sufficient lung capacity.

I suppose it is the more to their credit as clever utterers of " patter " and of quips and cranks that they could make it all so attractive without great volume of sound. But if Grossmith was no Boanerges, he had at least one capacity which was of inestimable value for the rendering of such words and music as Gilbert and Sullivan put into his mouth. He could bring the words out, racing after one another with a most terrific speed, and yet each one vocalised so distinctly that even a deaf man could not miss it. That was a much more useful gift for songs of just that kind than the voice of a Caruso would have been.

Of course the ladies had delightful songs, too, and sang them delightfully : " Three little maids from school are we," and so forth. But my concern is not with them. They were young, and doubtless are still alive. Grossmith was the Puck-like creature who held this stage, playing antics on the solemn background of Rutland Barrington—solemn, be it said, only as solemnity fitted the humour of the piece, for a person more bubbling with fun never was seen. Grossmith has left us sons, with something of his own special gift. His brother, Weedon, a real comedian, in quite another line, died only in 1919. There was a fairy godmother hovering near, at the christening of all these Grossmiths, as we must think. Weedon, of whom I have heard men say that no one on the stage ever amused them so much—he generally took the " fool-of the family " kind of part—was a painter of much merit before he took to the stage, and had pictures in the Academy. Besides his genius as a player in those rôles for which Gilbertian opera gave him his opportunity, George could compose his own songs, both words and music, and when he took to drawing-room entertainment, after he severed connection with the Savoy, his own compositions made quite a useful part of his repertoire.

Speculation on what might have been if things had happened differently is always interesting, though always perhaps barren. It is scarcely possible to conceive of the Savoy operas played without Grossmith, or at least without the tradition that he bequeathed to them, in the chief rôle. Presumably they would have been played successfully, on their own merits, if some other than Grossmith had been in the parts which he created. That would have happened, no doubt ; but it is very difficult to imagine in what manner it would have happened, and how those parts could have been played much otherwise than as Grossmith played them. Played successfully they might, and probably would, have been, but they would have been played quite differently. Grossmith's genius was peculiarly a personal one. We should have had quite a different conception of the Gilbert and Sullivan series from that which he so helped to give us. And we do not want it bettered : we may be grateful that we had it as it was.

Incidentally, and chiefly as a foil to Grossmith in Leslie Ward's picture, I have mentioned Corney Grain. He is deserving, however, of an honourable niche of his own among the entertainers of the Eighties, for he really set a fashion. He was among the first to go round—" Piano and I "—and give his recitals in private houses. He was, if I remember right, among the army of the comparatively briefless at the Bar, and realised that he had talents which he could turn to better account than seemed likely in his profession. He was welcome everywhere, whether in the new profession of his adoption or as a friend, for he was the most cheery of companions. The " funny without being vulgar " label is one that can hardly be applied without a smile at its cruel ironic use by Gilbert, quoted a page or two back, but it fitted Corney Grain's songs and " patter " to admiration, and it was an age when the one without the other was rather novel. He set the vogue for a host of followers, Grossmith himself among them; and perhaps with the single exception of Grossmith none have quite rivalled him. The big man sitting down at the piano, before a room full of people, with an assumed solemnity on his face, and in a very few minutes reducing a fashionable assembly to helpless laughter, was a sight of wonder. The gaiety of one nation, at least, suffered serious eclipse through his comparatively early death.

CHAPTER XXII

IT is hardly possible now to credit the existence of those people, the " Æsthetes " of the Seventies and Eighties. One can hardly believe them real. The young person of to-day, looking over the pages of *Punch* in the golden days of Du Maurier, may say, after his or her manner, " Oh, this is tosh ! Of course there never were people at all like that."

We who are older know better. They were exactly like that. They were so like it, that although we call those pictures of Du Maurier's " caricatures," we know quite well that they were not caricatures at all, in the sense of pictures exaggerating the peculiarities of their originals. You could not caricature these folk : they had done that for you, of themselves : themselves were caricatures of human beings living the reasonable life. Du Maurier had no need to do otherwise than draw them as they were. He could not exaggerate their absurdities.

What these people claimed for themselves was a sensitiveness to the artistic impression entirely superior to that of the members of the common Philistine herd by whom they were surrounded. This lovely sensitiveness expressed itself in the standing in affected attitudes before any picture or thing of what they chose to call beauty, which appealed to their taste, or of which they thought that by affecting the pretence of its making such an appeal they would get the credit of being persons of a peculiar sensibility.

272

The correct attitude to express this beautiful sensibility of soul was a drooping, a languid one. They could not hold the head upright : they must droop it or hold it sideways, like the heads of figures in Burne-Jones's pictures or like a lily bloom too heavy for its stalk. Everything about them must fall and droop. Their hair must be worn long—I write this of the men, of course—the drapery must be flowing and falling ; it must not seem as if it was fitted to the figure at all—this is to be said of both women and men, for though the former could most easily so modify the existing fashion as to let the garments fall in the manner of a bath towel carelessly thrown upon the shoulders and allowed to trail, still the men could do something in this line too, by wearing a long frock coat, a collar cut low, flowing tie, and baggy (a word calculated to make their delicate frames shudder) trousers.

The men did their best, but the women had unfair advantages, even in the possible form of the garments ; and when it came to a question of their hues, of course the mere male had no chance of competing. Something he might do in the way of curiously dyed tweeds, and possibly might affect some chaste jacket in velvet or other pleasing material as dinner jacket or for indoor wear at all times ; but the ladies, with their hues—not of the rainbow as commonly understood ; that would have been outrageously crude and glaring ; but of the lunar rainbow rather, or worked out in faded reflection of the true solar effect —they had their opportunities, which they did not neglect, of creating harmonies such as were impossible for the man unless he would run the imminent risk of being carried off and shut up in a lunatic asylum. Even as it was, some, " for Art's sake," ran peril of it ; and there were few but looked as if they had escaped from some such place.

18

A curious thing is that at the back of all this mass of posturing and affectation and absurdity there was an honest, sincere, hard-working zeal to bring some greater beauty into a world which had in truth grown very ugly. I do not mean that there was any reality at all about the people whom Du Maurier sketched by the names of Maudle and Postlethwaite : they were *poseurs* and *poseuses* and little more. They affected a kind of hyper-æsthesia towards Art that was very nearly sheer nonsense. The only thing that redeemed it at all from nonsense pure and simple was that even such ridiculous pretence of appreciation as this was almost better than that open and unabashed indifference of the normal people of that day towards things artistic. Better perhaps to make the sacred name of beauty ridiculous than not recognise it at all.

And then these people, whatever we may think of them in themselves, were really the artistic posterity of very genuine and sincere ancestry. I do not know —I wish I did—what William Morris had to say about them. His comments would have been interesting. But though they must seem very remote indeed from that never-resting, never self-satisfied spirit which possessed, like a demon, William Morris, they really did inherit from the Pre-Raphaelites. They believed themselves to be living the life beautiful, in the garb beautiful and within the house beautiful, and to have attuned their minds to express, by sighs and gasps and words of appreciation which had scarcely more definite meaning than these suspirations, their intensity of feeling. The singular attitudes of body were designed to testify to the same enthusiasm. It was really a lovely ideal which they worshipped, although their ritual was flagrantly absurd.

By far the most gifted of the devotees, and almost the most extravagant in pose, was that morbid and

ill-destined genius Oscar Wilde. Unquestionably he
was a genius ; unquestionably, too, as I think, there
was in that genius a strain of madness. Madness
is a term admittedly difficult of definition, but,
without the necessity for definition at all, the very
fact that a man should be so utterly unable to bring
his conduct into any conformity with the conventions,
not only of the society of which he was a member but
of all civilised human societies whatsoever, is in itself
full justification for pronouncing him mad. If this
be not an example of madness we hardly know where
to look for it.

Enough said on that score. On the other side of
his very singular mentality, the saner side of that
border, so often perilously narrow, which divides
genius from madness, his gifts were quite extraordinary.

It must have been just about the beginning of the
Eighties that he left Oxford. I must have been " up "
with him for about two years, but it was either part
of his pose, or a result of athletic disability, that he
disavowed all interest in the games and sports which,
no doubt, absorbed a great deal more of my own
attention and that of my friends than they should
have done. We, on the other hand, had extremely
little sympathy, far less than it behoved us to feel, for
the arts, and least of all for that exaggerated and
affected sensibility to them which was the mark of
the æsthete. We heard of Wilde as decorating his
rooms at Magdalen with peacock feathers and other
strange adornments, but very few, I imagine, suspected the great intellectual light which he obscured
under these fantastic bushels. In 1878 he gave some
evidence of his poetical power by winning the
" Newdigate," and when he left Oxford there were
some at least of the examiners who suspected something of his genius, for his paper on Greek history

in " Greats " was said to have been quite remarkable.
He had travelled in Greece, I think with Professor
Mahaffy—his fellow countryman, for Wilde, of course,
was Irish—and his paper bore witness to a personal
knowledge of the places referred to in classical story,
as well as a brilliant interest in the stories themselves,
which examiners, harassed by the hackneyed sentiments of the ordinary undergraduate writing on this
much worn theme, must have welcomed as most
refreshing.

When he left Oxford and went to London his place
among the æsthetes was already assured by his
adoption of their most extreme fads, quite apart
from the position to which his literary gifts entitled
him.   He was recognised even then as a brilliant
and original, though tiresomely affected, talker.   He
was reputed to be an unblushing thief of other men's
good sayings—the *à propos* retort of Whistler to him
in that connection has been told too often for yet
another repetition.   In truth, his conceit was so
colossal that it was impossible to abash him.   The
ordinary *poseur* endeavours to conceal his pose :
often he is even a *poseur* unwittingly, not knowing
himself.   But Wilde knew himself perfectly for a
poseur, and made no effort to conceal it.   He deliberately adopted the rôle, and may be said to have
actually posed as a *poseur*.   Evidently that is a
position from which no ridicule or sense of shame can
shake a man.   With his self-conceit, and as a very part
of it, was mingled a great dose of obstinacy.   He
judged himself not only to be cleverer and to know
better than most other men, in which he was perfectly
correct, but also to be wiser and to know better than
the collective wisdom of men who had spent their
lives in special studies.   Thus he was at times the
despair of the actor-manager when he began to write
his brilliant plays, because he would accept no

OSCAR WILDE.

guidance from their stored knowledge, but would insist on situations and dénouements which all the history of the stage had proved to be impossible of favourable presentment. George Alexander complained of him to me most bitterly in this connection, speaking of his " damned Irish obstinacy." Wilde's view of his own opinions and his own productions was that they were above rules. Rules, confirmed by the experience of ages, might serve as useful guides for other men. He, Wilde, was above them. Really it was very like a kind of megalomania, and was destined to be a large element in his ultimate undoing.

The first play of any importance which he ever did write was, so far as I know, *The Duchess of Padua*, especially designed for Mary Anderson, though she never produced it. This was as early as 1883. It was a five-act tragedy. Apparently he had yet to discover his brilliant capacity for comedy which he demonstrated triumphantly in *Lady Windermere's Fan* and *The Importance of being Earnest*. The dialogue was unfailingly sparkling and witty. Its artifice was often quite obvious, and he worked very hard his favourite trick of giving a turn, the most opposite to expectation, to very trite comments. " Never buy a thing you don't want because it is dear " may serve as a type of many of the kind. Still, they were delightfully entertaining plays, despite the tricks, and how excellent was the fooling in *The Importance of being Earnest* was effectively proved quite lately in a very recent revival.

In conversation he would often affirm the most impossible theories, as that no modern literary work of any worth had been produced in the English language by an English writer, and would support it by argument of extraordinary and original whimsicality. " I will make one exception," he said ; " I will grant you *Bradshaw*."

That his wit was always *impromptu* would be too much to assert. Often it bore witness of being long elaborated, but he had a genius for leading conversation to his cue. When some *Nonsense Rhymes*— that admirable invention of Lear, followed by a host of imitators—were being quoted, Wilde said, with all the air of composing the lines as he spoke, " I think this would make a good one :

> There was an old man of St. Bees,
> Who was very much stung by a wasp ;
> When they said, " Did it hurt ? "
> He replied, " No, it didn't ;
> I thought all the time it was a hornet."

It was only long after the laugh had subsided that some one recalled the fact that Wilde, doubtless with this priceless composition already rehearsed and polished, had started the quotations !

No one, I imagine, seeing Wilde for the first time, would have given him credit for quick wit or ready brilliancy. His round, heavy, pallid, and moon-like face, clean shaven at a time when moustaches were in universal vogue, gave the impression of a slow thinker. He had plenty of cranial capacity for brain, but he looked like a man far more likely to produce some weighty volume on German philosophy, if he produced any intellectual output at all, than ultra-modern comedy scintillating with a wit that was Gallic rather than Teutonic. Of all his varied work, perhaps the most sincere and the most really worthy of him was that piteous *Ballad of Reading Gaol*, wrung from the depths of his tortured and penitent soul.

CHAPTER XXIII

W. G. GRACE

IT used to be said, in the Eighties, that the best known man in England was the then Prince of Wales, later King Edward VII, and the second best known, W. G. Grace. I do not think the statement was exact. It might serve for London, where the heir to the throne was a familiar figure, but taking all the country over, towns and villages alike, I believe that that royal personage would not have been recognised, in spite of all the picture papers, nearly so readily and generally as " W. G."

Of course " W. G." had an immense advantage, if it be an advantage to be thus recognised by the multitude, in his singularly recognisable figure—you could not forget him if you once had seen him. He was immense, both in height and bulk, taller in reality than he looked just because the bulk disguised the height. And then he had that big red face, and that big black beard. He would serve quite well for the figure of the ogre in a child's picture book—a very kindly ogre withal.

I heard two in a Club—the sort of place where you do hear pernicious nonsense—debating who had deserved the better of his country, who had given more delight in his generation, " W. G." or " W. E. G." Is it necessary to remind a modern audience that the latter were the initials of Mr. Gladstone ? Of course the debate was futile : it is as vain as the assertion we have seen that Pitt was

a greater man than Shakespeare. The two " great-
nesses " are not comparable, in the one case more
than in the other : there is no common standard of
measurement. One of my men in the Club said,
" Go to the Reform—you will there hear that
Gladstone is the greatest man the world has ever
known, that Disraeli is the most pernicious. Go into
the Carlton, there they will tell you that Disraeli is
the great man of the world and that Gladstone is
everything that is evil. The opinions balance each
other, so that the sum total is zero to the credit of
either. But go into any Club that you please, along
St. James's Street and Piccadilly and Pall Mall, ask
them about ' W. G.,' and every one of them will tell
you the same story about him, that they are grateful
for his existence, that he is a real benefactor, that he
has given joy to thousands."

That at least is true, and on that count we may
rank " W. G." with the *prima donna* and the great
actor. He was an actor, the finest we have ever had,
on the twenty-two yard stage between the wickets—
tragic, for the bowler and the side opposed to him,
yet with an element of comedy always about him.
You never hear any one speak of " W. G." even now
without a smile of amusement curling up the lip
both of speaker and listener. He was both to be
laughed at and to be laughed with ; but perhaps you
had better do the former, at all events, with discretion.
He was too big a man to be trifled with, and though he
was kindly he was quite self-assertive. Sometimes
they said that he was inclined to be rather too assertive
of his rights, if not of a shade more than his strict
rights, in the cricket field, but we have to remember
that all that side of games, even of our greatest game,
is governed by tradition, and that the tradition in
which " W. G." and his brothers had been reared in
Gloucestershire and the West was not precisely the

(*From a photograph by Lionel Wood, Brighton.*)

DR. W. G. GRACE.

same as that which prevails at Eton and Oxford, or
Harrow and Cambridge, and so on.   There was just a
little of the " win, tie, or wrangle " business about the
game in the provinces, especially perhaps in the West,
and it was all considered perfectly fair business, and
" all in the game," so to say.   " W. G." really was
not unsportsmanlike in insistence on points about
which an Eton or Oxford captain, let us say, would
not have insisted, because it was only part of the
custom of his county and of the game as he knew it
to be thus insistent ; and he would not have resented
at all a like insistence on the part of another.   In fact
I am not quite sure that he would not have thought
another rather a fool if he did not insist.

I have heard many a young cricketer say how
kindly he has been to them, how he has encouraged
them by a word and even condoled with them in a
kindly way after a missed catch.   He would be
charitable to everything except slackness.   That was
the unforgivable sin in his eyes, and one that he
never was guilty of.   He would be, to all appearance,
just as keen in some county match or some friendly
Free Forester affair as in an All-England Test match.

I remember him well at a Free Forester match at
Esher, on the ground that Mr. " Charlie " Clarke,
the " Conductor " of the Stock Exchange, and his
brothers used to control more or less.   I remember
it the better because it was a very high and rare
honour for me to find myself in an eleven of which
" W. G." was a member.   It rained furiously most
of one day, and we sat indoors, and after we were
tired out with trying who could tell the biggest stories
we began, on Mr. Clarke's suggestion, to play a game
of which I think the name was " tip it."   It consisted in passing a threepenny bit from hand to hand
under the table, while one of the party had to guess
in which hand it was, at a certain moment.   It was

not a very intellectual game, but what has fixed it
indelibly in my memory was the sight of the threepenny bit in the centre of " W. G.'s " palm. It
looked so small, in that immense expanse, as to be
hardly visible to an eye fixed at the focus which took
in the whole hand. Everything about him was on
the massive scale, everything except, curiously enough,
his eyes. It was singular how little of them showed,
considering how exact and quick their sight must have
been. They were like slits in his great face, black
slits, in a red face fringed with black bushy beard and
whiskers, slits slanting very curiously upwards,
from the inner corners to the outer.

As his eye was quick, so were his movements,
marvellously quick for his bulk in the Eighties,
though when he played against an All-England Eleven
at fifteen years of age we are told that he was long
and slim. It seemed hardly credible later. But what
was also hardly to be believed was his pace. He was
very seldom run out, both because he was such a good
judge of a run and also because he was so quickly
across to the other wicket. In his youth he won
sprint races and hurdle races, he excelled in all forms
of athletics in which he took a hand, and he kept
himself in condition till well up in years by running
with beagles in the winter.

I suppose that his really greatest year was a little
before the Eighties, in 1876. It was then that he
made that almost incredible score of 400 not out,
against Twenty-two of Grimsby. Four hundred,
with twenty-two men in the field to get the ball past !
Then, in the same year, came that extraordinary
succession of scores—first, 344 for M. C. C. v. Kent
at Canterbury ; next, two days later, 177 for Gloucestershire v. Notts ; finally, two days later again, 318
not out for Gloucestershire v. Yorkshire. That
amounts to 839 in the three innings.

Take now a later year, shortly after our decade (as
this was before it), namely 1895. He was then 47.
He scored 2,346 runs in the year, of which over a
thousand were made in May alone. It was in that
year that he made his hundredth century, and in his
whole career he scored over a hundred runs one
hundred and twenty-one times.

I do not think that he scored quite so largely as
this in any of the Eighties, but on the other hand his
bowling was very effective, and he scored quite heavily
enough to satisfy most people. Thus, in 1885 we find
him scoring 1,688 runs and taking 118 wickets ; and
the following year scoring 1,846 and taking 122
wickets. Apart from his ability as a cricketer, these
are figures which bear witness to extraordinary
physical strength and endurance. He did not know
what it was to be tired, and he did not know what it
was to be ill. He had a great constitution in that
great frame. I remember a most amusing story of
him at Oxford, some years after I had gone down.
I think it was in 1886. He had been invited to dinner
with the " Phœnix " Wine Club the night before the
match, and instructions were issued to the most
valiant members of the Club that they should all
drink to Mr. Grace, until finally he should be reduced
to such a condition that it would be humanly speaking
impossible for a man to be in any good fettle for
cricket on the morrow. The instructions were very
faithfully followed. All round the table, from one
after the other, came the invitation. " A glass of
wine with you, Mr. Grace ; your good health ; no heel-
taps." Every challenge was very readily accepted,
even to its final clause, and at the end of that entertainment I do not know precisely the condition of the
members of the Club—that did not greatly matter,
for if any of them were in the Eleven they had been
careful in their cups—but as for the great hero of

the occasion he went rolling home, with his rocking gait from side to side as, but no more than, usual, and the members, as they watched him depart, congratulated themselves, saying, " Well, I think we've done it all right. We've settled him. I don't think he can be very much good to-morrow."

And on the morrow, I am not very sure what happened if and when he went in to bat. I think they got him out for something just under the three figures, which was cheap. But I do know that on the morrow of that dinner he took all ten wickets in the 'Varsity's first innings, and that, from that day to this, those diners have been a little sensitive to any chaff about their well-meant efforts to wash all the cricket out of " W. G." by the champagne that they poured down him the night before.

How did it happen ?　How was it that, in a game which we all play, there should arise this one man so masterfully better than all his fellows ?　That is a question to which it is not likely we shall ever find an answer.　One thing is quite sure, that it is a question which " W. G." could not have answered.　Never was there a man less prone to theorise.　The practice of the game was good enough for him.　" What's the best thing to do, ' W. G. ' ? " some one asked him, " with those tricky balls of —— ? " (I forget the bowler. It does not matter.)　" I should say," was the answer, " put the bat against the ball."　It is very sound advice, no doubt ; whether it went far enough to be very helpful is another matter.

" Have you read Fry's book ? " some one asked him.　" No," he said, " I was afraid to read it.　I was afraid if I was to read it that Charles would bowl me out while I was trying to recollect what to do with a long-hop."

I remember poor Alfred Lyttelton telling a story of " W. G." at a cricket dinner. Alfred, always

most generous of opponents, was keeping wicket ;
" W. G." batting. " Wait a moment, ' W. G.,' " he
said, " there are some fellows moving in the pavilion
behind the bowler's arm."

" Never mind, Alfred ; never mind," was the
answer. " I don't mind what they're doing in the
pavilion ; I keep my eye on the ball." That is a
story that some fussy batsmen might do well to lay to
heart.

" How did it happen ? " Lately a " Memorial
Biography " of this greatest of cricketers has been
published containing a thousand and one good stories
about him from many pens. I am not sure, but I do
not think that this, brought to my recollection by
this phrase which I thoughtlessly wrote, is told there.
It was on the voyage out to Australia, and amateur
theatricals were among the pastimes of those weeks
of leisure. " W. G.," who was not a practised actor,
was cast for a part in which he had to say " How did
it occur ? " He always did pretty well in the re-
hearsals until he came to this sentence, which he
invariably paraphrased, " How did it happen ? "

" Well," he said, when the stage manager corrected
him. " It means the same, don't it ? "

And so it does—only, unfortunately, the sentence
next to follow was " It was not a cur ; it was a very
well-bred dog." I hope I hurt no feelings by the
suggestion that it was not exactly a very high-class
drama.

So the man with his " cur," but sadly at a loss for
his " cue," expostulated bitterly after being thus left
en l'air in the third rehearsal running. " Ah, well,"
said " W. G.", " I'll do it all right on the night when
it comes to the match ; this is only practice at the
nets." " I bet you don't, ' W. G.,' " called out
Briggs. And " Done with you " was the response.

On the great night, as the drama worked up to

the point of " W. G.'s " speech, all attention was concentrated in the interest of hearing whether he would deliver it correctly, and how the unfortunate man with the cur would follow him. To the gratification of the audience and the relief of his fellow-player he delivered the speech with perfect exactness, but followed it up with the pronouncement, not found in the book of the play, and not at all to the assistance of the next speaker—" and that's half a crown to me, Johnny Briggs ! "

There were those who said that he ought to be rated as a professional, and of course we all knew that he took money for playing over and above the amount of his expenses by way of reimbursement for the fees he might otherwise have been earning in his profession. But, after all, he could not have played had he not done so ; and if he had become a professional, the Gents *v.* Players matches of his time, and how long a time it was we know, would have had little interest. There would have been but one side " in it." With the professionals he was always popular ; and he would travel long distances to play in a match in which one or other of them was taking his " benefit " —to the certain enhancement of the gate-money.

In the evening of that life which seemed to most of us much longer than it really was, because he had come so early before the public, it must surely have been gratifying to him to reflect that in the playing of the game which he loved and in which he was the acknowledged master he had given such great pleasure to many millions.

CHAPTER XXIV

THE " SOULS "

SO far as I have acted on any definite principle in the selection of the originals for these attempted sketches, one of the principles has been to refrain from the portraiture of people still alive. I know what a shock it is to come unexpectedly on a mirror in a strange house, and to be confronted of a sudden with a face and figure that for a moment you take to be that of some one perfectly unknown until you recognise with a shudder that it is yourself, and exclaim in a mental perturbation destructive of all fine grammatical sense : " Good gracious ! Is that me ? " I have no desire of administering any such shocks to persons still alive and sensitive to them.

It is scarcely possible, however, to present even the most sketchy gallery of people of this daté without any reference whatever to that really very remarkable little set commonly known as the " Souls," which flourished—in the phrase dear to the historians—during the Eighties. It was a title or nickname, or whatever it should be called, applied to them at first—in gentle and not at all unfriendly derision—by some Philistine who did not profess himself of their sect. Never was there a label which stuck more adhesively—the members of the coterie so named were even content to accept it for themselves—and never was a label, designed to be, if not descriptive, at least suggestive, less apt in its suggestion.

The distinctive characteristic of these people—for of their distinction there can be no question whatever —was almost anything rather than that which could be described as " soulful." They were peculiarly lacking in that quality ; and it is possible that a moderate infusion of it might have done them good. " Soulful," in the most extravagant degree, is an epithet which might well fit that of the society of " æsthetes," now withering or already withered to death under the frosty irony of the Gilbertian opera or the pictorial ridicule of Du Maurier's pencil in *Punch*. They were indeed soulful, intense, yearning : any epithet of the kind that you chose to pick might suit them ; but emphatically none of these terms were at all adapted to the case of these whom the Philistine heathen in his blindness named " Souls," and by so naming them miraculously conferred a title which survives in history. These so mis-called " Souls " were not in the least soulful or æsthetic in the very mildest form of that emotional disorder. They had not such a creature as an artist in their number, if we except Lady Granby, with her delicate pencil portraits. They had Arthur Balfour, with a quite uncommon knowledge in an amateur of the theory of music, but they had no musician. They had none with any literary gift or bent at all out of the common, unless we except Henry Cust, sometime editor of the *Pall Mall Gazette*, and with at least one notable poem to his credit.

The truth is that a title far more apt which the friendly Philistine might have found for them would have been the " Brains." They had no very remark- able gifts, as a set, on the æsthetic side, but on the purely intellectual count they had gifts that were quite astonishing. Of course it was a title which the Philistine could not be expected to bestow on them, for it would amount to a confession of a superiority in their brains to those of himself and his fellow-citizens of Gath. However accurate such an admission would have been it is evidently one which he was not likely to concede, for the view of the Philistine in regard to the persons whom he gently derided under the name of " Souls " was that his own brains, if only he cared to use them in the same manner and to the same ends as these others, were quite equal to theirs. The difference, as he conceived it, was just this, that he did not choose to use his brains in such unprofitable exercise as that of social conversation. He kept them for serious things, such as sport or business. He regarded these others, in fact, rather as we may imagine some wise old sporting dog regarding the antics of one of his own kind performing " parlour tricks "— taught to " sit up and beg," to "die for the Queen," and so on. All this he could do if he chose, but he knew a great deal better than to choose to do it.

That, or something like that, was the attitude of mind of the ordinary Philistine towards this little coterie of not at all ordinary people. That the attitude was in large measure a mistaken one is quite another thing, but an obviously true one. It was his greatest mistake of all to suppose that they had no more than the normal share of intellect. The mention of a few of their names, and a consideration of their later record, will show this beyond all doubt. Even those already mentioned would go far to prove the point—Arthur Balfour and H. Cust to start with. There were also—whom shall we say?—Asquith, George Curzon, St. John Brodrick, Haldane, Lady Granby (later Duchess of Rutland), the Elchos, Mrs. Horner, Lady Frances Balfour, Alfred Lyttelton, Gerald Balfour and Lady Betty ; perhaps Miss Maxse, Evan Charteris, Miss Balfour (who became the second Mrs. Alfred Lyttelton)—others of course, but above all, and as the pivot and inspiration of the whole group,

there were the sisters Tennant.   Many went and came
on the circumference, so that one hardly knows
precisely in what arc or how widely to describe it ; but
though there be this doubt about the circumference
of the set, no one, I imagine, could hesitate to say
where lay its centre—in that astonishing quartette of
sisters, of whom one is now Mrs. Asquith, another
Mrs. Graham Smith, a third was Lady Ribblesdale,
and a fourth the first Mrs. Alfred Lyttelton.

I have always regarded my own life as distinctly
the poorer in that I did not have the privilege of
knowing Miss Laura Tennant, the first Mrs. Lyttelton.
By the common and, as I think, unanimous consent
of all she was the bright particular star of that
constellation.   As one of the set, not a sister, nor a
relative, said to me very soon after her lamented early
death : " She was a flaming spirit."   Put together
all that we know of the other sisters, the charms, the
wit, and the audacity, we still, as I suppose, have to
add to these some attribute over and above—perhaps
spirituality would be as nearly descriptive a name for
it as we shall find—to complete the very extraordinary
attraction which all who knew her realised and lauded
in this lady : so beloved of the gods, dying so young.

The story of the attack and conquest of London by
the sisters Tennant is like a fairy tale.   In no novel
would it be in the least degree believable.   In solemn
history it has to be believed only because it is true.
Mr. Tennant, the father, was a Glasgow manufacturer.
He made money.   He speculated in Mysore Gold
Mines.   He made a great deal more money.   He
bought a property in Peebleshire, " The Glen."
" Little Glenny " was the name that he went by then
in Scotland.   He came to London.   Whether it was
the Mysore Gold Mines or his daughters that brought
him there I hardly know.   Immediately, in a single
campaign of the Cæsarian *Veni, Vidi, Vici* character,

these ladies forced the social defences of the town, which capitulated without conditions.

The weapons with which they achieved the surprising conquest were perfectly manifest—there was no mystery about them—audacity, charm, and wit. No two of these, without the complement of the third, would have sufficed, but with the three they were irresistible. One and all, they were innocent, some said innocent to a fault, of the vice of self-consciousness. They knew no fear. In any and every society they were equally at their ease, their wit outflowing, their charm beguiling. So the town fell, and so they conquered.

Always it is difficult, speaking of people " rising in society," as it is called—rather as though they were aeroplanists seeking record altitudes—to avoid the suggestion that they were in some degree or other more or less deftly concealed snobs. There was nothing in the very least in the nature of snobbism about this sensational rise of the Tennant sisters. They did not, in fact, rise, for they floated in at once on top ; they had no lower strata to penetrate ; but, apart from this, anything with the taint of snobbishness about it was not in the nature of Sir Charles Tennant, as he was soon created, nor of any member of the family. I used to be told by people who stayed at " The Glen " constantly, that you would often meet there, jostled up with the London society guests, a sprinkling of the old Glasgow friends of Sir Charles's earlier days. These were never allowed to feel " out in the cold " at all : they were always brought into the circle and into such of the talk as they could understand. What they said about " The Glen " when they went back to Glasgow and compared notes, history does not tell us. The silences of history are very tantalising. It is ever the most interesting points on which that Muse will be the most secretive.

They were Glasgow people, and therefore shrewd, but it is no reflection on their shrewdness to suggest that the talk sometimes went over their heads. To say truth, it was talk that very often went right over the heads of the talkers themselves. I have claimed for these people that the title of " Brains " was far more appropriate for them than that of " Souls." I do not ask for any fuller or clearer witness to the claim than is afforded by that list of names which I have drawn up as tolerably representative of the members of this set. The men there named had not done a great deal perhaps at the beginning of the Eighties. They had gone through Universities with very high distinction. But they were for the most part in the stage of promise rather than of fulfilment. They were in process of fulfilment right through the Eighties, and, of course, far beyond that period. Arthur Balfour especially did his most distinguished political work, in my judgment, during that decade, when he took on the office of Irish Secretary at a moment when a man took it to the imminent peril of his life ; he carried it through to the astonishment and admiration of all men, especially of those who had held the office with conspicuous ill-success before him ; and of the Irish Party themselves, whom he treated in the very manner to win their respect and to appeal to their humour—that is to say, that he listened with profound attention to all the statements and arguments, even the most extravagant and absurd, which they chose to bring forward, and then proceeded on his own course precisely as if such extravagancies had never been uttered. This lowland Scot, of nature as alien to that of the Celt as even their own Parnell, understood these children of a warmer temperament, and understood their right treatment, by virtue of some mysterious faculty of insight which has never, so far as I know, been explained, and which never

seemed to serve him so faithfully in after years and in
higher office. My own guess at the explanation is
that it was the natural disposition of his peculiarly
cool and equable judgment to look upon all others,
not Irish only, as children of unbalanced impulse.
It was treatment which suited the Irish admirably,
and which they did not resent, but which was destined
to give cruel pain now and again to the more serious
English nature at moments when the very being of
the nation appeared in danger and when Mr. Balfour
—verbally at all events—played with the scorching
fire as if its menace were of no importance. In spite
of which, that wonderful common sense of the nation
never failed in due gratitude to Mr. Balfour for his
great services to his country, his long holding of office,
nor in giving him all just credit for absolute honesty
and for disdain of all ambition and self-seeking. Its
only quarrel with him was that he disdained too
much : that he disdained not only his own advancement, but also that his heart would not beat with a
rather more zealous pulse for the advancement of the
people within the nation and of the nation within the
world-unity of nations.

The other men of the group were younger, ripening
for office. Some were at the Bar. But always, it is
to be noticed, it is for political distinction that these
were ripening. Never is there a hint of other kinds,
æsthetic kinds, of distinction aimed at by this society
called by a name suggesting soulfulness. It was a
society predominating, scintillating, with intellectual
gifts. " Brains were sticking out all over it," as
somebody said of it—with no great elegance. And
they loved to scintillate. They frankly tried to
scintillate and to out-scintillate each other. The
Philistine was perfectly correct in one of his criticisms
of them : they were always sitting up and performing
their parlour tricks. They were trying to out-talk

and out-vie each other all the while. They did not
pretend to conceal the effort of the rivalry, although
they lived in the comfortingly warm atmosphere of
a mutual admiration society. They were generous in
their mutual admiration and perfectly candid about
their mutual rivalry. This is to be said rather of the
ladies of the party than of the men. The men were
relatively lazy conversationalists—relatively to these
surprising ladies only. Some were of uncommon
fluency, measured by the masculine gauge. One of
the ladies would say, generally complimenting another,
" You were very great last night " : meaning that
she had talked to admiration. Or, discussing an
evening, they would say, " It was ——'s night,"
naming the one who they deemed had shone most
brilliantly. It is regrettable that George Meredith
was not of their company—what a picture he would
have sketched us of it ! One might almost fancy
that they had come right out of his pages, incarnated
Meredithian characters—though even he never drew
anything quite so bright and glittering.

And they *did* talk. Obviously, talking so much,
they talked of many things of which it was quite
certain—even before they began to talk about them,
and so put it to the proof—they could know nothing.
This it was that gave the Philistine occasion and
justification for his gentle friendly smiles. Inevitably
they came croppers—what a schoolboy would call
" howlers." That did not affect them in the least.
They were up and at it again directly. No fall could
shake them. That was all part of their courage,
their audacity, and it is all a version of the old story
that the person who is afraid of making mistakes will
make nothing. They knew no such fear : therefore
they made many mistakes. But they made abun-
dance of far better things, better than any of those who
went more prudently could possibly make. They

made brilliant comments and criticisms. It was all intellectual glitter, some of it very poor paste, but some real diamonds. And about it all not a trace, not a hint, of soulfulness.

Unless you like to call this constant intellectual striving and strain a pose, and I do not think it is quite a fair name to give it, these people had no pose, no affectation. They had no inclination, that I ever perceived in any of them,

> To walk down Piccadilly,
> With a poppy or a lily
> In their mediæval hand.

There was nothing in the least mediaeval about them. On the contrary, they were very much what is vulgarly called " up-to-date," or even quite ready to " go one better," as a poker-player would say, and be just a little ahead of date.

But yet again, they would be quite willing—it was indeed much in their way—to

> . . . lie among the daisies
> And discourse in novel phrases
> Of their complicated state of mind.

It was just that sort of discourse which made the poor Philistine, temporarily drawn within their circle, feel himself so very far from his ease. I have the keenest recollection of seeing one unfortunate outlander seated at dinner next one of these elect. The conversation was voluble on the lady's part, but I noticed a look of harassment growing on the face of my friend throughout the meal. When the ladies left the room he heaved a profound sigh. I asked sympathetically how he had fared during dinner. " I want to go away and lie down and rest," he said, " and not speak or be spoken to. I had never met her before, and she began talking faith and freedom with the soup." Thus it was that the Philistine,

accidentally caught up into an atmosphere so rarefied,
would soon be ejected as too opaque of spirit, or
would voluntarily descend from it and retire with
gratitude to the lowland peace of his native city of
Gath. There he would find a society congenial to
him, and friendly gatherings conducted on the
pleasant principle enunciated by an eminent London
banker, lately deceased, " Now let's be jolly, and
not talk."

Sir Charles Tennant, the father, was amusing in
his attitude of detached and charitable wonder and
interest at these strange things happening. He was a
very remarkable man, and well worthy a place in
any portrait gallery of the time. He was small, with
a grey, rather pointed, beard, and a face of uncommon
astuteness. Undoubtedly he was astute : the very
money that he made is a witness to it ; but he was
also something a good deal better than astute, he was
a very kind man. I know many an instance of
people whom he has assisted, young fellows whom
he has helped with a friendly " tip " of information
as to a stock which he knew to be likely to rise. So
many men in the City of London seem to make it
a point of jealous pride to keep these good things
closely in their own pockets, that this sort of kindliness
is worth noting. Of his more ordinary dealings in
the way of charity I know nothing, but should be
greatly surprised if they were not generous.

For his relaxation he played golf and he collected
pictures. He was very well advised in his picture
buying, and the walls of his house in Grosvenor
Square were almost like those of a museum. The
catalogue alone was a valuable work of art. Many
of these pictures are now in possession of his son Lord
Glenconner. I am reminded, by the way, that I
should certainly have named Lady Glenconner, then
Miss Pamela Wyndham, as one of the elect among

the " Souls." " Elect " is a word liable to possible misunderstanding, as if there were some vote or ballot for election to this exclusive circle. It is the more liable, because people who were not in touch with the set had all kinds of strange stories and beliefs about it. They were quite capable of supposing that, if no actual ballot and vote, there was at least some sort of more or less formal invitation to admission, as it might be to the I Z. Cricket Club. It needs hardly to say that there was no bond of the kind to draw these people together to protect their frontiers. They were quite capable of taking all necessary measures of protection for themselves.

I have heard it stated that the title of " Souls " was assumed with some mystical idea of each member of the group finding his or her " soul-affinity " within it. It is hardly worth saying that this is utter nonsense. There was none of this beautiful psychical fidelity about the group. Their way was rather a psychical polygamy and polyandry—community, in fine fact—as is the way of all the sane world. The other is the childish ideal of schoolgirls. And these people were as far from childishness as they were from soulfulness itself.

INDEX